EXTRAORDINARY SEX NOW

EXTRAORDINARY SEX NOW

A COUPLE'S GUIDE TO INTIMACY

Dr. Sandra R. Scantling

Doubleday

New York London Toronto Sydney Auckland

PUBLISHED BY DOUBLEDAY
a division of Bantam Doubleday Dell Publishing Group, Inc.
1540 Broadway, New York, New York 10036

DOUBLEDAY and the portrayal of an anchor with a dolphin are trademarks of
Doubleday, a division of Bantam Doubleday Dell Publishing Group, Inc.

Library of Congress Cataloging-in-Publication Data
Scantling, Sandra R.
    Extraordinary sex now: a couple's guide to intimacy / Sandra R.
Scantling. — 1st ed.
      p. cm.
    1. Sex. 2. Man–woman relationships. 3. Intimacy (Psychology)
I. Title.
HQ21.S27   1998
306.7—dc21   98-6771
                                                  CIP

ISBN 0-385-48955-2

*I dedicate this book to my extraordinary parents,
Joseph and Frances Wofe, who had 6 million
reasons to give up on life, but instead taught me to
cherish every moment.*

ACKNOWLEDGMENTS

Writing a book about the fabric of intimacy has been a unique challenge. The principles are simple, yet complex. They are finite, yet infinite. Through this process, I've crystallized insights that empower me in my personal and professional life. I've come to realize that I teach my patients and students what *I* most need to learn (or once needed to learn) and grow from the more difficult interactions. The same is true in intimate relationships—like two mirrors, we often reflect what we need to see in one another. There are lessons all around us, but we must be willing to receive them.

I am thankful for the lessons and efforts of so many people. It is to each of them that I offer my sincere gratitude:

To Ellen Geiger, my agent and friend, whose passion, intelligence, and valuable insights were irreplaceable. Thank you for sustaining me through the best and worst of times.

To Bruce Tracy for christening the proposal and being "Otter-ly" delightful.

To Frances Jones, my astute editor, who suggested changes with good humor and precision while remaining open to my point of view.

To Judith Kern, Senior Editor at Doubleday, whose expert advice was always wisely on target, and to her assistant, Theresa Pulle.

I will also eternally be grateful to the following teachers and friends. Although some of them have passed on, their words continue to inspire me: Dr. Elvin Semrad, Dr. Annie Hargreaves, Dr. Sue Bishop, Dr. Marshall Edelson, Drs. Natalie Lurie and Harry Fiss, Drs. David Singer and Roger Peterson, and a special acknowledgment to Dr. Phillip M. Sarrel and Lorna J. Sarrel for the ideas and concepts that influenced my early thinking about sex and relationship therapy.

I could never have completed this book without my caring family. I am indebted to my parents for their countless sacrifices and for being people I have come to so deeply love and respect. My stepson, Jesse Cooperman, has always been in my corner and is a source of great pride and joy. My daughter, Jennifer, is the consummate light of my life and I bless each day we have together. I thank her for her love, support, and wisdom that extends well beyond her years. And finally, I thank my loving husband and best friend, Robert J. Cooperman, for adding his inspirational genius to this work. Without his creative touch, the animal fables would never have been written.

AUTHOR'S NOTE

I have made every attempt to protect the privacy of my patients and to preserve the confidentiality of the doctor/patient relationship. The case histories in this book are composites of real cases. Names and other identifying information have been fictionalized to assure anonymity. None of the examples in this book describe actual people or events; any similarity between these stories and an actual couple or individual is purely coincidental.

CONTENTS

PREFACE: WHY THIS BOOK?

Your passionate future is in your hands. Take a moment. Why did you pick up this book? What are you searching for in your love life? And *why* is satisfying sexual intimacy so elusive? The answers await in the pages ahead.

Let me warn you. I don't have a linear formula for creating extraordinary sex, but I do have a wealth of information and experience, countless clinical examples, exercises, and personal anecdotes from my years as a clinical psychologist, sex therapist, educator, wife, and mother.

Sex has always been somewhat of a mystery to me. When I was eleven, I mustered up the courage to ask my mother, "What's a period? The kids at school keep asking me if I've gotten mine." My mother's face turned a bright shade of red and she replied, "Yes, honey, that's something you'll get when you're older." That was the sum total of my home-based sex education. I had the distinct feeling I had stumbled into a forbidden zone. Given my inquisitive nature, I was intrigued and determined to find out more.

What my parents couldn't tell me, my friends were only too happy to. Abraham Bowers, my six-year-old buddy, showed me how boys and girls operated differently. As I watched in amazement, he demonstrated how he could change the color of a large rock by deftly urinating on it with apparatus *only boys had.* He then announced authoritatively, "Babies are made when the boy pees inside the girl after both people say 'I do.'" Abraham, who I understand is now a prominent New England cardiologist, was my first sex educator. I'm certain that I was hesitant to say "I do" for years after that—and decided never to have children if it meant having someone *pee* inside of me.

I was equally unprepared for puberty and the range of confusing feelings I'd encounter while dating hormone-driven teenage boys. Somewhere I got the message to "be careful" because boys only want "one thing." I quickly learned that kissing led to other things, things I didn't feel ready to do, so I curbed my burgeoning passion and focused on my studies instead.

And so it goes. Bits of misinformation and innuendo provide the backdrop for our sexual choices. Typically we find ourselves with partners who offer us important lessons about ourselves—that is, if we're prepared to receive them.

In my case, it was no coincidence that I was attracted to lovers who were safe, emotionally nonintrusive, and somewhat constrained. It's hard to know with any certainty whether my earlier lovers were actually unenthusiastic or whether I was merely unprepared to recognize the depth of my own sexual passion. Until we're ready to receive love, we may not notice its presence.

The end of my first marriage coincided with the beginning of my search to answer the question "How do we create lasting sexual intimacy?" My wonderful husband, Robert, has been my partner in this quest. Together we've faced the daunting challenge of keeping intimacy alive by appreciating that the mechanics of sex are much easier to master than the nature of enduring intimacy.

There is no doubt that the need for lasting intimacy is universal, but the fear of daring to be intimate is equally intense. Reconciling this "need-fear dilemma" is essential to discovering and enjoying extraordinary sex.

My first book, *Ordinary Women, Extraordinary Sex* (1993), reveals how ordinary people bring a variety of pleasures into their lives. Shortly after writing it, I created the best-selling video series *Ordinary Couples, Extraordinary Sex.* The three-volume series shows actual couples demonstrating the lovemaking techniques and ways of relating to each other that make sex extraordinary. As I've toured the country lecturing and sharing the ingredients of my Extraordinary Sex program, I've been repeatedly asked whether there is a book describing the points in more detail.

This book was written to offer what I've learned so far. *Extraordinary Sex Now* isn't intended to be an explicit sex manual, advising how and where to stroke the clitoris or how to give the best fellatio. There are already a number of excellent books that do that. Mechanical sex is fairly straightforward. Intimacy is another issue entirely. Without intimacy, sex is flat—two-dimensional—and void of meaning. Like fast food, mechanical sex serves an immediate purpose, but leaves us unsatisfied and longing for something more substantial.

The questions that this book addresses have to do with creating extraordinary sex: *the intrinsic blend of sexuality and intimacy.* Topics like: Why do we become attracted to partners who are unlike ourselves and then spend the rest of our lives trying to change them? What's your sexual style and the style of your partner and how can you capitalize on the best qualities in each of you? How can you have extraordinary sex with the same partner year after year?

When it comes to extraordinary sex, I've found that small changes can have far-reaching impact. Ironically, so-called simple gestures, like an appreciative look, a lingering kiss, or other loving expressions are the most complex and difficult to sustain in long-term relationships. Soulful smooches are replaced by perfunctory pecks as intimacy fades.

But be forewarned, this journey will not be easy—nothing that's worthwhile ever is! I've included some poignant real-life case histories and an assortment of exercises that you may find unsettling. Some may stir memories or feelings you thought you had resolved long ago. Others may inspire. But don't be discouraged, and most of all, don't give up on your own happiness. You deserve it. I've found that the sweetness of lasting intimacy often grows out of the rockier terrain of self-discovery.

There are still so many questions about intimacy that remain unanswered. Of one thing I'm certain—to be intimate with another, you must first be honest with yourself. Few of us live up to our intimacy potential. Begin today!

In the immortal words of the Jewish sage Rabbi Hillel:

"If I am not for myself, then who will be for me? If I am only for myself, then what good am I? And if not now, when?"

—Dr. Sandra Scantling
Farmington, Connecticut
1998

EXTRAORDINARY
SEX
NOW

PART 1

INTRODUCTION

"To give style" to one's character—a great and rare art!
He exercises it who surveys all that his nature presents in
strength and weakness and then molds it to an artistic plan
until everything appears as art and reason, and even
weaknesses delight the eye.

—FRIEDRICH NIETZSCHE, 1887

CHAPTER 1

EMERALD EARRINGS

"A loaf of bread, carton of milk, and orange juice," Adrienne said without preamble. Bob always gets the same phone call on Friday. The weekends are times to restock the cupboards for the kids and their hungry friends. He had thought tonight might be different; after all, it was their anniversary.

"I'm on my way, Adrienne," trying not to sound too disappointed, "Be home in about forty-five minutes."

"Did you hear what I said about the bread, milk, and orange juice?" she asked impatiently.

"Uh-huh—be home soon."

Hanging up the phone, he thinks back and flashes on their honeymoon. It had been ten years, but he could remember it vividly—smooth skin, dancing cheek to cheek, cool Caribbean breezes, her incredible warmth . . . The thoughts quickly evaporate, replaced with the mantra "bread, milk, orange juice . . ." Picking up his briefcase and reaching for his coat, he feels the accumulated fatigue of the week and the familiar tension moving up his neck.

One good thing about leaving the office at eight o'clock is that there is very little traffic. He and Adrienne used to love rainy Fridays. The windshield wipers beating out a rhythm took him back. They'd leave for their weekend retreat that was simple, but oh so romantic. A small cabin in New Hampshire—making delicious love in front of the fireplace, her breasts so full and welcoming—anyplace with Adrienne was heavenly then. That was before the kids, the bills, and the two jobs. Lost in thought, he almost drove right past the grocery store.

With the ordered essentials in hand, Bob heads toward the express checkout line. It always amazes him that there is so much late-night shopping. "Bob Jenson, please come to the customer service desk," the loudspeaker echoes his name over the grocery-filled aisles. "What could be the problem?" he wonders. "Your wife left this for you," the clerk explains as he hands Bob an envelope.

As he opens the note, Bob thinks: last-minute groceries, or maybe a pickup at the late-night cleaners. "Dear Bob, hope you don't mind, Aunt Helen is coming into town unexpectedly. Would you please meet her at the airport? It's Delta flight 261, arriving at 9:15." It is signed "Love, Adrienne," and there is a PS: "Be a darling and pick up some strawberries for dessert, Aunt Helen loves fresh fruit."

Bob feels the heat rising from his collar again. "Just what I need, a twenty-minute drive to the airport and then a weekend of entertaining Adrienne's relatives. Oh God," he mutters, "I can't cope." . . . He imagines her aunt waiting at the Delta terminal. Better hurry.

Nine-fifteen sharp and Bob scans the airport terminal for Adrienne's aunt. Just then he feels a tap on his shoulder.

"Hi there, looking for someone?"

"Adrienne! I don't understand— What's this all about?" he asks.

Adrienne looks fabulous in a gray trench coat and high heels. She's carrying their overnight cases and has a sly grin on her face. "Take a guess . . . Surprise, sweetie! Happy tenth anniversary! Hope you brought the strawberries!"

"What?! Where's your aunt?"

"She's at home watching the kids and *we're* going to the Bahamas for *three days!*" She hands him two first-class tickets and kisses him passionately.

Later that evening, feeding each other strawberries as they look out at the waves from their balcony suite, they reaffirm their love. Although it has been many years since their honeymoon, the romance feels brand-new. The

sound of the ocean crashing against the shore and the smell of the salt air
. . . it is all too perfect for words.

"You thought of everything, Adrienne. You're the best. You know, I
haven't told you lately, but you really are everything to me." He reaches for
a small box in his briefcase. "I picked up a little something for you, too," he
adds, looking deeply into her eyes. "Happy anniversary, darling."

"They're gorgeous! But emerald earrings—these must have cost
a . . ."

Taking her face in his hands, he looks into her eyes and gives her a long
smoldering kiss. "Take a walk on the beach?" he asks with a wink.

"Love to," she whispers.

Although it may seem hard to believe, Bob and Adrienne aren't some
fictional couple out of a hot and steamy Danielle Steel novel. They are actual
clients whom I treated in my sex therapy practice over six years ago. In
many ways, they are an ordinary couple who learned how to have extraordinary sex.

You're probably saying to yourself, "Sure, who couldn't be romantic in
the Bahamas!" And although it would be great to be able to take an exotic
vacation or shower your lover with emeralds whenever things get dull, it's
not necessary. It's just the icing on the cake.

Bob and Adrienne have lives that are far from leisurely—they have a
hefty mortgage, three young children, and an overburdened schedule filled
with soccer practice, school events, and social commitments. Like so many
couples, they had placed their relationship at the bottom of their priority list
and forgotten how to be intimate.

By following the steps of my Extraordinary Sex program, they learned
how to make their time together special in dozens of little ways. By blending
intimacy and sexuality they've re-created a passion-filled marriage that continues to get better with each passing year.

By counseling thousands of couples over the past twenty years, I've
discovered how to keep the sexual excitement burning. *Extraordinary Sex
Now* shows men and women how to regain their "vital connection"—the
original magnetism that attracts partners to each other. By following the
step-by-step guidelines and straightforward exercises in this book, your lovemaking *can* become extraordinary. There are only two requirements for
success—a committed relationship and a willingness to make a change.

SOME GENERAL POINTERS

1. IF YOU WANT IT, YOU HAVE TO WORK FOR IT, BUT WORK *CAN* BE FUN

Everyone longs to have a love life that's romantic and sensual. But what would you do to get it? Would you read erotic books? Talk to experts? Change some of your behaviors? Consistently great sex doesn't happen by accident. The couples who have memorable sex year after year have worked to keep it that way. But as the old expression states: "They haven't just worked harder, they've worked smarter." As with any proficiency, developing satisfying intimacy involves finding a teacher and being willing to practice some new skills. Success doesn't come easily—whether it's in your career or in your marriage. But when it comes to sex, practicing can be fun!

2. DON'T SET YOUR SIGHTS ON PERFECTION

Nothing spoils sex more than striving for perfection. If you expect to achieve some *perfectly* orchestrated scenario, complete with multiple simultaneous orgasms on a bed of rose petals each and every time, you're likely to be disappointed. Going for the perfect erection or ultimate no-hands orgasm is a surefire way to dampen your ardor. And unfortunately we're continually bombarded with utterly unrealistic sexual standards and expectations by movies, books, television, and all manner of erotica. Now don't get me wrong, I'm a staunch supporter of erotic film and literature—assuming it doesn't offend your personal sensibilities. But it's important for each couple to distinguish for themselves what fantasy they might find enticing to consider and what is realistic or comfortable to expect in their own bedrooms.

Focusing on pleasure and not measure is key. If you do what you love, you'll love what you do. Extraordinary sex isn't about another set of techniques—so put away your calendar, ruler, egg timer, and illustrated volumes of the *Kama Sutra* and just enjoy yourselves.

3. ALLOW YOUR PLEASURE AND INTEREST TO LEAD YOU

Tastes are variable and unpredictable. Human beings fluctuate in their body temperatures, biorhythms, appetites, and patterns of arousal. One moment we crave chocolate chip ice cream and the next moment it's the spicy salsa that beckons to us. The same is true about sex, that's what makes it so exciting—and frustrating. One day light playful stroking may hit the spot, the next you may find yourself welcoming a fast and furious romp in the hay. If you think you can find the exact formula and simply repeat it ad infinitum, you're wrong. That is a formula for disaster! Don't assume you already know what each sexual experience will bring. Instead, welcome the differences, expect each time to vary, and decide to follow the pleasure wherever it may lead.

4. CHALLENGE YOURSELF . . . A BIT

Each of us has a security zone—an area of comfort and familiarity that doesn't challenge the status quo. To expand your sexual enjoyment, find your sexual security zone and stretch it just a bit. For instance, if you're only comfortable making love in the dark, light one candle. It's the same principle that bodybuilders use—they increase their weights and repetitions gradually. Stretch, don't strain, and your improvements will be steady and lasting. Or let's assume that you feel uncomfortable or awkward expressing intimate feelings. Begin to stretch your security zone by making one phone call or leaving a message on his voice mail to say you're thinking about him or can't wait until he comes home. Don't plunge ahead and buy that G-string complete with a CD titled *Music to Strip By*. If you overwhelm yourself with unrealistic expectations you'll be afraid to try anything new. Start small, and you'll be amazed at the far-reaching results.

5. ASK FOR WHAT YOU WANT

If you ask for what you want, you're much more likely to get it. Remember the lists we wrote for Santa Claus? It didn't take us very long to figure out that telling someone made it more likely that we might find one of those toys under the Christmas tree. Asking can be very powerful. Especially if we learn *how* to ask, *when* to ask, *whom* to ask, and *what* to ask for.

Don't assume the worst or jump to conclusions by saying things like: "What's the use of asking him to take a relaxing soak in the tub with me, he'll just say no" or "I'd just like to cuddle tonight but I'd better not tell him because he'll assume I want sex." Keep an open mind. Couples who play mind reader and are *certain* they know what their partner feels or thinks are often wrong. Certainty closes off opportunities for experimentation and keeps you stuck in that familiar rut.

6. REMEMBER, IT'S NEVER TOO LATE FOR GREAT SEX

People often say, "Let's be realistic, we're both getting older, isn't it too late for us to rekindle our passion?" Let me tell you a story.

One day I picked up the phone in my office and an older woman's voice asked for my help. "My name is Alice and I just turned seventy-eight," she began. "I was hoping you could tell me where I could get my vagina stretched." A most unusual opener. "I heard you talking on the radio about painful intercourse, and I think I have that problem . . . I think you called it vaginismus . . . I can't be sure, because I've never really had intercourse." She went on. "You see, dear, I was married for forty-three years to the sweetest man who was a very heavy drinker and he had problems keeping his erection. We did just about everything else, but we never had intercourse. I had some great orgasms, though." She laughed. "But poor Arthur died, rest his soul, and now I've met an older man, his name is Gus. He's eighty-one and he has really firm erections. He's a sensitive and patient lover and we'd like to have intercourse, but I feel some tightness and discomfort when we try."

I asked Alice when she had her last pelvic exam. "Oh, not for years, dear," she replied, apparently unaware of its importance. "I'm long past menopause." I suggested that she do two things: first, she must make an appointment with a gynecologist, who would take the necessary time to perform a gentle but thorough pelvic exam to evaluate any structural or hormonal problems that might be contributing to her vaginal discomfort; second, she should get a tube of Astroglide (a terrific water-soluble lubricant that simulates the natural slippery secretions of the vagina) to incorporate into their lovemaking and genital touching. About three weeks later Alice called again. "Dr. Scantling, thanks so very much. The doctor you referred me to recommended some estrogen cream and said I just had some vaginal dryness, but everything else looked fine. The lubrication you suggested works like a charm. I just called to tell you that I'm not a virgin any-more"—she giggled—"and sex couldn't be better." She sounded delighted, as was I. So when you think you're over the hill at thirty-nine, remember the story about Alice and Gus and take heart.

7. BELIEVING YOU CAN CHANGE IS THE MOST IMPORTANT CHANGE YOU CAN MAKE

If you're frustrated about your sex life, let me ask you a question. Is there an area in your life in which you feel very successful? Maybe you're proud of your parenting skills, or you've earned a degree of success in your business or in a particular sport or hobby. Maybe you're an organizational dynamo who balances work and recreation with such aplomb that you make others turn green with envy. Your friends can't imagine how you do what you do—but you've never doubted you can. And that's the answer—thinking something is possible sets the stage for making it so. So, if you're having trouble believing your love life can change, it's time to change that belief. Try these mental tricks to begin visualizing success:

• First think of a sexual time between you and your lover that you'd like to improve upon. Picture the episode with all the clarity and vividness you're capable of. Spend a few moments filling in the details, including any emotions you might recall.

• When you're finished, take a deep breath, let it out gently, and imagine an eraser wiping the slate clean.

• Now picture the same scenario with a new, more satisfying story line and ending. You've just replaced one image with another.

Or try this:

• Visualize a large pink elephant sitting on your couch. A silly notion, but go with it. Now try to block out that image. Impossible, isn't it? The harder you try, the more difficult it is to erase that picture from your mind.

• Instead of trying to "not" think of the elephant, simply replace the image with one of a green donkey wearing a purple party hat. See how easy it is! The technique works just as well with sexual images.

Some people say, "I can't visualize and I never fantasize." Although some people are more imagery-prone, anyone can learn to develop their visualization skills. If I ask you to tell me how many windows you have in your home, you'll need to visualize the location of each window and then count them, and just about everyone can do that.

What's exciting about this technique is that you already have everything you need to enhance your sexual thinking. Instead of trying to block your worries about not having a firm erection or your difficulty having an orgasm, focus on pleasurable images, thoughts, feelings, or sensations. We can't hold on to two opposing images or feelings simultaneously. It's impossible to feel tense *and* relaxed. Fill your mind with a positive focus and you will provide no opportunity for distracting thoughts.

These attentional substitution and visualization techniques have been used for years in sports medicine and health psychology. By mentally rehearsing new possibilities, we actually design a way for desired behaviors to emerge or become intensified.

A few minutes before the next time you make love, take a minute or two to think positively about your encounter—every detail of it. In your mind's eye, watch yourself reaching for your lover and welcoming his or her touch. See yourself enjoying the strokes, smells, or tastes. Feel your lover's tongue move across your lips in the special way that you enjoy. Enlist all of your imaginal senses as you develop your picture as completely as you can. Practicing visual rehearsal in a comfortable relaxing way mentally warms up your arousal pathways.

In the same way that spying some scrumptious chocolate éclairs on a waiter's pastry cart whets your appetite, focusing on an erotic thought, feeling, or image can actually "whet" your sexual appetite. It doesn't matter if the "real thing" doesn't follow suit. Your mental rehearsal gets your blood pumping more and your adrenaline surging. It's a kind of sexual aerobics of the mind that *you* can choose to intensify.

By modifying your ways of thinking about yourself, your partner, and your capacity for loving intimacy, you will demonstrate how easy it is to change an ordinary sexual encounter into an extraordinary one.

CHAPTER 2

CHANGE MY WHAT?

When our inner situation is not made conscious,
it appears outside as fate.

—C. G. JUNG

Change isn't easy. If it were, there wouldn't be so many dissatisfied people. Think about your own situation. You may know that it would be good to start exercising, or stop smoking, or count to ten before losing your temper, but you don't. Why not? Years ago one of my supervisors told me that asking "why" is as effective as stopping a centipede by pulling off one of its legs. Why? Because merely answering the "why" question generally leaves us with a list of excuses that block change.

Couples often come to my office armed with a list of explanations that justify "why" they're so unhappy: "He's afraid to commit," "I'm a woman who loves too much," "She won't reach out because she's afraid of rejection," "I never saw affection expressed between my parents," and so on. It's typical for them to present their explanations or separate blaming perspectives as if I were a judge who would hand down a decision as to who's at fault. Many secretly long to be vindicated and hope the expert will agree that the *other* one must change.

I've found that explanations and psychological labels can provide excuses for staying the same. While there's a certain comfort in naming a problem, merely announcing, "I'm commitment-phobic" or "I have the Peter Pan syndrome," doesn't improve sex. Improvement happens when you learn to think differently about the same problem and take some action. Couples tell me that they feel it's risky to modify their sexual approach: "I know what I have now. If I try something new, I might lose it all." I tell them although there can be no change without risk, there is greater risk in making no change. In my workshops and therapy practice, I've discovered that the couples who are the most successful in learning to have extraordinary sex share two important qualities: first, they are puzzled or confused about something; second, they're motivated to make a change in themselves.

THE IMPORTANCE OF CULTIVATING CONFUSION

Have you ever argued with someone who is perfectly confident that his or her position is the *only* position? Frustrating, isn't it? If you're certain that you have the correct viewpoint, you've left no room for discussion or negotiation. Allowing yourself to be confused about an issue can be freeing. It gives you permission to look at it from different angles. Of course, it's natural to resist other explanations. It takes courage to listen to your partner and hear what they're saying. It takes courage to rethink your "truth."

Have you ever noticed how little listening actually occurs during an argument? Each partner desperately wants to be heard—that's what often triggers the frustration and raised voices.

Think about your own relationship. How do you disagree about something as trivial as the color scheme of the bathroom or whether to invite an annoying relative for a weekend? Do you listen attentively to what your lover has to say or do you make your case as convincingly as possible? The second approach can turn a minor disagreement into a formidable battle of wills.

One way to stop the struggle and strengthen intimacy is to *cultivate confusion* by *enabling empathy*. Say things like "Please help me understand how you see it that way" or "How did you come to that conclusion?" or "I'd really like to understand how you feel." Too many couples assume that they already know how the other person feels, so they don't bother asking.

The next time you find yourself hotly defending your point of view, *stop and really listen* to your partner. Take a breath before you make your point and try to see things from their perspective. You'll be amazed at how this one technique heightens your intimacy.

When it comes to sex, there's no "right" way or "wrong" way to do it, as long as no one is being injured. Yet, my guess is if we had a microphone planted in the bedrooms of couples, we'd have evidence of a range of struggles—overt and covert—reflecting their natural differences, and the difficulty negotiating so both partners feel heard.

Jim and Joan, married for eight years, used to argue endlessly about Joan's insistence that they only make love in the light. She could have wonderful orgasms as long as there was some light on in the room. Even a closet light would do. At first Jim found this to be fun. Looking at Joan's body was a real turn-on. But once in a while he longed for a "quickie in the dark." When they argued Jim called Joan "rigid," "inflexible," "controlling," and blamed her for taking the spontaneity out of sex. Joan would say that Jim was the one who was controlling, and this was just something she needed. Period. Jim fumed and never backed off long enough to give Joan the space to reveal her secret. The more he blamed, the more she defended herself.

One day Jim tried a different approach. Instead of lashing out, he decided to enable empathy by cultivating confusion. He selected a time when they were both relaxed and asked Joan to help him understand how this pattern started. Joan's eyes filled with tears and she broke down in sobs. As a young teenager she had been sexually molested by her uncle. Being able to see her husband's face when they make love reminds her that she is safe in his arms.

Joan's explanation literally put a new "light" on the entire problem. Jim no longer felt that his wife's preferences were arbitrary, and stopped pushing her in ways that made her feel more unsafe. And what do you think happened to Joan? As Jim worked to enable empathy, she felt more relaxed, affirmed, and willing to stretch her comfort level by experimenting with lovemaking at dusk and then gradually decreasing the lighting even further. The last time I spoke with them Joan excitedly announced to me that she had initiated sex in the middle of the night and it was "unbelievably freeing!" Her husband's patience helped her finally bury some old skeletons from her past.

Wanting "Things" to Change Isn't Enough

"Of course I want 'things' to change," complained Marilyn. She and Tyler were soon to be married and he "wasn't able to have an erection when it was time for intercourse." He had been evaluated by a urologist, who determined that there was no physical problem. "Coming to a sex therapist is our last hope," she emphatically announced. "Our sex life sucks!"

Marilyn, a television news editor, was very articulate as she described Tyler's problem in excruciating detail while he sat transfixed and red-faced. "Tyler isn't very experienced sexually," she continued, "and I'm at my wit's end." I had the distinct feeling that I was watching an interaction between a critical mother and her embarrassed adolescent son. I began to wonder how this mirrored the rest of their relationship.

Tyler, a quality-control engineer for a large company, allowed Marilyn to talk for him as he squirmed in his seat. When he did speak, his tone was apologetic. "It's been really hard on Marilyn, she's put up with a lot. As soon as things get hot and heavy she puts in her diaphragm and I just lose it!"

And did Marilyn think she was contributing to this problem in any way? Not really. "I love Tyler and do everything I can to turn him on, but it's *his* penis that's not working."

When I asked them to describe the last time they got together sexually, Marilyn offered the following:

"I started by going down on him in the car and he got really hard. We continued when we got home. He had a good erection right up to the time he was going to put it inside of me." When I commented that she seemed to be keeping close tabs on the hardness of Tyler's penis, she said, "Sure, I'm worried it's going to deflate at the wrong time."

And what about Tyler—did he know Marilyn was noticing the firmness of his penis? "Well, sure, I guess we're both watching it. It's not easy to have intercourse with a limp one." He laughed nervously.

When I spoke to Tyler individually, he revealed how pressured he felt by Marilyn. Her practice of giving him oral sex in the car feels like a "test" to him, but she seems to like it, so he doesn't refuse. Actually, all of sex seems like a test—a test that he usually fails. With a little more exploration, Tyler described his history of performance anxiety in school and his unsuccessful efforts to please his critical mother by getting good grades. Marilyn was a little like her, he admitted reluctantly. Ideally, he'd prefer to go more slowly and take more time touching her, but he senses her impatience to have intercourse. He'd like to tell her to back off, but worries that he'll hurt her feelings. So he just tries hard and hopes "things" will work out. Of course, the harder he tries, the softer his penis gets.

And what was Marilyn so angry about? Further sessions with her revealed a disappointment with men that started when her father left her when she was four. That traumatic event, and other events, had led to her becoming extremely self-reliant and disinclined to trust the men in her life.

This is a classic example of two people who want "things" changed without understanding how each of them keeps the problem going. Each of them is struggling with unresolved issues from the past that continue to repeat themselves in a variety of ways.

Patterns of behavior aren't easy to change—but it can be done. First there must be a willingness to change and an ability to look closely and honestly at yourself. Unless you take responsibility for reexamining your past, exposure to parental conflict, confusing messages about intimacy and sexuality, or unsuccessful attempts to please or be recognized by a parent will more than likely surface in your own love relationship.

But don't conclude that you're destined to repeat the mistakes of your history. By recognizing how your earlier experiences affect your current love choices, you can learn different responses.

Consider the following areas as you think about your own background, then begin a discussion with your special someone in a relaxed and nonjudgmental way:

1. Of your parents or caretakers, who was more dominant and who was more submissive? Which role did you assume? Which role did you marry?

2. How were you treated by your parents? Did you feel valued and respected? Could you share your private feelings with them? Did you feel you could trust them?

3. What made you feel hurt and angry at home? Think of some examples. How did you deal with your hurt? Did you retreat to your room, use drugs/alcohol, verbalize your anger, deny your feelings?

4. If you had a magic wand, what is the one thing you would have changed about your past?

Use these questions as a guide for sharing and enabling empathy. Take as much time as you need to discuss these areas with your partner. Practice attentive listening without interruptions. End the session by expressing caring to one another in some nonverbal way.

In therapy, Marilyn learned to stop blaming Tyler and Tyler learned to stop blaming himself. Instead he began to assert himself sexually and let Marilyn know about his wishes and timing. As Tyler asserted himself, Marilyn felt less pressure to orchestrate their entire sexual encounter. With practice, she learned to relinquish control and the responsibility for making sex "perfect." Both of them paid less attention to the hardness of Tyler's penis and focused more on their intimacy. It wasn't long before sex became better than they ever imagined it could be. They got back into the groove of feeling turned on from head to toe. But most important of all, they felt like soul mates again.

PART 2

DISCOVERING YOUR SEXUAL STYLE

"We never leave each other. When does your mouth say goodbye to your heart?"

—MARY TALL MOUNTAIN

First Kiss

I grew up in the sixties when nice girls didn't have intercourse or even get naked with their boyfriends. We didn't do the *nasty,* but we sure fogged up lots of car windows making out. My first love, Bill, had a green Ford Fairlane and we'd neck for hours until the shine of a policeman's flashlight dampened our ardor. I'd say we were experts at kissing back then. All kinds of kissing. Passionate, wet, playful, sexy, light, warm, and tender. As Johnny Mathis serenaded us, we'd reach erotic heights fully clothed.

Of course, there *were* girls that "went all the way," like Mo DiAngelo. Her name and phone number were whispered in the locker rooms. Mo wore white lipstick and had huge teased hair. She'd typically arrive late to French class in order to make an entrance. Mr. Renault's public censure of her conduct seemed to encourage her lateness all the more. All male eyes were transfixed by her tight sweater and short leather skirt. I liked Mo. I think I felt sorry for her. Her dad used to beat her and her mother. After her mom and dad divorced when she was nine, Mo rarely saw her mom, who worked as a cocktail waitress and brought home an assortment of men. Mo told me that she'd sometimes hear them having sex in the next room. The sounds were scary, but intriguing at the same time. She used to tell me how she'd listen for a while and then pull a pillow over her head to muffle the sounds. Mo wanted what we all want. Love. She just didn't know how to get it.

My friends talked a lot about sex. I remember a quiz we took called the Purity Test. You'd get a number for kissing, French-kissing, petting above the waist, below the waist, and so on. The total score would tell you how pure you were. I was rated "pure as the driven snow." I would have been "hot to trot" if only I French-kissed. In those days, the thought of French-kissing was unappealing to me. My first teen crush, Alan Singer, broke up with me because I wouldn't French-kiss him. I kept my teeth tightly shut and although he'd try in vain to pry them apart with his tongue, he never succeeded. I wrote him a letter with these closing remarks: "Someday you'll realize that sex isn't everything, it's a trusting relationship that's important." Even then, I knew intuitively that sex wasn't something to be casually shared; it was a special experience that included love and commitment. It's not surprising that I've spent most of my adult life conveying that message. Sex is more than physical release. Without the vital connection it's very *ordinary*.

Let your mind drift back to your own early crushes—necking in the back seat of that Mustang convertible, or kissing passionately on the beach after the senior prom or finding a few minutes in your boyfriend's rec room for some stolen pleasures. How easily the feelings return—the heat, the stirrings, and sweet memories. Putting his name and initials everywhere— scrawled on the bathroom walls, carved on trees, doodled on your school notebooks. Ah, love! It seemed so simple then.

I'm sure I fell in love with my husband, Rob, with our first kiss. My universe exploded when he leaned over the table and kissed me softly and sensuously. His lips brushed against mine, lingering long enough to stir my soul. Like Sleeping Beauty, I was awakened by love. I still feel tingly when I think about it. What made the kiss so special? I know it wasn't just his kiss. It was his whole focus on me. We were fully present for each other. The kissed lasted about six seconds, but felt like an eternity. I remember think- ing that I could go on endlessly, and when he looked at me in that unforget- table way, I swear I saw God in his penetrating blue eyes.

Why is first love so potent and how can we recapture it? It's really very simple. When lovers first meet, they think about each other, long for each other, focus on each other, and show caring for each other in dozens of little ways. When they touch, they don't do so absentmindedly while listening to the monologue of late-night television, they touch with all of their senses in high gear, actively tasting and absorbing each other's fragrance. It doesn't take much time to recapture passion—it only takes a willingness to immerse yourself in one another once again.

Most of us have accepted the notion that burning lustful passion comes to an end somewhere in the first year of marriage. For some, it ends even sooner. The skeptic, romantic, and clinician in me all believe this isn't true. I'm convinced that passion can get stronger over the years, as long as the connection between the two partners is nourished by care and attention.

Now, many years since our first kiss, I confess that there are times when I forget to remember the magic. I take him for granted, think there will always be time to make love tomorrow, and get swept up in my too busy life. Even a sex therapist can get lost in daily pressures and multiple responsibilities and feel like there's too little time or energy for love. But when I take just a moment to pause and remember, I can feel the first brush of his lips against mine as if it were yesterday.

"But he's not the same man I fell in love with," you might protest. "I try to be loving, but he's just not interested." What happens to the attraction of those early days? The next chapter will explore that question and suggest some answers.

CHAPTER 3

THE ATTRACTION OF COMPLETENESS

The meeting of two personalities is like the contact
of two chemical substances, if there is any reaction,
both are transformed.

—C. G. JUNG

According to Native Americans, each masculine side carries a feminine component, and each feminine side carries a masculine component. The ancient Greeks thought that lovers were like two halves of a puzzle—each incomplete without the other. Jung referred to these opposites as archetypes, dividing them into the anima and the animus. In Plato's *Symposium,* Aristophanes spoke of the complete human being containing masculine and feminine attributes in one body. This being was represented by a circle having four arms, four legs, one head, and two faces looking in opposite directions. In some marriage ceremonies, the ritual that symbolizes two individuals becoming one is the lighting of the unity candle. The couple lights one candle to represent their new union and then blows out their individual flames.

Relationships promise eternal fulfillment and completeness. Each person bestows or *projects* on the other positive images or expectations for an ideal partnership that will be *everlasting.* These projections are typically unconscious wishes that hold enormous amounts of information about qualities that are underdeveloped or desired in their partner or in themselves. Passion is dampened by disillusion when projections inevitably fall short of reality.

As the "ideal" lover reveals his human frailties, the first blush of disenchantment appears. The rosy glow of the "ideal" picture-perfect relationship fades. It's not unusual to feel like the very fabric of the union has been altered and you've made some horrible mistake. Now, instead of feeling complete or more whole with your special someone, you feel uneasy, dissatisfied, or strangely deceived.

This uneasiness is the first sign of the erosion of early intimacy. It may be expressed through blame, avoidance, criticism, or infidelity, as the trust, connection, and sexual excitement in the relationship spiral downward. Couples have told me repeatedly that this was the moment they identified as the "end of the honeymoon."

MAKING THE UNCONSCIOUS CONSCIOUS

One of the prime reasons relationships fail, again and again, is that *we are unknowingly attracted to and fall in love with an image of what is lacking in ourselves.* Until the unconscious factors motivating you to select a mate become conscious, this pattern is likely to repeat itself. Let me give you an example of this process:

Bethany couldn't believe she had done it again! Marriage number two was coming to an end just in time for her thirty-third birthday. Always considered attractive and with countless guys drawn to her beautiful face and great brain, she had met and married her first husband during her sophomore year at Stanford when they were only nineteen. She had thought he was perfect, "Tall, educated, a nice guy from the right family."

Bethany didn't have very many happy childhood memories. She was an only child of seven years old when her father died of a heart attack. Consequently, Mom provided for the family by working several unskilled jobs, and Grandma took care of her after school. All the women in her family were critical and controlling, and Bethany could never please any of them. Grandpa was a quiet man who didn't stand up to Grandma's intense verbal tirades. He comforted himself with several daily shots of whiskey and a good cigar.

For as long as she could remember, Bethany felt profoundly alone and unloved. Is it any wonder that she rushed into the safety of Raymond's arms the first time he proposed marriage? Nine years later, however, after two children and three moves with Raymond's company, she found herself with a quiet, emotionally unavailable man not unlike her grandfather, while she had taken on the role of a critical castrating female like her mother and grandmother.

Bethany fell in love with husband number two before she divorced Ray. Patrick, twenty-eight, was their landscaper and had never been married. One hot summer day, she caught a glimpse of his tanned body through the dining-room window. He had removed his shirt while mowing her lawn and the sight of his muscled physique took her breath away. It was such a contrast to Ray's pale thin frame. Sex with Ray had been dry and unimaginative. She never orgasmed and he never noticed. Bethany decided Patrick was different: a real man—powerful in a homespun workingman kind of way. She was drawn to his simplicity and sheer animal magnetism.

Ray's financial talents as a CPA had built them a nice nest egg, but Ray lacked passion. And what was marriage without passion? Patrick was an incredible lover and gave her the best oral sex on the planet. She experienced her first orgasm with him and it was transcendent. She was certain they were soul mates. She decided to leave her home, two children, and Mercedes 500SL to lie in Patrick's strong arms.

Not long after their six-month whirlwind romance, her divorce from Raymond was finalized and she married Patrick. But only three years later, Bethany was once again filing for divorce. She accused Patrick of being uneducated and boring. For her, his appealing simplicity had rapidly faded into mediocrity.

Now she finds herself, once again, attracted to what she believes is the "perfect man." Colin is an artist and a college professor who combines the intelligence of Raymond and the simple forthright nature of Patrick. But sensing she might be heading down the same dead-end path, she came to me to get some therapy before leaping into marriage number three.

HOW TO NOT MARRY THE SAME PERSON OVER AND OVER

Bethany's case illustrates a woman who unwittingly marries the *same* man in different forms over and over again. Although each husband is different in appearance, socioeconomic background, and countless other ways, they possess a similar essence that attracts her to them magnetically. What Bethany discovered in therapy is that she falls in love with men who have the qualities she's seeking in herself.

She married Raymond because she needed a family, love, a noncritical partner (unlike her family of origin), and financial security. She married Patrick because he represented passion, power, and the masculine protection that was absent in her father and passive grandfather.

The pull toward complementarity and wholeness explains much of the attraction in couples. Each individual is drawn to the person who enhances his or her sense of self. "He completes me," she might say. He might confess that he feels more whole with her and laughingly refer to her as "my better half." But you can't marry someone else to *complete* yourself. To the extent that attraction is based on the fulfillment of something that is lacking in ourselves, we will be continually disappointed. No one person can make up for our own shortcomings. If we are, in fact, falling in love with a missing piece of ourselves, then as the reality of our partner's humanness reveals itself, the sparkle of love fades and we become faced with the incompleteness within ourselves.

DISCOVERING YOUR ATTRACTION HOOKS

So how do we find our way out of this dilemma?

1. THE FIRST STEP IS TO IDENTIFY YOUR "ATTRACTION HOOKS"

Attraction hooks are usually areas outside of our conscious awareness that grab us and hook us before we know we're being hooked. Try this exercise. List all the lovers that you've been attracted to and *find* the common denominators. Don't immediately say that they're all so different. They're not. There are some unifying qualities that are eluding you. If Tom is quiet, and Dick is insensitive, and Harry is self-absorbed, perhaps they are all men who have difficulty expressing love. Search for the common thread and then ask yourself, "What do I *really* get from these partners? How do they complete me?"

2. SEE YOUR PARTNER AS HE REALLY IS AND *NOT* AS YOU WISH HIM TO BE

Idealization is a natural part of falling in love. During your first major couple's conflict, the "deep-set blue eyes" you used to adore become "beady little eyes," and the "strong nose" you admired is transformed into an "ugly protruding proboscis." How does this happen? Could we have been incorrect about our lover's appeal? Hardly. But the poets were right when they wrote that love is blind and it colors many of our senses and perspectives.

If you dare, ask a friend you really trust to give you an objective opinion of your Mr. or Ms. right. Ironically, our parents often see the problems on the horizon long before we do. In cultures where marriages are arranged, couples don't fare so badly. Don't get me wrong, I'm not suggesting we forgo love in favor of a more "sensible" choice. What I'm proposing is that we temper unbridled idealism with a healthy dose of reality.

Instead of spending hours *only* listing his or her virtues, make an equally long list of your partner's "growing edges." If you can't find them, you're not looking hard enough. Love resists careful scrutiny, so don't be lulled into believing you're the only one who has truly found perfection. Walking into romance with your eyes wide open will minimize the possibility of being blindsided down the road. How many times have you foolishly dismissed warnings from friends or your lover's exes, thinking, "They're just jealous," or "He'd never cheat *on me*—I'm different." Identifying and understanding your lover's limitations is a worthwhile challenge.

3. KNOW *YOURSELF* BETTER THROUGH YOUR PARTNER

After identifying your partner's predominant strengths and limitations, ask yourself whether those qualities are somehow wanting in yourself. There are numerous reasons we select our life mate and many of them defy logic. Remember, the key to a fulfilling relationship is an accurate understanding of who *we* are.

So now that you've discovered your fair maiden or knight in shining armor isn't all you had fantasized, what are you prepared to do? Are you ready to learn to be a bit more like your lover or do you plan to change him or her? If you picked the latter, be prepared for disaster. The quest to change him or her back to what you thought they were when you met is rarely successful.

There's nothing wrong with falling in love with someone who is different from you. In fact, opposites *can* attract. Fortunately, each time we select a partner, we have an opportunity to know ourselves better. For instance, if you tend to be passive and are continually attracted to overly controlling partners, perhaps you have to reexamine the power dynamics in your own background. Were there conflicts surrounding who was in charge? Or if you're work-driven and have difficulty relaxing, you may find yourself being drawn to spontaneous fun-loving types who despise list making and are poor organizers. These selections may be great in the short run, but can you go the distance with them?

By understanding what qualities you're attracted to, you are given a unique opportunity to see what's lacking in yourself. Once you've identified the parts of yourself that you had expected the other person to provide, instead of struggling to change your lover, you can learn from them and develop a more varied and richly textured *self*.

In Shel Silverstein's children's fable *The Missing Piece Meets the Big O*, he writes:

> "THE MISSING PIECE SAT ALONE WAITING FOR
> SOMEONE TO COME ALONG AND TAKE IT
> SOMEWHERE. . . ." THROUGH ITS JOURNEY IT
> DISCOVERED THAT AS ITS SHAPE BEGAN TO CHANGE, IT
> CONTAINED ALL THAT IT WAS SEARCHING FOR.

Some people may prefer to search endlessly until they find the perfect mate to supply their missing piece. Change carries with it a degree of risk, sacrifice, and uncertainty. But with the proper focus, each of us can achieve wholeness and independence within ourselves and the capacity to share in a mature, infinitely passionate relationship.

The key to wholeness is learning to develop flexibility and balance within ourselves and with our partner.

4. MAKE THE CHOICE TO FACE THIS *TOGETHER*

There's no question that a change in one person will alter the balance of the unspoken relationship contract. One of you can get the process going, but the other will undoubtedly be affected. As in the cooperation between two playmates on a seesaw, each partner has to learn how to adjust to the other's actions.

We've all heard of marriages that break apart because one of the partners claims he or she just "outgrew" the other. To ensure a dynamic and deepening intimacy, *both* partners must be invested in self-exploration and self-change.

No living entity can stay static and survive. Healthy relationships are no different. For intimate partnerships to remain vital over the years, they must contain mechanisms to accommodate a wide spectrum of changes—changes associated with aging, parenting, career responsibilities, illness, and the like. While it's true that each change destabilizes the status quo, it also offers an opportunity for restabilization at a more intimate level.

5. GETTING BEYOND "GOOD COP/BAD COP"

I'm always amazed at how many people would like me to "fix" one of the partners who has the supposed "sexual problem." She might call and say, "My husband doesn't want to come in. Couldn't you please just see me alone—*I'm the one with the problem.*" Assuming that there's no physical or traumatic basis for the dysfunction, sexual difficulties usually arise within the context of a relationship. Both partners are part of the problem and both must be part of the solution. To get beyond the blaming stance, try the following:

• *Agree from the start that* he's *not the problem, and* you're *not the problem—it's the* relationship *that could benefit from repair or revitalization.* After all, your relationship is a product of both of your efforts and both of you must work on it together. Don't just give lip service to this principle. It's important that you share in the responsibility of this journey from the start.

• *Think of your partner as an expert and your private tutor.* For instance, instead of thinking of him as a lazy so-and-so who is difficult to pry away from the television remote control, think of him as a *relaxation expert. Cultivate confusion:* Isn't it odd that somehow, in the midst of a zillion household tasks, he doesn't feel driven by overwhelming guilt or anxiety to do any of them! How does he do that? Don't you think you could benefit from a touch of his talent? Don't immediately say, "Oh, great, we'll both sit on the couch and no one will do anything!" Try to recognize that that's just your highly organized self getting very uncomfortable. Remember, if he has agreed to face this journey of self-exploration with you, he will also be working to learn to be a bit more like you and to understand how he can develop more of his own organizational expertise.

• *Drop the tendency to want to prove your way is the best way* long enough to face what *you* get out of being with him. Instead of thinking of him as overly cautious and pushing him to "let go," ask yourself, "What's my reason for selecting a cautious partner?" "How does he stabilize or complement me?" Is there something about caution you're puzzled about and could master for yourself? Ask him to teach you how he learned to be that way.

GOING FORWARD

If you both have considered why you fell in love with each other, you've probably remembered some of the magic of the first kiss. If you're clear on why you've become somewhat disenchanted with each other (and can articulate it in a nonblaming way), you've gone far toward enhancing your own maturity and the ultimate strengthening of your bond. If you've discovered areas for increasing your own sense of completeness, you have taken on the most important task of all—making the unconscious conscious and facing yourself with curiosity, courage, and the determination to change things for the better.

In the next chapter, we'll talk about how partners can develop the mental flexibility to access a range of exciting possibilities.

FLEXIBILITY: THE KEY TO EXTRAORDINARY SEX

The world is a beautiful place
to be born
if you don't mind happiness
not always being
so very much fun
if you don't mind a touch of hell
now and then
just when everything is fine
because even in heaven
they don't sing
all the time

—L. FERLINGHETTI, PICTURES OF THE GONE WORLD

If I had to point to the main goal of my Extraordinary Sex program, it would be to heighten *flexibility*. You might be surprised by that answer and wonder, "Other than being a contortionist and being able to assume a number of exotic positions, what does flexibility have to do with sex?" I'm not talking about the flexibility of your body (although that's certainly a plus), I'm referring to another kind of flexibility—the mental flexibility that allows you to tap into a range of possibilities.

Whether it's a young sapling bending in the breeze and stretching toward the sun, or a toddler's wide-eyed nonjudgmental curiosity, flexibility is critical to survival. We each enter the world inheriting a particular genetic template, but our choices are limitless. Have you ever wondered how your life would be different if you hadn't met your future husband in the bakery line and accepted his invitation for a cup of coffee? And what if you went to medical school instead of taking that job in your father's business? With each choice, we set an infinite number of variables into motion that refine our directions and shape our paths.

Over time, in response to countless developmental challenges, a preferred personality style emerges. As it becomes more fixed and defined, flexibility is compromised.

THE IMPORTANCE OF FLEXIBILITY

There's a familiar saying: "If all you have is a hammer, you'll treat everything like it's a nail." Being a one-trick pony limits your options. Whether we're talking about the physical flexibility necessary for a limber body or the capacity to stretch our thinking, flexibility is essential to good health and to great sex. Regardless of the situation, couples trapped in inflexibility relate in predictable ways that can be smothering, controlling, evasive, or distancing. Typical patterns emerge in their interactions which result in sexual relationships that are dull and unimaginative. There's a punch line to a joke that makes this point well: a long-married car salesman is overheard telling a colleague who's about to order lunch, "Don't get me a fish sandwich, Andy. On Fridays I can always count on two things . . . a fish dinner and sex in the missionary position."

When sexual flexibility is low, options are not considered, and it's difficult to include alternative styles. Invariably, frustrations mount—along with anxiety—as we tend to react instead of proact. We become unwittingly locked into predictable ways of thinking and doing that limit the freshness and appeal of sexual encounters.

Flexibility and balance make good sense physically, emotionally, *and* sexually. When it comes to learning to be more sexually flexible, your relationship is the classroom. With the right motivation you can discover a range of options that will heighten your flexibility *and* your sexual passion.

THE PARTNER DIMENSION

The age-old questions are: How can passion just fizzle out? Where does it go? How do we get it back? When you first meet your special someone, you're usually on your best behavior—and you're also much more flexible. People are much more willing to try a variety of new behaviors while dating. If he offers you some of his escargot on your first date, chances are you'll take a little taste even though the idea of eating snails makes you gag.

Dating offers an environment for adventuresome experimentation that continues throughout the enchantment period. This is the phase of early intimacy that Harriet Goldhor Lerner, in her book *The Dance of Intimacy,* calls the "Velcro stage of relationships." I've always loved that phrase because it describes how couples are powerfully attracted and "locked" together at their genitals. There's an exciting turbulence to this phase that is addictive. It's the rush of adrenaline we feel when new lovers stir, mix, and transform each other. The uncertainty of whether you'll blend, compete, or augment is part of the initial excitement. As soon as things settle into a more permanent arrangement, a more predictable sexual style emerges and the thrill subsides.

WHEN COMMITMENT REPLACES ENCHANTMENT

As commitment replaces enchantment, we begin to confront the fallacy of our idealizing projections. What emerges is the "reality" behind our wished-for ideal partner. As our new husband or wife falls from his or her pedestal of imagined perfection, we are often rudely awakened from the phase of enchantment.

Commitment often creates a climate of reduced motivation for experimentation and reduced flexibility in approach. After all, the chase is over. The partners imperceptibly recalibrate themselves toward their natural comfort zone. After the wedding vows are shared there's an almost audible exhale—"Now I can *finally* be myself!" Many couples actually date the decline of sexual heat to their wedding night, complaining, "Sex was so steamy before the honeymoon and then it just fizzled out!" There's a belief that after the wedding there's no need to try so hard to please or impress. The husband and wife assume they can now express themselves without fear of censure or disapproval. As the commitment phase evolves, we become more fixed in our preferred sexual styles and passion seems to evaporate.

BECOMING MORE FLEXIBLE TO ENHANCE YOUR PASSION

Diane and Bert fought every weekend like clockwork. During the week, Bert was usually on the road selling insurance. After five days without him, Diane wanted "contact." So as soon as he walked through the door, she would begin what Bert calls her "list of grievances." But Diane thought she was just communicating and reconnecting. Unfortunately, the more she kept at Bert, the more trapped he felt. He'd look for any excuse to escape— mow the lawn, weed the yard, sweep the garage, make a bank deposit at the locate ATM—it didn't matter. As you'd expect, the more he avoided, the more she pursued. A classic dynamic with a negative outcome.

This pattern repeated itself in the bedroom. Diane frequently initiated sex and Bert was often "too tired." So to get him in the mood, she'd give him oral sex. Although Bert enjoyed it, he also felt manipulated. Bert had trouble saying "no" because he was afraid that Diane wouldn't take "no" for an answer.

Diane and Bert were stuck. After a number of discussions, they came to the conclusion that their sexual relationship needed help. Diane called me and set up an appointment for them both. She wanted an appointment "immediately" and sounded upset when I wasn't able to fit her into my schedule that same day. As our therapy progressed, the major focus in treatment for her became apparent—becoming more patient and sensitive to the limits of others.

Bert's goal was different. He was too tolerant. He needed to work on asserting himself and his wishes more directly. Historically he had been afraid of disapproval or making waves, but he came to recognize how this fear had locked him into a self-denying pattern. In one of our sessions, after mustering up his courage, he said, "I'd like to be clearer with you, Diane, but I don't want to hurt your feelings." At that, Diane looked surprised. She had no idea that he had been holding back on *her* account. "I may not like everything you have to say, Bert, but I'd really like the opportunity to hear you—I want us to be closer and I promise to try to be less headstrong." They smiled at each other as Bert took her hand.

Bert told Diane he needed to decompress when he comes home from work and wanted thirty minutes of *silence*. He then promised to give Diane a *full hour* of rapt attention. This worked beautifully for them.

Now that Bert was no longer suppressing his feelings and avoiding disagreement, he could begin to look for opportunities to express himself. As he asserted himself more, he felt more loving and interested in reaching out sexually.

Since he rarely had shared his desires or feelings with her, Diane was unaware of the depth of Bert's discomfort. She vowed to accept his feelings and not argue him out of them. This wasn't easy for her, since she had been on her college debating team. This relatively simple adjustment made Bert feel empowered and satisfied Diane's need to connect more intimately.

Another way of stating this is that Diane, an expert in assertion, learned patience, and Bert, an expert in patience, learned assertion. By taking responsibility for modifying their individual emotional styles, their flexibility as a couple expanded as well.

When couples are stuck in a negative inflexible pattern, the way out is simply *to change something*. Granted, this is easier said than done. Patterns are often firmly entrenched and resistant to change. Nevertheless, try something new. It doesn't have to be a big change. It can be something as easy as smiling at your partner when he comes home and giving him a warm kiss instead of launching into a vivid description of how your boss is driving you crazy. It's like getting the first jelly bean out of a jar—after the initial one is dislodged the rest come pouring out!

Although couples lull themselves into thinking the major challenge is over once they're wed, nothing could be further from the truth. Keeping sex fresh is an exciting ongoing challenge—and it depends on a willingness to let go of the tried-and-true standards, stretch your security zone, and venture into less familiar, often uncharted territory. Remember, the more you increase your flexibility, the wider your potential sexual repertoire.

In the next chapter you'll see how sexual styles develop, how they go wrong, and how they can be modified.

CHAPTER 5

❧

SEXUAL STYLES

*Only in relationships can you know yourself, not in abstraction
and certainly not in isolation.*

—J. KRISHNAMURTI

We're all creatures of habit. Every human being expresses certain patterns, redundancies, or tendencies in the ways they've learned to think, feel, and behave. Just think about it, every day we brush our teeth the same way, towel off the same way, and drive to work the same way. In terms of our personalities, we find ourselves lecturing our kids in the same way we were lectured (and *promised* ourselves we'd never do). These response patterns were formed early on and generally become more fixed as we age. Without arguing the question of nature or nurture (because they're both important), we have learned how to relate in a style that's comfortable for us. Once we find that style, we use it over and over again. Even when it doesn't work very well.

How do these styles develop? They come about as adaptations to life's challenges, including the ability to trust ourselves and someone else, becoming independent and interdependent, and finding security, satisfying love, and sexual intimacy among others.

For instance, Kelsey, twenty-four, was raised in a nontraditional family. She referred to her parents as "perennial hippies" unwilling to face the realities of adulthood. Her father believed that fidelity was an affectation and made no excuses for his numerous open "affairs." Her mom was equally free with whom she decided to have sex and both smoked marijuana to "relax."

When Kelsey was eight, her father built an addition onto their modest home, where he opened a pottery studio. Mom was also a potter specializing in raku glazes. Although many of her parents' friends had gotten divorced, Kelsey's parents believed they had found a "style" that worked for them. Monetary security never motivated the Bakers; consequently there were some lean times. It wasn't unusual for creditors to call at all hours of the night. Dad told her to keep the window shades down in case the IRS should stop by unannounced. Although there was a part of Kelsey that admired the ostensibly free artisan lifestyle, she was constantly worried that their home would be foreclosed against or that Dad would be carted off to debtors' prison.

So what career did Kelsey choose? She majored in economics and minored in political science. Her boyfriend, Randy, a conservative Republican from a strict Roman Catholic background, is a high-powered bond trader in New York City. In terms of intimacy, they're both intensely energetic and determined to make their relationship a success—in the *traditional* way. Given Kelsey's background, one might say she moved to the opposite end of the spectrum to provide for her own emotional security. This was her way of adapting to life's challenges.

Styles can vary in different contexts. You may present one particular style on the job, another as a parent, and a third in your love relationships or you may express consistency throughout. For example, you might be an authoritarian leader on the job, but express a more laissez-faire attitude with your family.

When there is a rigidity in one's style, it can create interpersonal discord. What if you'll only consider making love when you're both fresh from the shower, whereas your lover enjoys an occasional sweaty romp? Or you thrive on sexual experimentation, but your partner is Mr. Conservative with the motto "If it ain't broke, why fix it?"

Stylistic differences are not problematic in and of themselves; in fact, they can be quite energizing. What becomes problematic is when we cling to our views although they have proven to be outmoded.

In Chapter 8 you'll have the opportunity to discover your predominant sexual style and the style of your partner, identify the relationship "fits" and "misfits," and see how you can improve your own sexual flexibility and the flexibility of your relationship.

SEXUAL ENERGIZERS, STABILIZERS, WORKERS, AND PLAYERS

Have you ever heard about how one lover wears himself out sexually—doing cartwheels in bed to please his partner, while the other just lies there, waiting to be turned on? What's going on here? How do these styles evolve and what attracts these couples to each other?

Over the course of taking thousands of sex histories and observing countless couples' interactions, I have identified four principal styles of sexual functioning. I call them: *Sexual Energizers, Sexual Stabilizers, Sexual Workers,* and *Sexual Players.* Each of us can identify our preferred sexual style in one or more of these categories. Imagine that the Energizer/Stabilizer and Worker/Player styles are located on opposite ends of intersecting poles. Some people are predominantly one style and may locate themselves on the extreme ends of the continuum, while others combine features of two or more styles and are closer to the intersection of the two poles.

When it comes to intimate relationships, it's not unusual for polar opposites, like an Energizer and a Stabilizer or a Worker and a Player, to get married or find themselves in a partnership of some kind. In evaluating your own sexual style and the style of your lover, don't fall into the trap of analyzing which style is more desirable. There is no perfect sexual style or perfect couple combination. Mates with similar styles can be as successful or unsuccessful as those with widely differing styles; each preference contributes to the balance of a relationship and contains certain strengths and limitations. As we know, opposites can complement one another.

As I mentioned earlier, when it comes to your sexual style and the style of your partner, *flexibility and balance are central to deepening intimacy.* When circumstances warrant it, the ability to access a wider behavioral repertoire by moving along the continuum from Energizer to Stabilizer or from Worker to Player is what keeps sex exciting and fresh year after year. When partners find themselves stuck in extreme stylistic positions, problems are not usually far off. Complaints of boredom, incompatibility, or irreconcilable differences usually suggest that partners have a low level of flexibility.

SEXUAL ENERGIZERS

Sexual Energizers are exciting lovers (if they choose to be). They can seduce the pants off of the most reserved lover and mesmerize him or her with their romantic charm. People who fall in love with a Sexual Energizer will often remark that they were swept off their feet and dazzled by his or her conversational ease and self-confidence. Sound great? Not always. What you might find out later about this sex partner is that when *you* orgasm, *he* takes a good deal (if not all) of the credit. Energizers are intense and powerful people magnets, but can also be quite self-absorbed. They're committed to being the best, most creative, or most passionate in whatever they do. Over time, when you make love to an Energizer you might feel like the supporting player to the star.

Making love with an Energizer male can be stressful because you know that even if you don't want an orgasm at that moment (and, yes, there are times when women don't), you had better go for it or *he'll* feel slighted. Partners of Energizers are often distracted by an awareness that his pleasure depends on the woman's sexual response. Generally women who find themselves faking orgasms are frequently paired with Sexual Energizers or Sexual Workers. They would rather lie to their partner than deal with their bruised ego. Even if you have an orgasm so powerful it rocks the bed, he'll still ask, "Was it good for you?" and you'll know he's wondering, "How was I?"

And let's not forget the Sexual Energizer woman who points to *your* erection as a measure of *her* sexual prowess (even if you happen to be secretly fantasizing about Sharon Stone the entire time). Sexual Energizers unintentionally steal the thunder of your sexual response by attributing your ecstasy to their exquisite technique.

Sexual Energizers can be strong-willed, emotional, and highly focused. Because of their competitive nature and high expectations, they can become anxious and have problems with erection or ejaculating quicker than they'd like, or female Energizers can complain of painful intercourse due to vaginal dryness. Moods may shift easily, and anger is rarely suppressed. Passion in all of its forms comes easily to them. There's never a dull moment if your Energizer partner is "in the mood." You never need to guess or ask about their feelings, because they'll always tell you (even when you'd prefer not to hear it).

Arguments can be foreplay for the Energizer: after all, aggression is one form of arousal. And by all means praise them after sex—just make sure it's sincere. At their best they can be exciting, frank, dynamic, and wild in bed; at their worst, they can be competitive, controlling, and pushy. Assertiveness is their forte. Unless you stand up to your Energizer partner, he or she can roll right over you.

SEXUAL STABILIZERS

And what about Sexual Stabilizers? They're the cooperative ones who don't want to rock the boat—the strong, sometimes silent types who express their power indirectly but undeniably. The Stabilizer supplies the ballast for the Energizer's hot-air balloon. Stabilizers are cautious, slow to anger and to forgive, and generally agreeable. When uncomfortable, they can get detached, cool, stubborn, and evasive. Because they have trouble identifying their own feelings and asserting themselves, it's difficult to read them emotionally. This is one of their power advantages. Instead of confronting you directly, Stabilizers express their anger *indirectly* by "forgetting" to do something, like get you a gift for your anniversary or pick up a carton of milk. Their sins are acts of omission, not commission. Apologies may be offered, but behaviors are harder to change.

Sexually, their technique can be predictable, with few surprises. When they find one position they like, they stick with it. Stabilizers don't crave constant variety or desire to try every posture in the *Kama Sutra*. For them, regularity is not boredom. In fact, they feel reassured by the predictability of sameness.

Stabilizers work tirelessly to give you an orgasm or a rock-hard erection, but have more trouble expressing their own pleasure. If you want your partner to moan and groan in delight, don't expect this from your Stabilizer mate. They may be having a great time—but it's difficult for them to let you know it. Stabilizers behave as if they're more interested in *your* pleasure than their own.

Sexual Stabilizers can be kind, generous, and nurturing. They are great supporters when they're not feeling threatened. When they're anxious, or feel painted into a corner, they can be difficult to budge. It's not unusual for a Stabilizer to bottle up anger for years and express it indirectly in the bedroom. An angry Stabilizer, female or male, who hasn't resolved their negativity may find themselves having difficulty reaching orgasm or ejaculating with their partner. The "make me orgasm" mood that gets enacted may challenge the Energizer's sexual stamina or creativity, but the Stabilizer is usually unaware of this dynamic. Although they often prevail in defeating their more outgoing partners, this is not intentionally hurtful.

When male Stabilizers experience sexual dysfunction, they may have difficulty getting and keeping erections or have difficulty with delayed or absent ejaculations. Female Stabilizers may report problems with sexual desire, feeling aroused, or having orgasms when they'd like them. Making love to a Sexual Stabilizer can make an Energizer feel like he's playing a game of Twenty Questions. Even a partner with boundless energy eventually grows tired of "doing all the work."

At their best, Sexual Stabilizers are wonderfully attentive lovers. They're interested in *your* pleasure and will bend over backward to please you. What they lack in imagination and spontaneity, they make up for in perseverance. They are unwavering in their love, usually easygoing (unless pushed beyond their breaking point), and well-intentioned. At their worst, they're stubborn, strong-willed, and lethargic.

HOW THINGS GO WRONG

Energizers and Stabilizers choose one another for a number of reasons, but many of these reasons are beyond their awareness. When Energizers and Stabilizers first fall in love, it can seem like a match made in heaven. Energizers need to feel important and Stabilizers enjoy making them feel that way. Some of these marriages do well, especially when each partner has the flexibility to modify his or her behavior. However, if they've selected one another to work out lingering issues from their own past, it's not long before problems emerge, including blaming, power struggles, and symptoms of sexual dysfunction.

When Stabilizers and Energizers come to see me because they have a sexual problem, it's the Energizer who usually makes the initial call and gets the Stabilizer to go along. Typically, what I hear in the first session is the Energizer blaming the Stabilizer, and the Stabilizer blaming herself or himself.

Relating to a Stabilizer partner may make you wonder where you stand. You feel insecure with him and that's *exactly* how *he* feels. The Stabilizer misinterprets suggestions from his Energizer partner as criticism or control tactics and often sees himself as a powerless victim. This perceptual flaw needs to be corrected. Stabilizers fear humiliation. They may have had a critical parent who could not be pleased, and they reenact this dynamic in their marriage over and over. By passively defeating their partner (while protesting they are doing their best) they undermine his or her authority without guilt. As you will learn later, the way to deal with your Stabilizer mate is to help him feel more powerful and confident sexually by setting clear expectations in a nonthreatening way. This is difficult to do when you're angry at him.

What kind of Energizer marries a conflicted Stabilizer? One with his own problems, of course. Energizers fear abandonment, in the same way Stabilizers fear rejection. If you're this kind of Energizer, you selected someone who will never leave you. By unwittingly eroding your partner's self-confidence through criticism and blame, you maintain your power position at the risk of diluted intimacy. By selecting a Stabilizer who has problems saying "no," Energizers are assured they'll never be left. After all, a person who can't assert certainly can't leave, can they?

Sex between an Energizer and a Stabilizer can go smoothly as long as everyone is comfortable with their respective roles. As soon as an Energizer changes the rules by expecting a Stabilizer to be more expressive, the battle lines get drawn.

TARA AND JASON

Tara and Jason, in their late twenties and married just eight months, find themselves in a classic Energizer/Stabilizer standoff. Tara, raised in a home where arguments were commonplace, never backed away from what she called a "good tussle." Jason, by his own admission, was a "peace-lovin' kind of guy." They came to see me because there hadn't been any intimacy for some time. During our first meeting, Jason said that things would be fine for a while until Tara started "picking" at him for not being romantic enough. "The more she demands, the less romantic I feel," he said. Their stalemate had begun when, in the heat of an argument, Tara threw Jason his pillow and said, "You can sleep on the couch until you're ready to love me the way I deserve to be loved." That was nearly two months ago. They continue to sleep apart.

Tara had hoped that Jason would get tired of sleeping on the couch, but she underestimated his disdain for conflict. Stabilizers are as well adapted to handling solitude as Energizers are to managing conflict. If she waits for him to tire of sleeping on the couch, she may wait some time! Chances are she'll provoke another brouhaha well before then.

The important thing to focus on in an Energizer/Stabilizer conflict is that the behaviors exhibited are not intentionally manipulative. Each unconsciously evokes the behavior in the other that makes him or her most comfortable *in the short run*. But in the final analysis, no one is a winner and each must learn how to modify their styles to create a win-win result.

Tara and Jason were determined to fix their miscommunication early on in their relationship. All that was needed was a simple but important adjustment in their approach to one another. On my suggestion, they set aside some time to discuss "romance" and what they each associated with feeling romantic. Jason listed things like a nonpressured dinner, sitting together watching a movie, and going upstairs to make love. Tara's list included personal conversation, a sensual massage, and a surprise dinner out. Together they designed a new list for the two of them that included items from both lists. When they followed this list, the anger was defused and intimacy was renewed.

DON AND SUSAN

To illustrate this struggle with another couple, let's meet Don and Susan, both twenty-five. Susan, a lively Energizer, and a print model who was called "the flirt" in high school, had never been at a loss for male attention. In Don, she discovered a Stabilizer who adored her. Susan had been raised in a physically abusive household. On several occasions the beatings from her father were so severe that there were visible bruises. Her mother and father divorced when she was seven and her mom never remarried. With the exception of a yearly birthday card, her father never contacted her.

In college, she dated lots of guys but nothing lasted longer than two months. Whenever things got serious, she got scared. Don was her first true love. They were friends before they were lovers and he proved his loyalty. Susan was convinced that he was a gentle supportive man who would always be there for her; he reassured that part of her that believed all men were unreliable and dangerous.

Don grew up in a small midwestern town, the only son of a Lutheran minister who had been trying to have a family for years. Don's mother was forty when he was born. What he remembers most is doing the endless chores on the farm and going to church. He never remembers any conflict at home and describes an "idyllic upbringing." When Don went through puberty, however, he didn't mature as rapidly as his peers. He was shorter than his male friends and was not suited for team sports. He was bullied by the bigger guys and wouldn't shower or walk around naked in the locker room because he was convinced his penis was smaller than his peers'. Dating was another disaster and Don feared he'd never find someone to love. Susan was the answer to his prayers. She was beautiful, popular, and she actually liked him. His greatest fear was losing her love.

Don and Susan came to my office considering divorce. Married just two years, Don said, "I can't do anything right, she criticizes everything I do. I'm not tall enough, ambitious enough, or confident enough. We rarely have sex, and when we do, I don't please her there either." Recently he'd started having problems with his erection that got worse the harder he tried. At that point, Susan had given him an ultimatum, "Get it up, or get out."

Sitting in my office, Don looked like a sad frightened little boy. As he "confessed" his shortcomings and his greatest fear—that he would lose the only love of his life—Susan sat stone-faced. As he spoke, he periodically glanced at Susan's face for some sign of acknowledgment or affirmation, but there was none.

Susan was angry. She misconstrued Don's lack of erection as disinterest in her. Instead of revealing her hurt and vulnerability, she berated him for not knowing how to touch her correctly, for not finding her attractive, and for not being a "real man." Susan didn't have a clue about how she contributed to the problem, and Don listened to her accusations like a condemned man awaiting sentence.

Over the next two months in therapy, Susan began to talk about feeling empty and unhappy with parts of herself, and a history of anger at men. She was unaware that she'd been struggling with not feeling "good enough" since her father left. She hadn't realized her hope that Don could fill her need for approval and acceptance. As therapy proceeded, she began to recognize that her anger covered feelings of helplessness and sadness about her father. She discovered she had been demeaning Don to render him powerless and incapable of repeating her father's actions. Don used therapy to become aware of his hurt and humiliation. He came to understand that he used his passivity and distance to express his pain, rather than talking to Susan about how he felt.

As they explored their individual issues and shared their insights, they enhanced intimacy and empathy. Susan faced her fears of being with an independent powerful man and worked to reduce her controlling behavior. She learned to accept "no" and not having her own way. She decreased her demands and increased her requests.

Don practiced saying "No" more often and faced his fears of rejection. He stopped thinking of himself as a failure and started believing in his own capability. As he took responsibility for his own emotions, his erections stopped being a problem and sex became more frequent. I recently got a photograph of their lovely new daughter, Leah, and a note saying that things were still great sexually.

Once you've developed a particular style, it's difficult but not impossible to alter it. I compare the shift in one's style to a fine-tuning knob on a television set. We don't actually change channels and select an entirely different style, but we can increase or decrease the contrast, modity the intensity by turning down or increasing the volume, and enhance or minimize a number of stylistic dimensions.

With the right motivation, guidance, and practice, each of us can stretch beyond our security zones and learn to enjoy a richer, more satisfying sexual connection.

THE WORKER STYLE AND THE PLAYER STYLE

In terms of the right brain/left brain literature, Workers are left brain. They're the logical, detail-oriented individuals who are great neurosurgeons and accountants. Workers prefer structure, like competitive sports with definite rules, and are product-driven as opposed to pleasure-driven. They have at least one personal scheduling system, use precise language, are very time-conscious, and are interested in efficiency. "Getting the most bang for your buck" would be the motto for Workers. They're great financial managers, wonderful providers, and their home is their castle.

Sexually speaking, Workers are (as the name states) hardworking! They aim to please and expect to be several standard deviations from the mean in sexual excellence. They're the patients who come to my office asking, "How long should I really be able to keep my erection before I ejaculate?" or "I've only had one orgasm and I'd like to have multiple simultaneous orgasms." When a Worker client reveals to me that he's worried because he only lasts four minutes and forty-five seconds before ejaculating, I know he's not focusing on his pleasure! Because workers are more concerned with your pleasure than their own, their partners often feel less than fully connected with them. When this happens I hear comments like "I want him to look into my eyes, to be there for me—I feel he's somewhere else, that there's this penis making love to me without a person attached to it."

Workers take pride in precision and technique. They'd love clear, un-ambiguous instructions (written would be preferred) showing the location of the most sensitive portions of their lover's clitoris and whether stimulation should be vertical, horizontal, or counterclockwise. They don't quite get the concept that there is variation in sexual preferences from time to time. After all, stroking you this way "worked" last time—why not every time? They are wonderfully determined, albeit unimaginative lovers, who'll try like hell to "give" you an orgasm. A Worker female would rather get lockjaw than give up on oral sex before you've ejaculated.

When it comes to sexual dysfunction, Workers are the ones who most often have problems maintaining erections or having orgasms. Problems with arousal develop, as it's often difficult to feel pleasure when you're focusing on technique. Also, sexual arousal and response are involuntary activities and cannot be willed—regardless of effort. A difficult concept for a Worker to grasp. Masters and Johnson's classic sensate focus exercises are tailor-made for the Workers (actually, Energizers and Stabilizers also bene-fit) because instead of focusing on performance and productivity, the objec-tive is enjoyment—a novel idea for a Worker who measures his importance by his achievements.

Sex therapy with Workers is focused on teaching them to become more aware of their own pleasure to the exclusion of everything else. To throw away their stopwatch, remove all cues of time passing, and discover how to have some fun. To take opportunities to recognize pleasure (of all kinds) and to expand it, Workers must learn how to enjoy, be a bit more self-absorbed, and relax.

Players, on the other hand, could be compared to right-brain-dominant individuals. They are more global and diffuse in their attention and notice the bigger picture before homing in on the details. They're easygoing pleasure seekers who have perfected the secret of enjoying just about everything. They're entertaining guests at parties, creative, often artistic, adventuresome, and curious. Players are open to experimentation in all forms. When Players go on a trip they don't plan lists of museums (like their Worker counterparts), they stay unscheduled and see what opportunities arise. If they want to spend the day collecting seashells or appreciating an inspiring Monet, so be it. Their mottoes are "Go with the flow" and "Carpe diem!"

Sexually, Players are thrilling—after all, they're pleasure experts. They're the ones who are not afraid to walk confidently into the adult toy shop and come out with a basket of titillating goodies. Guilt and embarrassment are strangers to them. They're never constrained by societal standards and their approaches are novel and refreshing. If you want a lover who is innovative, open to playing out your favorite fantasy, or who can leave you breathless with their sexy talk, find a Player. But you'd better be ready for a wild ride. The downside to this is that Players' tolerance for limits is low. They resent anyone structuring their fun and prefer a free-flowing spontaneous connection. If you're open to sex in the woods, in a parked car, between floors six and twelve in the elevator, or playing Sailor and Shipmate at a moment's notice—this is your perfect match.

Players often make the call to my office because they'd like their Worker or Stabilizer partners to open up more. They rarely see that *they* have anything to do with the relationship problems. Players can be so anti-authority that they don't respect anyone's limits, including their lover's. Sex therapy involves teaching them to listen and respect their partner's comfort level, to delay their need for immediate gratification, and to practice compromise. Sex for a Player is often "all" or "none." They need to learn that the gray zone can be very fulfilling, and that sex without all the bells and whistles can reveal a refreshingly different kind of intimacy that may never before have been fully appreciated. When Players take a break from the action and step back from their own desires long enough to reconnect with their partner's sensitivities, they discover a passion with their lover that's deeper than any they could create alone.

ALAN AND MINDY: A MARRIAGE BETWEEN A WORKER AND A PLAYER

Alan, a forty-three-year-old plastic surgeon from New Jersey, met his twenty-six-year-old Colorado ski instructor wife on his last vacation. She was the answer to his dreams—beautiful, physically fit, playful, easygoing, and adventurous.

Alan was the apple of his Jewish mother's eye. After all, he was a handsome doctor who visited regularly. The only thing missing for her was *grandchildren.* Alan's immediate family, extended family, friends, and business colleagues had fixed him up with dozens of attractive, intelligent women. The women had come from the best families, graduated from the finest colleges, and were usually attorneys, high-powered executives, or physicians, but there had never been a heart connection. Not until he met Mindy.

Mindy was nothing like the others. Born in Arkansas to an indigent alcoholic mother, she dropped out of high school in the tenth grade because she was pregnant. After giving her baby up for adoption, she never went back to school. Mindy's mother, who worked at a local diner, didn't know Mindy's father. She thinks she got pregnant during a "one-night stand." There were five other siblings. Three of them were from different dads. Mindy was the oldest and played "mother" to the younger children.

For as long as she could remember, it was her dream to move out West. Although she wasn't well educated, Mindy was bright and very athletic. She was a risk taker and a thrill seeker. Skiing down a dangerous double diamond slope, tempting fate, was her joy.

Mindy never thought she'd marry. Not after seeing what happened to her mother. But Alan was her Prince Charming, and he swept her off her feet. The seventeen-year age difference didn't bother her. He was a great skier and looked "much younger than forty-three." For his part, Alan was "blown away" by her loveliness. He felt he had captured the trophy of his dreams. After only two months of a long-distance relationship, he presented her with a flawless three-carat pear-shaped diamond. Alan's family was less than exuberant about Mindy, but delighted that there might, at last, be grandchildren.

The problems began after the wedding. Alan purchased a $750,000 home in Scarsdale, complete with a three-car garage for his Ferrari and Range Rover and Mindy's BMW. Mindy was ecstatic at first, but after a while she began to feel like a fish out of water. All of Alan's friends were much older than she was, with children in college. The country club scene bored her, and Alan was too busy to go off to Colorado for ski trips. Mindy felt she had everything, but nothing. Without adventure in her life, she felt trapped.

Sex became boring, too. Alan was an unimaginative lover and rarely the initiator. Mindy thought about having an affair, and called me instead.

After only eight months, Alan and Mindy were considering divorce. He expected Mindy would feel grateful for all he had given her, and just settle down and be his wife. What he didn't understand is that he'd married a risk-taking Player who considered settling down the equivalent of death.

And what about Alan? He was a Worker through and through. His logical, analytical style had been comforting to Mindy at first, but she soon tired of his dry, mechanical, humorless approach to lovemaking. Unfortunately, neither partner was motivated to modify their style—each wanted the *other one* to change. After three months of therapy, Mindy left for Colorado and Alan filed for divorce.

It's difficult to predict whether Alan and Mindy's relationship could have lasted if she'd taken up some of Alan's interests and limited her impulsiveness, and he had worked on relaxing more and confronting his rigidity. Sadly, they were unwilling to look at, and work on, themselves, and that spells certain disaster.

WHAT DO I DO IF MY RELATIONSHIP IS A MISFIT?

What do you do if you're a Stabilizer who prefers to schedule everything, including sex, and you're married to an Energizer who's ready for sex anytime? Or what if you're an Energizer who always initiates sex and you're married to a Stabilizer who goes along with your invitations but never initiates? In both instances, you are probably aware of a misfit.

The trouble is that in many cases Energizers and Stabilizers are initially greatly attracted to one another. Over time, however, each begins to try to maneuver the other into his own camp. That's when the honeymoon is over—communication becomes strained and sexual problems arise.

Finding a solution to a misfit in sexual styles has nothing to do with deciding who's right and who's wrong. It involves learning to understand our basic differences. By learning that your lover is an Energizer and you're a Stabilizer you can go a long way to stop blaming and criticizing each other. Once you've recognized how you're similar or different and in what ways, you can each start to speak the other's language. As you foster understanding of empathy, intimacy grows and sex becomes extraordinary.

HELEN AND BOB

Helen, a thirty-two-year-old Ph.D. student in international diplomacy at Cornell, is a classic Stabilizer. She lives by her Franklin Planner and is intensely task-oriented. She knows how many calories she's consumed daily, how much her weight fluctuates from A.M. to P.M., and where to get the best price for top-grade sirloin. She's a devoted mom, a ready listener for her friends, and the consummate hostess. Her parties are well known for their attention to detail, fabulous food, and impressive guest lists. Unfortunately, Helen is usually a nervous wreck at these gatherings because she's so worried about everything going off without a hitch.

Sexually, Helen rarely has orgasms *or* pleasure. She's usually thinking about a project that's due or how long it seems to be taking her. When she does orgasm, it's more like a hiccup or a small sneeze than a full-bodied release.

Helen's partner for six years is an Energizer. Bob is in sales and could sell snow to the Eskimos. He's charming, effusive, but quite self-absorbed.

During their dating, Bob was the choreographer and Helen was the appreciative audience. She loved his enthusiastic initiative and felt comforted by his love of the spotlight because she was so good offstage. Her mom had been the quiet, dutiful, stay-at-home parent who had sacrificed career for kids. If her mom was ever upset, she certainly never showed it. Helen had been groomed to be the "wind under Bob's wings." Bob was the firstborn male and the apple of his family's eye. Attention, gifts from grand-parents, and praise were lavished upon him.

Initially, their sexual styles gave the impression of the perfect fit—until they were married. Not long thereafter, Bob began to feel insecure because he became aware of the fact that Helen rarely initiated sex and didn't seem to enjoy it. She was quiet during their lovemaking and, although he hadn't missed it before, he expected more sexy talk during their passionate moments. One day, after routine sex, he remarked, "I'm tired of putting on the show all the time. Why can't you contribute to the excitement?" Helen was crushed. Bob had suddenly changed the rules and now she felt an immense pressure to perform. Instead of dealing with her fears of failure openly, she kept her feelings inside (the way her mom had done) and busied herself with school and community projects, Little League games, and throwing gala parties for Bob and his firm. With such a schedule, she was often too tired for sex. Bob reacted by getting loud, angry, and critical, accusing her of having an affair with her dissertation chairperson.

In therapy, Helen learned to see how her pattern of trying to please others backfired by closing her off from what *she* wanted. She had become so focused on others, she had lost track of herself and her sexual desires. Bob came to realize that he had the opposite problem. By focusing solely on himself and what he wanted, he had lost touch with Helen. No wonder sex felt so lonely for him.

As they each listened to the other, their defensiveness diminished and they allowed themselves to consider alternative approaches. Helen discovered ways to be more playful. She made space in her schedule to invite Bob to a sensuous lather in the shower and other impromptu sexual surprises. Bob focused on being more supportive and appreciative of Helen's efforts. Developing patience and an interest in another person's point of view wasn't easy for him, but it paid off in a big way.

As couples often find it difficult to talk, particularly without the aid of a therapist, one of the ways I've found to make it easier is by describing the Energizer, Stabilizer, Worker, and Player in nonthreatening "animal" language. The next chapter will introduce you to the Lion, Bear, Bee, and Otter and help you identify your own style and that of your partner.

CHAPTER 6

LIONS AND BEARS AND BEES . . . OH MY!

*From the oyster to the eagle, from the swine to the tiger, all
animals are to be found in men . . . sometimes several at a
time. Animals are nothing but the portrayal of our virtues and
vices made manifest to our eyes.*

—VICTOR HUGO, LES MISÉRABLES, 1862

Comparing personality styles to animals is not new. Animal archetypes and
metaphors have long been used by the Native American and Mayan tradi-
tions to represent the four poles of the universe and countless authors from
Aesop to Estes have done so as well. Astrology refers to the four polarities of
fire, earth, water, and air and connects animal symbols like the bull, ram,
fish, and scorpion to its signs.

The idea of using animal typologies emerged for me serendipitously a
number of years ago.

As I played with the Energizer/Stabilizer model and worked on ways to
clearly express it to my clients, I found myself associating an *animal* with
each sexual style. The Lion is the Energizer, the Bear is the Stabilizer, the
Bee is the Worker, and the Otter is the Player. Each animal archetype
contains a symbolic richness and complexity that extends beyond words like
Energizer or Stabilizer.

Selecting the most appropriate animal equivalents was a bit of a challenge! There was no question that the Lion was "king" and the most fitting
animal to represent power. The Bear is equally powerful and its image

evoked feelings of stability and contemplation. Finding a "playful" image took more effort. I dismissed "puppy" because it represents a stage of life and all young creatures are playful. I considered the cricket, inspired by La Fontainne's fable of the fiddling "Cricket and Ant" but thought couples might have trouble identifying with those specific insects. I settled on the hard-working, yet lovable Honey Bee and the thrill-seeking spontaneous Otter and found they were intuitively perfect.

I then developed my own inventory and use it as a part of each couple's clinical assessment. The twenty items appear on pages 77–80. Once clients discovered their own animal styles, they began to refer to themselves as "Otterly" or "Lionly" in our sessions. I was delighted that I had apparently stumbled upon a simple and non-threatening way to communicate some very complex personality variables.

While at first it may seem childish to think about yourself and your partner in animal terms, it serves an important function. Talking about sex and intimacy can be difficult for many people. Having a nonpathological way to understand your style and the style of your partner has proven to be an effective way to enhance communication.

Instead of complaining about his mate's "kinky" sexual fantasy, one very conservative Bee partner laughingly said, "That's a little too Otterly for my tastes." Naming the particular style as Lion, Bear, Bee, or Otter became a shorthand way to highlight a cluster of specific behaviors.

I also find that couples can more easily identify with the "Lionness" or "Bearness" embedded in their personalities in ways that aren't stigmatizing or pejorative. Instead of saying, "I have to stop being such a controlling nag," you can smile and say, "There's that Lion again, not wanting to take 'no' for an answer."

Couples who use animal labels lighten the seriousness and avoid the blaming that often accompanies injurious labels like passive-aggressive, avoidant, or controlling. Animal metaphors are a shortcut way to talk about some difficult interactions. It's important to be careful about what you say to your lover and how you say it. Once words are expressed, they can't be retrieved. When couples call each other lazy, boring, or uninteresting, it's not long before a self-fulfilling prophecy emerges. So instead of labeling your would-be fiancé as "commitment-phobic" try thinking of him as expressing his strong Bearlike qualities. When you talk to each other in the language of the Lion and Bear, you'll become less defensive and more willing to hear each other. You'll be surprised at how a shift in your thinking will improve your feelings about your lover and pave the way for more satisfying intimacy.

THE FOUR POLARITIES

Broadly defined, there are four principal sexual styles. We're some combination of Lion, Bear, Bee, or Otter. Figure 1 shows how Lions and Bears are at opposite sides of the Energizer/Stabilizer continuum. Figure 2 shows how Bees and Otters are at opposite ends of the Worker/Player continuum.

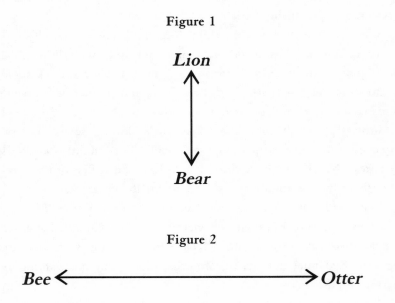

Figure 1

Lion

Bear

Figure 2

Bee ⟵————————————⟶ *Otter*

These animal images have proven their worth by undergoing the test of time. As people become less attached to the belief that there's only one right way to feel, think, or behave, solutions begin to emerge. If you're an Otter and prefer playful spontaneous sex, and you're married to a Bee who likes to schedule everything, the problem is clear from the get-go. This doesn't mean the Otter/Bee relationship is doomed; it only means some understanding and compromise will be required.

When animal types interact (Bee with Otter, Lion with Bear, or a variety of other pairings), they confront a number of their ideas and beliefs about what constitutes great sex. (See Figure 3.) **Remember, there's no one correct standard.** Sexual styles in relationships can be complementary and harmonize, or they may conflict. The important thing is to recognize your own style and that of your partner, and to bring the strengths *of both* to your passionate intimacy.

Figure 3. Characteristics of the Four Principal Animal Archetypes

Lion (Energizer)

- Communicative
- Controlling
- Critical
- Intensely caring
- Assertive
- Energetic
- Demanding
- Risk-taking

Sexually a Lion . . .

- Initiates sex
- Prefers center stage
- Takes credit for lover's orgasm
- Enjoys sexy talk
- Can be a passionate partner if in the mood
- Can be hard to please sexually

Bear (Stabilizer)

- Cooperative
- Agreeable
- Avoids conflict
- Thoughtful
- Stubborn
- Expresses anger indirectly
- Nurturing
- Generous

Sexually a Bear . . .
- Has difficulty asserting and initiating
- Works hard to please partner
- Is not orgasm-focused
- Prefers to ignore a problem rather than confront it
- Likes to hear sexy talk, but isn't as comfortable talking

Bee (Worker)

- Practical
- Analytical
- Well organized
- Perfectionist
- Precise
- Orderly
- Hardworking
- Planner

Sexually a Bee . . .
- Is subject to performance anxiety
- Measures orgasms and times ejaculations
- Enjoys creating an outstanding experience for a partner
- Strives to be technically "perfect"
- Orchestrates sex carefully
- Has difficulty relaxing or being spontaneous

Otter (Player)

- Playful dreamer
- Artistic, fanciful, creative
- Impulsive
- Rebellious
- Disorganized
- Fun-loving
- Risk-taking
- Not driven by material gain

Sexually an Otter . . .
- Seeks pleasure and thrills
- Lives for the moment

- Connects to passion
- Is spontaneous
- Is a sexy-talk expert
- Has a low tolerance for indecisiveness and restrictions

COMBINATIONS OF SEXUAL STYLES

When the four principal styles intersect, the following ten combinations occur:

LION

BEAR

OTTER

BEE

LION/BEAR

LION/OTTER

LION/BEE

BEAR/OTTER

BEAR/BEE

BEE/OTTER

I'm not suggesting that these four categories reflect the totality of sexual style possibilities. You might compare the four principal sexual styles to the primary colors of a color wheel; when the colors are added or subtracted from one another in various proportions or intensities, they produce virtually all other colors.

In the same way, while there are some people who tend toward a relatively "pure" expression of Lion, Bear, Bee, or Otter, most people express characteristics of two or more styles. As the primary styles combine and influence one another, a spectrum of possibilities emerges.

Imagine that the "pure" tendencies (Lion, Bear, Bee, and Otter) are located at the poles of a compass. (See Figure 4.) At the intersection of the poles, four quadrants are created. As you spin the needle, it passes through a wide range of possible combinations. Quadrant I combines features from

Lion and Bee, resulting in a hard-driving professional. Quadrant II combines Lion and Otter, resulting in expressive creative types, Quadrant III is the Bee/Bear who combines analytic thinking with a cooperative spirit, and Quadrant IV is the Bear/Otter who dislikes rules, restrictions, and deadlines of any kind.

Sexual Styles and Quadrants

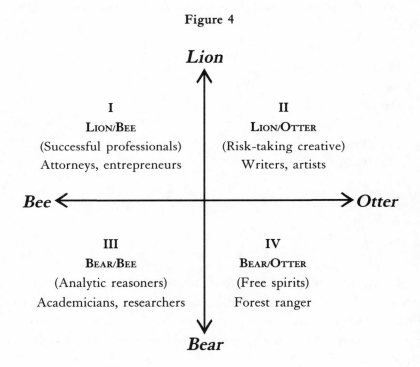

Figure 4

Lion

I	II
Lion/Bee	Lion/Otter
(Successful professionals)	(Risk-taking creative)
Attorneys, entrepreneurs	Writers, artists

Bee ← → **Otter**

III	IV
Bear/Bee	Bear/Otter
(Analytic reasoners)	(Free spirits)
Academicians, researchers	Forest ranger

Bear

Keep in mind that styles can be situation-specific. It's not uncommon for you to be a Lion/Bee in the office (orderly and hard-driving), but a Lion/Otter when it comes to sex (risk-taking and spontaneous). Although you'll find some uniqueness from one context to another, when you look at your behavior over time, in a large number of situations, you'll discover certain overall patterns and preferences.

Based on the information in this chapter and in Chapter 9, you might want to take a guess about your own style or that of your partner. In Chapter 8, you'll find a test that will tell you if you were correct.

CHAPTER 7

HUMOR, METAPHOR, AND FABLE

Mirth is like a flash of lightning, that breaks through a gloom of clouds, and glitters for a moment; cheerfulness keeps up a kind of daylight in the mind, and fills it with a steady and perpetual serenity.

—JOSEPH ADDISON, 1712

From as far back as I can remember, I've incorporated humor, stories, and metaphors into my clinical practice. When I was a girl, my favorite corner of the library was the fairy tale and mythology section. Perhaps the tales provided me a necessary escape into a world where there were no limits. Some of my teachers thought I should broaden my literary tastes, but I found myself transfixed by the world of make-believe. I'm certain that I learned some valuable lessons from the ghosts, gremlins, and princesses: From the princess and the pea I learned to value my sensitivity, and from the tortoise and the hare, I learned to persevere; but most important of all, I learned to believe that anything was possible if you wished and worked hard enough.

The symbolism I've discovered in the four sexual styles expressed through the Lion, Bear, Bee, and Otter is entrancing. Very much like characters in a fable, they dynamically portray human qualities and diverse interactions. With these archetypal characters in mind, we can identify aspects of our own personalities and see in them both limitations and possibilities.

In many ways fables are like sexuality. They awaken in us a childlike wonder that is unquestioned—like the animation of a toy doll or the magic of Tinker Bell. The use of fables is an opportunity for reenchantment. Lovers often talk baby talk and give each other sweet pet names. Playfulness releases passion in all of its forms.

These fables illustrate the importance of flexibility for couples and the requirement that we let go of absolutes regarding what is possible. If you believe that you're a Bee, and only can do Bee things, or your partner is a Lion and only does Lion things, you've limited your flexibility and emotional growth as an individual and as a couple. Rather, if you learn to appreciate your partner's style, empathize with it, and ultimately decide to incorporate aspects of it—you've created the vital connection, and extraordinary sex emerges.

The following fables illustrate the four principal sexual styles and the dynamic complementarity of their vital connection. They offer an opportunity to enter the lives of these creatures and see how their worldview shifts through something or someone who impacts them. Let the fables speak to you as they take you on a journey of self-discovery that stirs your imagination and taps the richness of your creativity.

The Lion and the Bear

In a beautiful place of clear rushing streams and bountiful lakes, beavers and moles built dams and turned the soil from dawn to moonrise. The great rivers teamed with salmon swimming upstream, airborne, defying gravity and the thundering rapids. Ten thousand salmon stood on their tails in the white foam, their eyes fixed on the next cresting wave.

Suddenly, like summer lightning, four golden paws lit on the elephantine back of a black boulder that effortlessly parted the unruly current. Those golden paws paced in circles atop the rock.

"Where is Bear?" growled Mountain Lion to the salmon, her tail snapping and eyes flashing. "Has Bear gone to sleep again, leaving me to rule alone?" The salmon said they did not know, their own way being so demanding.

Mountain Lion sprang away and strode through the forest, finally bursting out from a stand of aspen that faced a towering sandstone wall peppered with caves. The mouth of Bear's cave was thickly carpeted with rich fragrant moss and wildflowers.

"Come out, Bear. Sleeping is done," Lion called. "The Great Spirit bade us to rule together, and you leave me to do it alone." A long, low moan emerged from the womblike darkness as Bear stretched languorously. "You need not awaken me," Bear said. "We are to *discover* how to rule together in harmony—it is a mystery not yet fulfilled."

Lion slowly rubbed her body against Bear's, moving from head to tail against his massive form. "My eyes are more keen than yours, but I need the wise vision that comes from deep within you. Come along, dear Bear, let us once again combine our strengths and lead together. I will make certain that you don't return to your den to sleep, for I grow restless when you do."

"Your hand is strong and sure, Lion," said Bear. "Your vigilant eye sees all that must be done in our domain."

"You bring me comfort in your quiet consolation," said Lion.

They left the cave and crossed a bubbling stream where sunlit stones warmed the pads of their paws. Dragonflies darted around their heads as wrens and chickadees serenaded them from low branches heavy with moss. Bear hugged the restless Lion.

"I'll spend less time hibernating," Bear said. "If you try to temper your relentless work for our kingdom with some play."

Lion just smiled, silently absorbing Bear's admonition. Throughout their day and for many months, they walked together, greeting the animals of the woods. Before long, however, Bear grew slow, napping frequently, and daydreaming while Lion called forth their subjects. All came forward: brilliantly plumed water birds, rabbits and other furry creatures, snakes and lizards, wolves and deer, all sharing the bounty of the woods. Lion reminded them how lucky they were to live in such a rich and wonderful forest. Although they were appreciative, something was amiss. Lion's ears pricked up and heard murmuring from her subjects and her sharp eyes caught glimpses of their saddened expressions.

One day, a hedgehog with the gift of prescience came before Lion. The hedgehog told Lion how the animals missed Bear's inspirational stories and tales. Some even considered Bear an oracle of whom they could ask spiritual guidance. While they loved Lion's decisive strength and agile power, they felt impoverished by Bear's absence. The other hibernating animals understood that Bear could not be true to his own nature without his winter rest to digest his year's experience in the presence of the Great Spirit. The hedgehog had learned that during Bear's brief naps, he yearned for the warm and welcoming cave where the eternal sea of dreams would rock, nurture, and replenish his soul. There had been, in fact, times when Bear told Lion of his wish to hibernate again.

Lion was, however, a very practical sort of creature and believed in experience as the only true teacher, and so, thanking the hedgehog sincerely for his concern, she moved on to the matters of the moment. In Lion's own thoughts, although there was a subtle awareness that Bear needed rest, they were drowned out by the practical response: "A little honey and fresh salmon and he'll be as good as ever."

The hedgehog went on his way. Later that evening, as the sun set over the sandstone cliffs in cascades of lavender and peach, and the moon rose over its reflection in the ebony lakes, Lion fell into a deep sleep and had a vivid dream.

Lion saw a great wooden boat, hewn in the shape of a giant hand, its palm upward with fingers gently outstretched pointing downstream. This hand was so huge that it carried in its hollow all of the inhabitants of Lion and Bear's domain. "This," thought Lion in her dream, "must surely be the hand of the Great Spirit holding and protecting us all."

In her dream, Lion was at the bow with a great paddle powerfully propelling the craft faster than the mighty current. Yet the hand-boat felt curiously unsteady and unstable to Lion. Looking back, she discovered that Bear was not in the hand-boat and the rudder aft was unattended, causing the boat's instability.

With all of her might, Lion drew the boat to the shore and landed in front of the peaceful mouth of Bear's cave. At that moment, Bear emerged from his long winter's rest, eyes luminous and clear. Springing mightily into the aft of the hand-boat, Bear seized the rudder, and calling out to Lion and others, exclaimed, "I see the Great Spirit's design. I shall steer as Lion propels us. That is how we shall reign in harmony."

Upon awakening, Lion said to Bear, "The Great Spirit has spoken through my dream. I have been shown that you possess what I am missing in myself. You have such quiet strength, Bear—you are my rock and my stability." Bear smiled and replied, "And I have learned from you to be less hesitant in my ways. I am not just a leaf carried on a stream floating wherever the current leads. My energy is episodic, but powerful nonetheless. Now we shall be like the hand-boat in your dream, with one propelling as the other steers, sharing the work and joys of the journey."

DONNA AND CHARLIE: A LION AND A BEAR

"So what brings you here?" I asked. It was my first session with Donna and Charlie, who had come for sex therapy at Donna's suggestion. I glanced at Charlie and then at Donna, who immediately started her saga. She was sitting directly across from me in an aquamarine tailored suit that complemented her thick auburn hair. Her eye contact was intensely penetrating and she had a worried look on her face. Her body was turned away from Charlie's and it erected a barrier that excluded him from our twosome.

In a shrill voice, Donna began to recite her litany of complaints about Charlie. It seemed to me this wasn't the first time she had gone through her list.

"We've been to other therapists," she began. "They listen and listen and don't do anything. I hope this time is different." Donna had put *me* on notice.

"What are you hoping I'll be able to do, Donna?" I asked.

"I need you to fix our decrepit sex life," she said sternly.

"In what way is your sex life decrepit?" I explored.

"In what way isn't it!" she replied, exasperated.

Without taking a breath she continued, "Charlie is irresponsible. He comes home from work at six o'clock and disappears into the garage to fiddle around with his tools or whatever. He doesn't ask me how my day was and neglects the kids. If he isn't in the garage, he's at the gym working out."

As she spoke, Charlie sat silently. His closely trimmed gray hair and conservative wire-rim glasses framed his expressionless face.

"When Charlie disappears into the garage and you feel neglected, what do you say to him?" I asked.

"I usually open the garage door and tell him that I need to talk to him. I might tell him that he left the towels on the floor of the bathroom after he showered, or that he forgot to put out the garbage this morning, and that

I'm sick and tired of being his mother. But he just walks away, ignores me, or tells me that I'm making a big deal out of nothing. I get so frustrated and angry I don't know what to do." Donna's voice began to crack as the tears ran down her cheeks. "Then he wonders why I can't turn off my rage and just give him a blow job whenever he's horny."

Charlie hadn't said a word. He looked surprisingly cool and unaffected by Donna's comments. I turned to Charlie and asked him to tell me what made him decide to make an appointment with me. Charlie took a few moments to consider his reply. He spoke carefully in a well-modulated voice that obscured any emotion. "I'm really not sure how you can help, Doctor," he began. "I came because Donna made the call. Donna's been unhappy with me for as far back as I can remember. It doesn't seem that I can do anything to please her. She's always finding fault with everything I do, and I never get told I've done anything right. If I don't ask for sex I'm being passive, but if I do then I'm not touching her in the right way. If she'd stop pressuring me about everything, things would be fine."

It was apparent to me that Charlie was a Bear who couldn't see his part in this marital problem and Donna was the Lion.

"Are you saying that Donna is the whole problem?" I inquired.

"No, not entirely," Charlie responded. "But if she'd just back off and not get so upset about every little thing, things would be so much better. I don't feel she ever cuts me a break. If I don't do everything according to her time schedule and in her way, I'm criticized and attacked. I feel on guard with her and I don't look forward to our times together."

"Can you give me an example of the last time you felt she attacked you?" I asked.

"That's easy. Yesterday," he said. "I had wanted to surprise her by buying a camel-hair jacket I've had my eye on. She's always saying that I don't have any new clothes. I went to a fashionable men's store and the salesperson picked out a designer shirt and tie to match. I put the outfit on and walked into the bedroom to show her the outfit. She shrieked, 'That's hideous!' I felt two inches tall."

"And what did you say? Did you tell her you felt put down?"

"No, I just walked out of the room."

Donna immediately interjected, "You should have *seen* that jacket. It was camel-colored but had an olive cast to it and he was wearing a sea-green shirt and an orange tie! It was awful! I've told him a hundred times to take me with him when he goes clothes shopping—he has no color sense."

Donna didn't seem to have a clue about her hurtful "maternal" approach and Charlie was similarly clueless about how he retreated and excluded Donna from parts of his life.

Believe it or not, Donna and Charlie love each other. They've been married for twenty-one years and there are countless things they admire and respect about one another. Their problem will sound familiar to many couples because they've gotten trapped in a typical chase pattern that spells disaster. Each one thinks, "If only the other would change, things would be great."

Donna has taken on the role of the huntress and Charlie behaves like the hunted. Donna stalks him with her Lionly precision and Charlie hides in the garage or at the gym. Instead of standing up to Donna, he, in his Bearish way, avoids, and behaves like her prey. Unfortunately the more adept she is at her pursuit, the more skillfully evasive and unavailable he becomes.

"IF ONLY HE/SHE WOULD . . ."

It is worth repeating that *trying to change your partner spells disaster.* The exact qualities that attract us to our lover are often the things we later complain about and try to change. Donna, for example, was attracted at first to Charlie's calming, carefree approach. He had a way of comforting Donna when she became distraught about a problem at work or struggle with her family. Charlie was taken by Donna's effervescent style and bubbly personality. There was never a dull moment when he was with her. He once told her lovingly, "You're my Energizer bunny!" Donna's emotional sensitivity balanced his placid persona beautifully.

Unfortunately, if Charlie relies on Donna to express his emotions and if Donna relies on Charlie to provide stabilization, *they never learn how to do these things for themselves.* We all want a complete package in our mates. Even though we're initially drawn to partners who "complete" us, it's not long before we want a partner who can also reflect the behaviors we admire, value, and respect.

For example, let's assume you're a Bear and you're most content when you can please your partner. You dislike confrontation and are generally pretty easygoing and slow to anger. Small matters are unimportant to you. It takes a lot to get you upset. You find yourself attracted to a person who can do anger and responsibility pretty well. They have an intensity that fires you up, and when that anger isn't directed at you, all is well. Unfortunately, over time, the worm does turn and you become the object of your Lion's wrath.

The same is true for your Lion counterpart. The Lion is fired by the power of the hunt. The emotionality of the Lion is drawn to the stability of the Bear, who soothes and contains her volatility and passion. In time, the soothing is insufficient, and the Lion longs for another challenge, feeling unsatisfied with the status quo.

When Lions and Bears get stuck in this way, the chase gets expressed first out of the bedroom and later in the bedroom. The Lions want the Bears to be energizing and emotionally available, and the Bears want the Lions to stabilize, relax, and let go of their emotionality. Soon we have a situation that becomes worse the harder you try to fix it. The more the Lion "attacks" the Bear, the more hiding places the Bear will find to elude her. The solution is simple—*each of you has to learn from your lover*. In seeking to be a bit more like your lover, you will succeed in balancing the qualities in yourself that will offer each of you more flexibility.

ENERGIZERS AND STABILIZERS: LEARNING FROM YOUR LOVER

What do the Bear and Lion archetypes teach us about intimacy? To the Lakota and Sioux, the Lion symbolizes leadership, insight, and control. The Lion is courageous, forthright, and uses her power to influence others. The shadow side of a Lion is in her difficulty expressing vulnerability or indecision. Listening is not her strength—roaring is.

Lions shun uncertainty and inactivity in the same way that Bears shun the path of direct action. The strength of a Bear lies in his introspective wisdom. He represents the silence that brings calm and stability to the Lion's energetic nature. Bear also represents the power of sustenance and self-preservation, but often to the exclusion of others' needs.

The wonderful thing about learning from your lover is that *your teacher lives with you.* He or she demonstrates the behaviors, thoughts, and feelings *you* need to learn.

Instead of pursuing your Bear mate in an aggressive relentless way, ask yourself, "How would my Bear suggest that I handle this?" You'll probably think, "He'd want me to avoid it altogether." Don't jump to that extreme position. A Bear would take a little time (or a lot of time) to cool off and consider whether all the hubbub is really worth it. Not bad advice for a Lion. And what about you, Oh Bear, how might you learn from your Lionly lover? A Lion would march forward with confidence and alacrity—thinking, "He who hesitates is lost." Not a bad message for a Bear to learn.

The tale of Lion and Bear may seem metaphoric and even far-fetched, but I see these couples struggling with love, sex, and intimacy on a daily basis. Marriages are threatened, families are in danger of being fractured, and patience wears thin as the same battles are waged again and again.

ONE AND ONE = THREE

It's paradoxical that we're initially drawn to the same qualities that later pull us apart. His "quiet stability," so attractive at first, becomes criticized as "boring and evasive." Her "excellent organizational skills" become redefined as "rigid overcontrolling compulsivity."

It is not by accident that we get together as partners. Each person brings a different set of strengths to a relationship and offers a perspective we are unable to give to ourselves. Through the Bear and Lion fable, the message of balance is clear. I find it most valuable in understanding the importance of not attempting to change the immutable nature of our partners. *Our task should not be to alter each other's uniqueness, but to appreciate and grow through the dynamic complementarity.*

In my practice, each partner wishes that I could transform the other to his or her liking. If this were possible, the marriage undoubtedly would fail. In "sameness," creativity stagnates. Instead of seeking to change our partners, we should learn from each other's strengths. After all, that's why we married them to begin with. The inability to learn this lesson is what causes the decline of sexual energy in relationships.

Passion unfolds in the union of opposites. But I'm not referring to the kind of union that makes us lose our individuality. *A relationship should be greater than the sum of its individual parts.* The remedy for assuring vitality and excitement in relationships rests in your ability to identify the salient differences between you, celebrate them, and learn from one another to be more than you ever dreamed you could be.

Let's look at a fable of Bee and Otter and their unique chemistry.

THE HONEYBEE AND THE OTTER

In another corner of the kingdom, far from the thundering river and the sandstone cliffs, there was a meadow by a merry brook. Light danced on the surface of the crystalline water as it swirled around polished stones and fallen branches, and meandered to the nearby sea. Alongside the brook, rich summer flowers, each one an intricate mandala of petal, pistil, and stamen— laden with perfumed nector and rich pollen—wove a carpet that sweetly colored the meadow.

There a honeybee toiled in droning dedication to swarm and hive, dashing from blossom to blossom, hovering and brushing each masterwork, collecting his prize, then calculating, plotting, and vectoring off to another and another. Honeybee's efficient zeal impressed even the hummingbird, whose efforts to chart the treasures of a nearby flowering tree paled in comparison.

At the same time, in the nearby brook, the shining surface of the water was broken by the sleek lines of an otter as she rolled and tumbled around rock and branch, buoyantly playing in the water's rushing coolness and the intoxicating fragrance of the summer's air. Even the graceful dragonflies hovered in their darting flights to enjoy Otter's comic choreography. Otter grinned at the dragonflies, reeled and dipped, then snatched a fish from an unwary school and gyrated away. Weaving and tumbling in apparent abandon, again and again, she repeated her fishing acrobatics until she was stuffed full.

As the afternoon passed, Honeybee steered himself toward the hive, like a precision craft. On Honeybee's itinerary was a certain stream that he crossed each day. As Bee crossed the stream, he also knew he would encounter one lovely but distracting Otter, who, he remembered from long experience, at the busiest times of the year would entice and cajole him, jokingly calling him stuffy or dull. Or, Bee remembered, Otter would lure and seduce him away from his responsibilities. Bee had, in fact, taken many wonderful rides on Otter's luxurious back over rapids and around serpentine curves of the stream. They had laughed together and sung songs until dark. They had shared drops of sweet honey that Honeybee secreted away from the hive just for picnics with Otter.

But those days were over, thought Bee. The hive depended on his work and though dear Otter was great fun, Honeybee could not tarry. As Bee traversed the creek, sure enough, there was Otter, bobbing on her back with her plump welcoming tummy pointing upward, just where Bee had to fly. And sure enough, just as Bee expected, Otter started right off with a sweet entreaty.

Otter said:

"Bzz, bzz, my Bee,
come play with me!
Get off your track,
ride on my back!
Here are billows
for our pillows.
From all your toil
I just recoil.
Look all around
God's gifts abound.
In colder times,
we've southern climes.
Don't be a drone.
Your life's your own.
There's just today.
We two must play!"

Honeybee made a careful circle, close to the water and near Otter's ear, and said:

"Brother, Otter,
I just can't bother.
I just survive
to serve the hive.
If you could see
our lives as bees
as examples

of making ample
cold weather stores
when bloom no more
God's seeds planted
not for granted."

Honeybee then went back to work, and Otter to fishing and play. And so it went for many seasons, with Bee, of course, secretly missing the picnic times and riding the rapids together with Otter and Otter wishing for a play companion.

When the cold weather came, the bees in the hive were tucked away with ample provisions. As for Otter, it was just a matter of riding the stream to the sea, where the favorable currents took her south to more abundant fishing grounds. So she bid a sad farewell to her tearful dear Honeybee and set off for southern waters.

That autumn, as bitter winds began whipping at the dried flower stalks of the ocher meadow, Honeybee was making the last run back to the hive. Upon crossing the familiar stream, he glanced down and saw a sight that made his heart skip a beat. There was a hungry-looking Otter, home unexpectedly. Bee dove close and asked why Otter had returned from her rich southern feeding grounds. Otter replied that there were no more fish to eat where there once were many. She now had to rely on Bee's love and kindness for her very life.

Bee was delighted to have his sweet playful Otter home. It was at that moment that Bee realized how much he loved his playtime with Otter. "I will never again deny myself my playtime with you," said Honeybee to Otter. "From now on, I will work for my hive *and* be with you every day!"

Bee led Otter back to his hive located in a great hollow tree. The community of bees, being a generous group, invited Otter to live with them as a guest for the winter and share their honey. Throughout the cold season, Otter pledged to her beloved Honeybee that she would not just cavort and play, but would work alongside the bees to keep their stream and meadow a sweet home forever.

JOANNA AND CHRIS: A BEE AND AN OTTER

They met at a feel-good personal enrichment seminar in Esalen during the late seventies. How could anyone not fall in love in Big Sur, California, with messages of love, peace, and togetherness all around?

Joanna was a thirty-one-year-old administrator of a halfway house for adolescent girls in San Diego, and Chris was an out-of-work aspiring actor in Los Angeles. Joanna was sent to the workshop by the halfway house CEO to "stretch her consciousness." Although she was excellent in running the business end of things, her staff had accused her of being stiff, rigid, and out of touch with her feelings.

It was Joanna's first group enrichment experience and she didn't know what to expect. Walking into the conference room, she saw almost two hundred men and women sitting on the floor of a large carpeted ballroom. Some of them were talking, others doing what appeared to be some Yoga stretching, and some were sitting alone with their backs propped up against the wall. Joanna felt uncomfortable. She didn't know anyone and didn't know what to expect.

Over the public-address system she heard the workshop leader introduce the first exercise. It was a warm-up called "blind milling." Participants were to walk around the ballroom and greet each other nonverbally. They could hug, shake hands, or do whatever they felt comfortable doing. "How odd," Joanna thought. "What if someone grabs me?" She wasn't sure she wanted to greet anyone, after all—they were strangers.

As some nondescript background music played, people began to walk around silently. She decided to wait and see what other people did before she ventured off on her own. And then she saw him. Chris was about six feet tall with dark hair and a pleasant face. He smiled at her from across the room and began to walk toward her. As he approached, there was something about him that she liked immediately. And as suddenly as that, her fear disappeared.

Chris moved toward her and ran his fingers lightly across the top of her hand. With her hands outstretched, she received his touch. She had cut her thumb earlier that morning and had a Band-Aid wrapped around it. Chris stroked the Band-Aid playfully, and communicated his concern without uttering a sound. He then gestured a goodbye and continued on to greet another person.

"This isn't so bad," she thought. "I can do this."

In the next fifteen minutes or so, Joanna met about twenty or thirty people. No one grabbed her or touched her inappropriately. The awkwardness faded, and she got into the spirit of things.

It was time for the next exercise. It was to occur in small groups of ten or twelve people. As she entered the small discussion room, her mystery man was there.

The group leader told participants to select a partner they didn't know before the workshop and touch each other's faces. "Oh my God," Joanna thought. "I can't do this with someone I don't even know." Just then, Chris moved over and signaled, "How about us pairing up?" She nodded.

People were instructed to take turns touching and receiving. The room had enough space for the pairs to spread out and find some privacy. She and Chris went to the far corner and sat down on the floor facing each other.

"Hi, I'm Chris, what's your name?" he asked.

"I'm Joanna," she answered. "What a captivating voice he has," she thought as she looked into his green eyes.

"Would it be okay with you if I touch your face?" Chris asked.

"I guess so. I'm kinda new at this sort of thing," she answered nervously.

Chris smiled a comforting smile as he reached up very gently and ran his fingers across Joanna's forehead, down her nose, and across her cheek. "Smooth skin," he commented. Joanna tipped her head demurely, allowing her long, straight, dark hair to fall across her face. She felt exposed and uncomfortable being looked at so closely.

"Why doesn't Joanna like Joanna's face?" Chris asked innocently.

Joanna was moved by his directness. "I guess I don't like my face very much," she answered, surprising herself with her candor.

"Why?" he asked. "It's a wonderful face."

She's sure she fell in love with him right there and then. It had been years since she had let herself be so vulnerable to anyone. There was something about Chris's gentleness and sweet honesty that made her trust him instantly.

In the weeks that followed, they saw each other often. Chris showed her how to skip stones across a pond, sail, and go backpacking in the Rockies. Sex was splendid under the open sky and she had never felt more in love. For the first time she understood what was meant by the expression "The earth moved!" Chris's lips were the most delicious she had ever tasted and they couldn't get enough of one another.

Every day was a surprise. Chris would never fail to pick wildflowers for her or express his love through his own guitar compositions. He taught her how to play, laugh more, and worry less. Chris introduced Joanna to the simple pleasures she had been overlooking for most of her life.

Ten months later, they were married. Joanna was the primary provider as Chris looked for acting jobs. This was fine for the first six months, but it wasn't long before Joanna became upset that Chris spent his days playing guitar or going to an occasional open audition.

Joanna, I'm sure you've figured out by now, is the busy Bee in this couple who had found herself a free-spirited Otter. As you'd predict, the trouble only escalated as she expected him to become a bit more responsible and well organized—like herself. "When are you going to get a real job and start taking some of the burden off my shoulders?" she demanded one day. Chris was crushed. He felt her limiting his spontaneity and became resentful.

Chris, a playful pleasure seeker at heart, expected Joanna to drop her financial budgets and briefcase at the door. Being an Otter, he would want to pack a picnic lunch or go away overnight at a moment's notice. This was not Joanna's style. Her Bee temperament required that she take the time to plan a trip "properly," considering all of the options.

By the time their second anniversary rolled around, Joanna and Chris were in my office. He had developed a problem with his sexual desire and they were rarely having sex. When they did have sex, Chris felt it lacked enthusiasm and fire. Joanna worked on making him feel good, but he felt her heart wasn't in it.

The turning point in therapy was when they realized that they were criticizing the same qualities in their lover that had initially attracted them. By remembering to appreciate what she loved about Chris, Joanna began to awaken his desire for her.

Chris decided to learn from Joanna's expertise as an administrator. He took her advice in organizing his job search. He drafted a clearly focused résumé and was soon getting several callbacks. The best part of this story is that Chris landed a substantial role in a feature film, so the tables were turned financially.

And what about Joanna? She still managed the money and kept the details of their home in order, but decided she needed to remember to "smell the roses." She made sure to interject a solid dose of fun into her daily schedule. After all, isn't that why she married him? By learning from their lovers, Chris and Joanna became more complete as individuals and an unbeatable team.

WORKERS AND PLAYERS

The Honeybee and the Otter teach us about the important balance between work and play. In the fable, the song of the Honeybee awakens the flowers. Its diligent, tireless efforts propagate the meadows with blossoms and provide the hive with sustaining nectar. Honeybees shun a lack of purpose in the same way that Otters shun organized activities. Bees thrive on scheduling, order, and thoroughness.

The Otter, on the other hand, loves spontaneity and fun. Neatness and order are unimportant to him. Creativity, responsiveness, and spontaneity are what matter. The Otter's motto is: "If you can't turn work into play, then it probably isn't worth doing at all!"

SEXUAL COMPATIBILITY

For sex to be meaningful, Energizers and Stabilizers—Lions and Bears, must learn to communicate in each other's language. Energizers must improve their listening skills and slow their pace. Energizers can feel unloved if their Stabilizer partner doesn't reach out at the "proper" time, or isn't as talkative as he or she would like, when it's simply a difference in preference. Energizers need to be careful not to talk too much during sex. They have a tendency to overstate points that will seem redundant and unnecessary to their Stabilizer lover. Stabilizers, on the other hand, need to learn to say "something" during sex—*anything*. If you're a Stabilizer who hesitates to speak your mind, begin with one loving word and go from there. Your Energizer partner values hearing your voice. Your silent reveries may be interpreted as boredom or disinterest.

And what about Worker and Player couples? Workers are more comfortable when they plan sex. "Saturday evening, after the dishes are done and the sheets are changed." This is the kiss of death to the spontaneous pleasure-seeking Player who would rather be grabbed in the hallway or have an impromptu lovemaking session on the kitchen counter. If you're a Worker, try to go with the flow *just once*. Give your partner a spontaneous squeeze under the table at the restaurant, or surprise her with a romantic voice-mail message for no particular reason other than you're thinking of her. And for the relentless pleasure-seeking Player, a little organization never hurt anyone. Go along with a scheduled time for sex and add your own creative flair.

And let's not forget the likes who marry likes; they're less common, but they *do* exist: Lions who marry Lions and approach everything as if it were a competitive event; or the Otters who pair up with Otters and are wonderful party types but can't do much else. Bears who hook up with Bears typically function in low gear (it's not unusual for the less Bearlike of the couple to complain of stagnation), and the two Bees find that all work and no play make for a very boring sexual relationship.

JANET AND RICK: A LOVE STORY BETWEEN BEE AND BEE/OTTER

Janet, a forty-one-year-old financial analyst, a classic Worker Bee, thought she had lived a very orderly life before she fell in love with Rick, her adorable Bee Otter companion. The first time she saw him he made her smile. While presenting his plans for a large housing development to the board of directors, he dropped his transparencies all over the floor. As he collected them, unruffled, Janet was impressed by his confident style and his ability to make light of a situation she would have found intolerable.

Janet's tidy office reflected her methodical Bee-like existence. A place for everything and everything in its place was her motto. She rarely acted on impulse and was the queen of the flowcharts. If a project required a firm deadline, Janet was appointed to the task. To look at her, there was no question she had it "all together." Her straight honey-blond hair, stylishly cut, was never out of place. From head to regularly pedicured toes, she was the picture of perfection, or so it seemed—wardrobe, makeup, the works.

Janet had never been married, but dated often. The ardor typically faded after a few months because of sexual "differences." Men were initially captivated by her easy smile, full sensuous lips, and confident manner. But, as you might have guessed, Janet's confidence was only skin deep.

Love wasn't openly expressed in Janet's family. Dad was conservative in dress and demeanor. His friends described him as reserved, emotionally unavailable, honest, and hardworking. One of the few times he showed passion was when he was annoyed. When she was young, she learned to tiptoe around Dad to not get him upset. Although he was slow to anger, when he'd finally blow it would be scary. "I remember forgetting to wipe my feet after coming home from a high school field hockey game," she said. "Dad saw the mud on the kitchen floor and slammed his hand so hard on the kitchen table I was afraid he'd break it. He was unpredictable like that and could explode at any time."

Sex was a taboo subject. Her mom made it clear that sex was a "duty" and not something to be enjoyed. Dad warned her that boys "were out for one thing, so be careful!" Janet learned to be cautious and shut down her sexual feelings. When she got older she couldn't turn her feelings on. Sexual desire became a problem for her.

Rick, forty-four, was a different story. Although he was also a Bee, he had a lot of Otter in him and could be carefree and fun-loving when the mood suited him. About twenty pounds overweight, he enjoyed food, good music, and wild sex with gusto. His motto was to work hard and play hard because you could die at any time. His father was killed in a motorcycle accident when Rick was seventeen. Rick was convinced that he would follow suit and "go out in a moment of madness." He liked watching erotic videos, and experimenting with sexual toys and some light bondage.

After two failed marriages, Rick was reluctant to do it again, but wanted a woman to "love intensely." Rick had lost his mom to cancer when he was only twelve. "She was a good Christian woman with a loving heart. Whenever you get close to someone, they leave," he offered sadly. "I miss my dad too. He was a great guy. After he passed away, I think a part of me died."

Early on, Rick and Janet said they were a great fit sexually. She was open to sexual experimentation and it didn't seem to matter that she didn't feel any real desire. But sex without desire became arduous and unrewarding. She became tired of Rick's complicated sexual extravaganzas and would participate only in straight "vanilla sex." Rick resented Janet's boundaries and felt his passion being smothered. Janet realized she'd never please Rick and pulled away emotionally and physically.

With Rick and Janet, one partner carried the warmth, spontaneity, and excitement, while the other was in charge of analytic detail and order. Rick was able to tone down the Worker Bee and free his Otterly passion. Unfortunately, Janet felt uncomfortable with what she perceived as Rick's impulsiveness. The problem came to me when they both felt locked into their respective inflexible positions.

IMPROVING YOUR SEXUAL FLEXIBILITY

The therapeutic goal for Janet and Rick, as it is for so many couples, is to develop more flexibility in their interactions. Each one shared, examined, and confronted their own fears and expectations for satisfying intimacy. Janet was a master at controlling herself and her environment by keeping her emotions in check. As a girl she lived in fear of Dad's outbursts, and as a woman she made sure she held her passion under tight rein. Instead of feeling her own passion, it was safer to express her emotions through her partner. But this becomes tiresome after a while.

Rick was delighted to be the "party planner" at first, but he had hoped they would come to share the responsibility. He admired Janet and loved her efficiency, but wanted to be "let inside"—emotionally.

They came to one of my seminars to find a way through their impasse. After identifying their individual styles and listing their strengths and growing edges, they discovered that each of them was an expert in what the other one must learn. Between them both, they possessed all the elements necessary for healthy intimacy and sexuality.

By completing the test in the next chapter you and your partner will discover your own sexual styles and the strengths and limitations of your sexual fit.

๛

FINDING YOUR SEXUAL STYLE

If you press me to say why I loved him, I can say no more
than it was because he was he and I was I.

—MONTAIGNE

I've used the following sexual styles inventory with hundreds of couples in my practice. I've included it for you and your partner to help you identify your individual sexual styles.

You may already know whether you're a Lion, Bear, Bee, or Otter, but this will help you validate your hunch.

- **Read each of the following twenty items and select the *TWO*** answers that *BEST* complete each sentence.
- **Don't spend too much time thinking about each response.** Your first response is usually the best response.
- **Remember that there are no "right" or "wrong" answers here.**
- **Pick only two answers, even if there are more than two that apply** to you.

SEXUAL STYLES INVENTORY

1. When I'm stressed or anxious, I prefer:

A. Closeness

B. Solitude

C. Doing something like gardening, playing a sport, or using my computer

D. Daydreaming, hiking, or just getting away

2. What I fear most is:

A. Predictability

B. Humiliation

C. Chaos

D. Abandonment

3. During sex I like:

A. Silent appreciation

B. Sexy talk

C. Knowing how to give my partner a great orgasm

D. Experimentation

4. During sex I'm thinking about:

A. My fantasies

B. What my partner wants

C. What I should be doing

D. What I want

5. When it comes to sex, I usually:

A. Initiate

B. Wait to be invited

C. Schedule lovemaking

D. Am a spur-of-the-moment kind of person

6. When it comes to anger, I tend to be:

A. Slow to anger and slow to let go

B. Quick to anger and quick to move on

C. An impulsive fighter who argues from my "gut"

D. A logical fighter who argues the facts

7. I think of myself as:

A. Sharing and emotionally available

B. Agreeable and cooperative

C. Fun-loving and creative

D. Rational and well organized

8. People have described me as:

A. Intense, demanding, or controlling

B. Hard to read, playing my cards close to the vest

C. Perfectionist, time-focused, and productivity-centered

D. Adventurous and pleasure-oriented

9. I find myself attracted to or marrying partners who are:

A. Exciting daredevils or artistically creative types

B. Intelligent introverts

C. Success-driven hardworking organizers

D. Passionate extroverts

10. It's harder for me to:

A. Give orders

B. Take orders

C. Shoot from the hip

D. Stay with a strict plan

11. During sex what's most important to me is:

A. How well I performed

B. My partner's pleasure

C. My pleasure

D. Sexual variety and excitement

12. When relationships end, I tend to be:

A. The one who leaves

B. The one who is left

C. The one who has a plan worked out

D. The one with another lover in the wings

13. During sex I like to talk:

A. Rarely

B. About techniques, not feelings

C. Before, after, and during sex

D. And make noises as the spirit moves me

14. When it comes to sex:

A. I just go with the flow, but the wilder the better

B. I ask for what I want

C. I approach lovemaking in a systematic or mechanical way

D. I'd like my partner to "know" my body and what I want without having to ask

15. On a vacation I prefer to:

A. Read the guidebooks and develop an itinerary that includes the important sites of interest

B. Make all the plans so I know things will be done right

C. Play in waves or browse, but never lock into a schedule

D. Trust my partner to make the plans

16. I prefer sex:

A. When I'm horny

B. When my partner is receptive

C. When it's planned and we've both showered

D. When it's spontaneous

17. When it comes to fighting, I:

A. Am a masterful debater and argue until I've won

B. Dislike confrontation

C. Stick to the facts and make my points logically

D. Use humor or some unconventional approach to disarm my opponent

18. I'd rather have my partner:

A. Yell at me than ignore me

B. Ignore me than yell at me

C. Tell me the feelings, not the facts

D. Tell me the facts, not the feelings

19. When it comes to problem-solving strategies, I:

A. Confront

B. Create

C. Analyze

D. Avoid

20. **My philosophy in relationships is:**
    A. Speak the truth
    B. Think before you speak
    C. Carpe diem—seize the day
    D. Actions speak much louder than words

SCORING

1. After you and your partner finish the sentence completion, circle the letters of the answers for each item in the styles key on next page.
2. Count your total responses in each column.
3. The two highest totals are your preferred sexual styles.

STYLES KEY

	YOU						YOUR PARTNER			
1.	A	B	C	D		1.	A	B	C	D
2.	D	B	C	A		2.	D	B	C	A
3.	B	A	C	D		3.	B	A	C	D
4.	D	B	C	A		4.	D	B	C	A
5.	A	B	C	D		5.	A	B	C	D
6.	B	A	D	C		6.	B	A	D	C
7.	A	B	D	C		7.	A	B	D	C
8.	A	B	C	D		8.	A	B	C	D
9.	B	D	A	C		9.	B	D	A	C
10.	B	A	C	D		10.	B	A	C	D
11.	C	B	A	D		11.	C	B	A	D
12.	A	B	C	D		12.	A	B	C	D
13.	C	A	B	D		13.	C	A	B	D
14.	B	D	C	A		14.	B	D	C	A
15.	B	D	A	C		15.	B	D	A	C
16.	A	B	C	D		16.	A	B	C	D
17.	A	B	C	D		17.	A	B	C	D
18.	A	B	D	C		18.	A	B	D	C
19.	A	D	C	B		19.	A	D	C	B
20.	A	B	D	C		20.	A	B	D	C
Totals:						Totals:				
	LION	BEAR	BEE	OTTER			LION	BEAR	BEE	OTTER

SCORES (YOU)

Lion _____

Bear _____

Bee _____

Otter _____

SCORES (PARTNER)

Lion _____

Bear _____

Bee _____

Otter _____

STYLES GRAPH

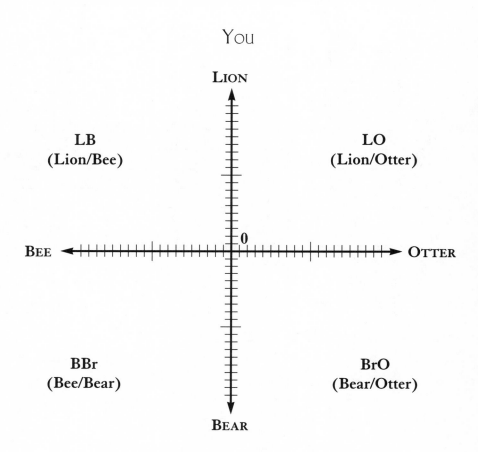

YOU

LION

LB
(Lion/Bee)

LO
(Lion/Otter)

BEE ← | | | | | | | | | | | | | | | | | | | | | | | | 0 | | | | | | | | | | | | | | | | | | | | | | | | → OTTER

BBr
(Bee/Bear)

BrO
(Bear/Otter)

BEAR

Most people can identify stylistic tendencies in more than one area. Remember, your responses suggest only personality tendencies. There are no fixed "truths." Each response can vary depending upon the specific situation, partner, or context.

Each style is on a continuum from mild to extreme. Remember, the goal of all *growth is the development of flexibility and balance.*

Before you read further to discover more about your individual and couple sexual styles, use the graphs and place a mark at the number that corresponds to each of your scores.

YOUR PARTNER

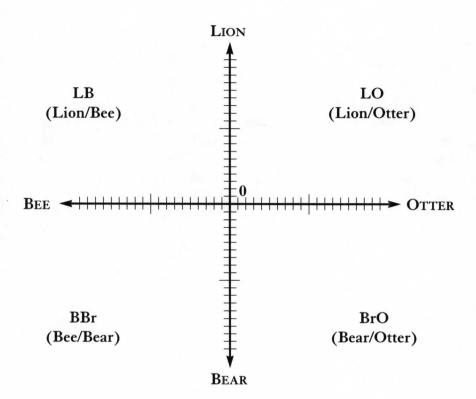

After completing your graphs, you've probably discovered that neither of you is *exclusively* Lion, Bear, Bee, or Otter. While you may have one predominant style, it's typical to find more than one style exerting its influence.

You may be a Lion Bee, Lion Otter, Bear Bee, and Bear Otter combination; or you may have three areas represented.

Connect the dots on your graphs and compare the shape of your graph to your partner's graph. Look for areas of overlap or similarity. The overlap areas signify your shared styles. Now look for areas that are different. **Those areas you do not share become your personal challenges and growing edges.**

The next five chapters will tell you more about your individual styles, the way your styles complement or oppose each other sexually, and your ongoing "life lessons."

Once you've become attracted to the partner of your dreams and have found that special fit, remember that *flexibility* is the antidote to boredom and the key to Extraordinary Sex.

The secret to making the *vital connection* depends on your willingness to face the hidden parts of yourself, confront the fears that accompany intimacy, try out an unfamiliar response, risk an unexpected reaction, and challenge your typical sexual style.

The following chapters will familiarize you with your usual sexual style and the style of your partner. By understanding what makes Lions, Bears, Otters, and Bees tick, you'll be better able to predict the trouble spots before they happen and be prepared to handle them more creatively.

CHAPTER 9

WHO ARE THESE LIONS?

*It is possible to have a strong self-love without any
satisfaction, rather with a self-discontent which is the more
intense because one's own little core of egoistic sensibility
is a supreme care.*

—GEORGE ELIOT, 1876

ANITA: A LION WHO NEVER HAS ENOUGH

Anita, a thirty-year-old assistant vice president for a multinational firm, is a proud Lion who describes herself as "high profile." Ever since she was four years old and got her first pair of black patent-leather tap shoes, Anita felt most comfortable with an audience. The spotlight was her favorite place to be. Whether it was on the job, at a social gathering, or in her intimate relationships, she felt best when she was center stage.

"I'm the kind of person who can't slip into any room unnoticed," she said. "Even if there are five hundred people in an auditorium, people look at me." I wasn't sure if she was bragging or complaining. In her tailored haute couture emerald-green suit and stylish gold earrings, she was the picture of poised self-assurance. Anita walked into my office with the confidence of a newly crowned Miss America greeting the eagerly awaiting paparazzi. No one would have guessed that her self-esteem was anything but impeccable or that she felt desperately alone.

When I asked her what she enjoyed about the attention she received, she said, "I'm not sure I enjoy it all that much—I'm comfortable in the center of things, but it's a lot of work. Sometimes I envy people who are okay just fading into the woodwork. There's a price to being so highly visible." An interesting response from a woman whose flame-red hair and matching personality screamed, "Look at me, world."

THE LION PERSONALITY

Lions are people who take charge in situations where others cave in. People admire their strength and leadership abilities, but often resent their power.

Anita was a natural-born leader. As a young student, she'd be one of the first to put her hand up in her classroom with the answer to a teacher's question. If you wondered where she would sit, that's easy—she'd be in the first row, right in front of the teacher. If volunteers were requested for a community project or for an extra-credit opportunity, Anita was the one to step forward. She was the editor of her high school yearbook, a Latin scholar, and a Big Sister to an inner-city girl.

But beneath all of the activity was a young woman who felt outside the real action. Like a child with her nose pressed against the candy-store window, she felt empty and deprived. "I always felt like there was a party going on and I was never invited," she said. I could never understand why the other kids didn't like me, because I tried so hard to be nice to them.

Lions underestimate their intensity and may not have a clear sense of how they're viewed by others. If they're told that they're too intense or too forthright, they're shocked. "I'm just trying to do my best," they'll say, or "I'm only being honest!"

Lions are perceived as strong, confident personalities who are independent and responsible. But inside, where no one can see, many Lions are lonely, insecure, and afraid of being unlovable. Instead of reaching out and asking for assistance, they feel more comfortable doing things themselves. Dependency isn't easy for a Lion. If you rely on someone to help you, they will have power over you—and Lions don't trust easily.

Like many Lions, Anita ached to be popular, but wasn't. Although she had one or two good friends, they were considered to be "nerds" and the in crowd shunned her. They found her attention-seeking behaviors annoying and off-putting. The sad part of all of this is that Anita didn't have a clue about why she wasn't liked. Ironically, the harder she tried, the more she distanced others. Because showing vulnerability wasn't her strong suit, she kept her softness and sensitivity hidden along with the possibilities for real intimacy.

Lions may be labeled as "flirts" but just see themselves as "friendly." If you don't invite a few well-selected Lions to your party, it will be a bore. Otters are fun, but no one can energize a party as well as a Lion. They are extroverted, gregarious, and have a penchant for entertaining conversation. Their candor can be refreshing or shocking, but is never mundane. If you want someone to keep a secret, don't tell a Lion. They share opinions and information easily and often indiscriminately. Unless the Lion is fortunate enough to have a solid dose of Bee on board, they may suffer from "foot-in-mouth syndrome" on a regular basis.

Lions are very giving, but expect others to give just as much. Their high expectations lead to frequent disappointments. Sexually their motto is "If you can't do it right, don't do it at all." Sex partners of Lions may feel so pressured to prove their adequacy, they become overwhelmed with anxiety. In trying to impress their Lion with their sexual talents, some Bears or Bees develop problems with erection, ejaculation, or orgasm.

If you know someone who has to be the first one to wear the hottest fashions right off the Paris runways, you can bet that person is a Lion. A person whose personality is dominated by Lion tendencies is driven toward conquest and attainment. They are more materialistic than Otters or Bears and are rivaled only by Bees. Bees are driven to accumulate wealth and security for their hive, but "having things" and status is important to the Lion's sense of pride. But Lions aren't selfishly materialistic. They can be very generous. Knowing how painful it is to do without, they are one of the first to champion a worthy cause or donate their time and resources to help those "less fortunate."

Another intriguing quality of Lions is their quixotic nature. There is never a dull moment if you live with a Lion. It's as if one moment the sun is shining, and the next minute a rain cloud rolls in, changing the Lion's mood dramatically. Fortunately, the moods pass quickly for the Lion, unlike the Bear, who can stay ensconced in a thunder cloud for days.

Lions dislike tedium in all forms. It's common to find them working on several projects at one time. If you're taking a Lion out to dinner, keep in mind that Lions love buffets because choosing just one entree is difficult for them. They'd prefer to sample a number of the items on the menu (or from *your* plate). After they've ordered the salmon *en croûte,* they wonder if they shouldn't have tried the lobster instead. Lions want it all. They want to go everywhere and do everything with boundless enthusiasm. Their love of travel and the exotic leads them to appreciate eclectic diversity and they allow themselves the freedom to try just about anything—at least once.

WANTING TO BE WANTED

At the center of it all, Lions just want to be wanted. Having the right designer label on her sweater made Anita feel better, but only momentarily. She spent all the money she had saved from babysitting on clothing, but no matter how much clothing she accumulated, it was never enough.

"At fifteen I was desperate to have a gray cashmere sweater just like Hadley Carrington's," she said. "Hadley, whose parents were both physicians, was the most popular girl in the school. I used to sit in English literature class and just stare at that beautiful sweater, and her perfect strand of white pearls."

As Anita spoke, her eyes began to fill with tears. "I knew I could never afford one," she continued. "One day I went to Pringle's department store and picked out their most expensive cashmere sweater. I took it to the fitting room and tried it on. It was beautiful."

Anita was having difficulty continuing her story. "And then what happened?" I asked.

"I've never told anyone this," she said. "I remember my heart pounding and this funny feeling in the pit of my stomach. The next thing I knew, I put my old sweater over it and just walked out of the store . . . just like that! I had never stolen anything before or since. I just *had* to have it."

"And what did you do with the sweater?" I asked.

Anita smiled. "The funny thing is that when I wore it to school the next day no one even noticed it. All of that for nothing."

When Lions are hungry or needy, they rarely let anything stop them. They'll relentlessly pursue a goal long after others have given up. A skillful Lion stalking her prey is reluctant to be distracted from her course. If they have some Otter features, like Anita, they aren't averse to giving in to their impulsivity and breaking the law to indulge their passions.

THE FAMILY OF A LION

There are as many families of Lions as there are Lions. However, there are some ingredients they have in common. Anita grew up in a traditional Italian home with a highly emotional father and passively compliant mother. Her mother and father were born in Sicily and spoke very little English. Her mother worked in a factory as a seamstress, kept the five-room apartment clean as a whistle, and catered to her father's every whim.

Her father was a strict disciplinarian and forbade Anita to wear any makeup or nail polish. When she was fourteen years old she decided to grow her fingernails and painted them bright red. She'll never forget his reaction. "It was Sunday evening," she said. "We were sitting down at the dining-room table for supper. I hid my hands in my lap, hoping he wouldn't notice my nails. But then I felt his eyes on my hands."

"What's that?" he demanded.

"What?" I asked innocently, pretending not to understand.

"Don't play with me!" he said, raising his voice. "Show me your finger-nails."

I held up my hands and heard my mother starting to defend me in Italian. "She didn't mean it, Mario, she'll take the polish off."

"No, I won't," I said defiantly. My father's eyes burned and his nostrils flared as he slammed his hand on the table and shouted, "Cut those nails, now!"

He told me to leave the table, but I knew only too well what was to follow. When I walked by him, he lunged at me to grab me, but missed. I ran upstairs and he was right behind me. I thought I was safe when I locked myself in the bathroom, but he got a screwdriver and opened the door. Anita began to sob. "I'll never forget that face of his as he came at me with his leather belt. I had strap marks and bruises across my face, arms, and back. But no matter what he did, I wouldn't cut my red fingernails. They were my 'red badge of courage.' "

Anita perfected a tough exterior to survive. "I felt I had two choices," she said. "I could give in to my father's tyranny and lose my identity, or stand up for my beliefs and risk being ostracized. I chose the latter."

Although Anita was an excellent student, her parents never noticed or commented. She used her studies as an escape and would spend most of her time in her room with the door closed, trying to avoid an altercation with her father. The kids called her "teacher's pet." Mrs. Marlow, her kindly fifth-grade teacher, was her savior. She sensed Anita's pain without actually knowing the details and spent hours after school just listening, offering her wisdom, and taking a genuine interest in Anita.

"I still have the Valentine's Day card she gave me," said Anita. "I wonder if she knows how important she was to me."

Lions and Their Lovers

Anita needed someone who would love her. She found herself attracted to quiet unassuming guys. Given her emotional past, she longed for someone who was "nice" and "wouldn't hurt" her. Many Lions are attracted to the solidity of a Stabilizer mate while others either avoid intimate relationships altogether or seek the familiar in a partner who replicates their challenging past.

Passion and aggression are closely linked physiologically and emotionally. They both lead to rapid heart rates, intensity, and the expression of emotion. Being yelled at or beaten can unfortunately be confused with the excitement of passion. It's not uncommon for individuals who have been hurt to confuse love with pain. If a relationship is a challenge and filled with strife, it *must* be love! The consequences of this kind of thinking can be disastrous.

Anita and Brian: A Lion and a Bear

When Anita was fifteen she met Brian, who was nineteen. He was a sophomore in college and had his own Harley-Davidson. He was the white knight who would take her away from all of the pain. This was the perfect rescue for the unhappy maiden. Brian was loving, agreeable, and pleasant—but most of all, he adored her.

Brian was a Bear from an emotionally distant home. His father was remote and his mother was stern, expecting unquestioning compliance from him. This set the stage for his attraction to strong-willed insatiable women, whom he tried to please—but rarely succeeded.

In falling for strong women, Brian could maintain his passivity and Anita could be assured of a partner who wouldn't hurt her or leave her. These were Anita's greatest fears: abuse and abandonment. Of course, what she thought would make her happy at eighteen did not satisfy her at twenty-eight.

Brian, like many Bears, wasn't especially ambitious. Because of Anita's reluctance to depend on others, she married a person who would let *her* take the lead. However, she soon grew tired of doing "all of the work" in the marriage. She was the one to initiate sex, and complained that Brian never showed "passion."

It was then that the criticisms began. Anita accused Brian of being irresponsible, lazy, immature, and aloof. She was angry at her Bear partner for not being more of a Lion! At one time, Anita had been abused, but now she had become the abuser. She was unaware that she was replicating the early lessons of her upbringing.

In his typical Bear fashion, Brian retreated more and more into his den. Sex came to a halt. They lived as roommates. Then one day he could take no more. During one of Anita's verbal tirades, Brian grabbed her by the throat and threatened to kill her. Anita was terrified, but Brian's physical assault was strangely familiar.

At the time they came to therapy, they had been sleeping in separate bedrooms, speaking to one another only when necessary. Anita was unwilling to take any responsibility for provoking the eruption. Her solution was easy—Brian had to change. Although there was no doubt that Brian had behaved abusively, Anita was also part of the problem.

In our sessions, Brian became more vocal about the hurt and anger he'd suppressed for years. He learned to verbalize his feelings and not act them out through avoidance or rage.

Anita eventually saw how she fed into their dilemma. She talked about her past, her pain, and her feelings of worthlessness. Instead of lashing out at Brian, she found ways to acknowledge and manage her anger and insecurity. By appropriately asking for what she needed, she made much more headway than by lashing out.

It's not necessary to have a crystal ball to predict the future of a marriage like this. Unless Brian and Anita were willing to take responsibility for healing their own wounds, they'd probably divorce and find themselves in another therapist's office years later with different partners but a similar saga.

OTHER LION FAMILIES

I don't want you to think that all Lions come from abusive backgrounds, because they don't. Lions, just like the other sexual types, emerge from a variety of settings and parenting styles. Many Lion families provide capable, competent role modeling and what psychologists refer to as "good enough" parenting. Other families may display either indifference or self-involvement—both contribute to a child's feeling that he has to fend for himself.

These self-involved parents often view their children as extensions of themselves. We might say that these children wind up "parenting" their parents. The child's accomplishment fill the parents' insatiable neediness. In the child's futile attempt to please the self-involved parents, he or she is left feeling empty, invisible, and ripped off.

CINDY AND KEITH: A LION AND AN OTTER

Cindy, now forty-two and married to Keith, a forty-five-year-old Otter, is one of these Lions. Her father died of brain cancer when she was twelve. "I remember the day of my father's funeral," she said. "My father's sisters and brothers were grief-stricken. There were close to two hundred people at the cemetery. He was a beloved man. One thing my mother said to me at the grave site keeps echoing through my mind: 'How could your father do this to *me?*' To *her?* What about everyone else's pain?

"I don't think I ever faced how alone I've felt for most of my life," Cindy continued. "It hit me the other night. Keith and I were making love and he was going down on me. It feels good when he runs his tongue across my clitoris, but there's something about oral sex that makes me feel sad—it's the feeling of being all alone up there. No eye contact. No body contact. Just a mouth on my genitals," she said. "After it was over, I asked Keith to hold me. I put my head on his chest and wept with joy. Keith understands how important it is for me to connect with a person, not just a penis or a tongue, and he is loving and secure enough to give me what I need."

THE QUEST TO CONQUER

The Lion's quest to conquer reflects a need for nurturing and affirmation. Some Lions tell of families that had angry confrontations, alcohol abuse, or drug use. Other Lions grew up in families that role-modeled passion and accomplishment at any cost. And still others were the product of very competitive, hard-driving, upwardly mobile families in which no achievement was deemed to be good enough. Whatever the historical antecedents, Lions learned to *count on themselves.* A very important and adaptive style unless it is taken to the extreme.

Whether one's temperament is a product of nature or nurture is uncertain. Siblings from the same family can differ widely in their personalities. Temperamental differences are discernible from birth. There are those babies who have a sensitivity to sound and startle at the slightst provocation, while others sleep soundly through the loudest clatter. There are babies with Otterlike personalities who are easily entertained and others with Bee temperaments who resist the slightest change in their feeding or nap schedules.

Lions make their wishes known boldy; Bears are more cautious; Bees prefer order; and Otters retreat into playful reverie. Keep in mind that there is no definitive family dynamic that produces a Lion, Bear, Bee, or Otter. Whether you're a Lion, Bear, Bee, or Otter or some combination, your preferences reflect a response pattern that has distinct strengths and limitations. In familiarizing ourselves with the pluses and minuses of your style, you're in a better position to make choices that enhance your intimacy.

᪥

TO SUMMARIZE SOME OF THE SALIENT FEATURES
OF A LION:
LIONS ARE PEOPLE WHO:

1. Consider themselves to be "people persons" and good communicators.
2. Love a challenge and the "hunt."
3. Prefer to chase, but enjoy being followed.
4. Are short on patience and, once they make up their mind, move quickly to action.
5. Prefer to take the initiative in all things.
6. Are great at a party and facile conversationalists.
7. Would volunteer for a solo role, but not for the chorus.
8. Share private thoughts, feelings, and opinions readily and speak before thinking.
9. Are excellent leaders, assuming they have the right followers.
10. Are quick to anger, but also quick to recover.
11. Can be intense and demanding.
12. Find themselves in the roles of rescuer or caretaker and drawn to help those who are "less fortunate."
13. Were labeled "flirt" or "ladies' man" in their dating years.
14. Usually do the walking when relationships end.

THE ATTRACTION OF A LION

What passion, what intensity, what power. It's easy to identify the body language of a Lion: confident, strutting their stuff, working a room with ease. Lions maintain good eye contact and may reach out and touch you as they speak. Appearance is important for them. The dapper guy with the designer tie is probably a Lion (or is married to one). If first impressions count, the Lion has got you hook, line, and sinker. That's their specialty. The bait and capture.

When you meet a Lion you're either drawn in by their captivating intensity or put off by their arrogance. One thing is for sure, there will never be a dull moment if a Lion is your mate.

WHAT YOU NEED TO KNOW ABOUT YOURSELF IF YOU'RE ATTRACTED TO LIONS

If you find yourself attracted to Lions, ask yourself, "What does my Lion do for me that I could learn to do for myself?" If he makes you feel important or needed, examine that more fully. You might like being in the wings for the moment and playing in the supporting cast, but ask yourself whether you'll grow tired of this routine.

Lions and Otters are very sensual types. They flirt and play easily. If you rely exclusively on your Lion mate to pique your desires, you'll never learn to ignite your own passion and give yourself a good time.

Maybe you enjoy the vicarious power you feel in your Lion's presence. The attention or respect they receive is attractive to you. As you bask in your partner's glory, walking proudly arm in arm, don't forget that this adulation is borrowed. If the Lion leaves, it goes with him.

SHERRI AND TODD: A BEE AND A LION

Sherri, twenty-four, was married to Todd, a gorgeous hunk of a man. He was a professional hockey player and exactly as you'd imagine—strong, powerful, and an egomaniac. Sherri was no slouch either. She had beauty and brains, but was much more reserved than her Lion husband. Stylistically she was a Bee, who managed Todd's career and kept things running smoothly from behind the scenes.

In the bedroom he liked sex on the wild side. Sherri's rational, somewhat restricted personality had to stretch, but she did it because she wanted to please him. Todd needed to know that he was the best sex partner she'd ever had, and Sherri reassured him that he was. Before long, however, she grew tired of the masquerade she was carrying on and settled into a more comfortable routine.

This didn't go over well with Todd, who rapidly lost interest. He was not an especially mature Lion and wasn't interested in compromise or cooperation. Without a challenge, he was bored. He wanted a woman who would cater to him, seduce him, and be his trophy. What Sherri had mistaken for love was merely convenience on Todd's part. As the excitement dwindled, he found himself a new honey and Sherri was out in the cold.

Fortunately, Todd's behavior isn't representative of all Lions. Nevertheless, Sherri's life in the fast lane was short-lived. After some soul-searching, she realized she didn't really love Todd—she loved what he represented. Before, she might have planned to attach her barnacle to another boat. Now she knew she needed to learn how to create her own success.

WHAT LIONS WANT FROM RELATIONSHIPS

IF YOUR PARTNER IS A LION, HERE ARE SOME THINGS YOU NEED TO KNOW:

1. They enjoy a challenge—mentally, physically, emotionally. Lions need to know that you look good together as a couple. If you're a Bee, Bear, or Otter, you may be less interested in your appearance than your Lion partner. Lions want to look fabulous and be seen with someone who looks equally fabulous. If you're invited to a party with your Lion, ask him or her what they plan to wear. Don't just show up in any old outfit and expect him not to notice. Coordinating your wardrobes at the same level of formality is a plus.

2. Lions prefer to chase and not be chased, although this is a difficult call. They like to feel desired and desirable, but they prefer to be at the control panel. If your Lion is also part Bee, control will be a *major* issue.

3. Remember that Lions don't trust easily and secretly fear being unlovable. Much of their bravado and confidence is merely smoke and mirrors. If they come on kind of strong or critical, recognize that they may be feeling threatened and this is one of their coping strategies.

4. Don't personalize your Lion's attacks, and whatever you do, don't run from them. Lions hate to feel abandoned. You may be tempted to leave the room, or the house, when your Lion starts his tirades, but don't. If you want to take a time-out to settle things down a bit, tell him that you'll be back in twenty minutes—and then come back when you said you would.

5. Lions respond to clear direction. Talk to your Lion. They can

be quite reasonable when approached in a forthright manner. Tell them you'd like to take turns listening and speaking. Once you have their agreement, the escalation will stop and the discussion will be more manageable.

6. If your Lion is critical of your Bear, Bee, or Otter qualities, tell them you're feelings are hurt. Remember that there is sensitivity beneath their growl and they don't want you to be hurt. Many partners of Lions play possum. They try to pretend they're unaffected by the Lion's power. This isn't a good idea. It fosters deception and distances both of you from your feelings.

7. Lions have trouble asking for what they *really* want. Many times they don't know what they want but have a vague sense that something is missing. Lions are difficult to please and frequently want "more." This may make you feel inadequate if your mission in life is to satisfy your Lion. Instead of reacting to your Lion in one of your usual ways, try saying, "Is there something that would make you feel better?" It's possible that there is nothing *you* can do and only the Lion can make himself or herself feel better. As you talk, reach out physically and stroke your lover's neck, shoulders, or back. Lions thrive on verbal and physical evidence that they're loved. If you can, writing a line or two of poetry will more than likely melt your Lion's heart.

8. Understanding your Lion on the *inside* will make it more likely that he or she will open up to you. It's a stretch and a challenge, but if you wanted it easy, you wouldn't have fallen in love with a Lion.

JOHN AND NATALIE: SEX BETWEEN TWO LIONS

Natalie, a thirty-seven-year-old homemaker, and John, a thirty-seven-year-old claims analyst, have been struggling with a sexual problem for all of their fourteen years of marriage. "I'm not sure why we waited so long to see you. I just hoped things would work themselves out alone," said Natalie. "Sex was good while we were dating and petting, but after we got married it's like someone turned off the heat and I didn't know where the thermostat was to turn it back on!"

Natalie was a Lion with Otter tendencies who had a colorful way of expressing herself. She was outgoing, spoke frankly, and had a great sense of humor. John was a Lion Bee combination. His comments were intense, but tended to be more logical and concise. "I think our problems began after Andrew was born, but I assume that's pretty typical." he said. "Natalie demanded so much attention, I just couldn't make her happy, so I stopped trying, I guess."

"So what are you hoping to gain from therapy?" I asked, turning to John. "I'm not sure," he replied. "Maybe you'll have some suggestions for how to make Natalie less upset, because I've run out of ideas."

So from the beginning it was apparent that John was in therapy to please Natalie, not to please himself. He wanted an end to the problems, not a more passionate love life.

Natalie grew up in a small town on Boston's north shore. Her father was a judge and her mom was a housewife. "Dad loved me very much," she said, "but he found it difficult to be physically demonstrative. He was a gentle man with a dry sense of humor, very Catholic, very conscientious about providing for the family, and in love with his cocktails!

"I hate to say this," she continued, "but my mother was really a very selfish woman." Natalie went on to say that she believed her dad would have divorced her mom but he feared the courts would have given her custody of the two children. "My mother was an only child of a severely depressed mother. I'm not sure what I ever did to incur her anger and disdain, but she never seemed to like me and told me so," said Natalie. "I think the worst story of all was when I was eight and she came right out and told me she wished I was dead. I learned later that she actually hurled herself down a flight of stairs to try to cause a miscarriage when she was four months pregnant."

John, the third of five children, was born into a middle-class family from Columbus, Ohio. His father was described as "domineering, unsuccessful, and cold." "My mother was a loving woman with a strong belief in Catholicism. She passed away two years ago and I miss her very much," said John.

"How did you each learn about sex?" I asked them both.

Natalie responded first. "I heard something about sex from the neighborhood kids and was stupid enough to mention it to my mother. Her words of wisdom to me were: 'Be careful you don't let your pussy get you into a scrape!' Natalie turned to me with an embarrassed look. "Can you believe a mother would say such a thing? For years I wondered what she meant.

"When my breasts started to develop she took me to a doctor because my nipples were swollen. She made me feel like sexual development was a *disease*. I'm lucky that the doctor reassured me that my body was growing normally."

"And what about you, John? How did you learn about sex?" I asked.

"I was raised to think that masturbation was a sin, but I did it anyway," John said with a chuckle. "The first time I ejaculated I wasn't sure what had happened, but it sure felt good, so I kept on doing it.

"The first woman I ever made love to was Natalie, and we were both twenty-two-year-old virgins. We didn't know what we were doing, but we figured it out." They both smiled.

"Anything I should know about your intimate times together?" I inquired. Natalie spoke. "Yes . . . I've always wanted sex more than John and that's been upsetting to me. John doesn't hug me or touch me very much. It's still the same now. He touches all the 'necessary spots' briefly and then puts it in."

John looked annoyed. "Well, what do you expect me to do? You just lie there like a dead fish." John and Natalie were demonstrating how easily they become embattled. Two Lions unwilling to back down.

When I spoke with John alone, he said he felt like a failure. "Whatever I do doesn't seem to be enough for her," he confessed. "She needs so much reassurance, I'm not sure I can give it to her."

Natalie told me she wished that John would talk to her and tell her he loved her. She didn't understand that John felt her repeated requests for loving assurances were excessively demanding. John assumed that Natalie knew he loved her—after all, why would he stay with her all of these years if he didn't? His actions should be enough proof for her.

For Lions, sex sometimes involves an out-front enthusiastic display peppered with talk, fantasy, and excitement; other times, being together, quietly and privately, can be equally satisfying. Natalie and John had gotten their signals crossed. Just because John didn't verbalize his feelings as often as she would have liked, Natalie mistakenly assumed he wasn't having any!

For sex to be satisfying, Lions need to learn how to ask for what they want in a less demanding way. They don't think there's anything wrong with their candid declarations—"Ouch, that hurts, you never know how to touch my clitoris the right way." Instead of jumping down your partner's throat, a Lion needs to try a more sensitive approach. Perhaps you could place your hand on top of your partner's and *show* him how you like to have your clitoris touched. Make sure to tell him what you like and not just what you don't like. "I like it when you brush your lips against mine like this." Even though you're both "strong" Lions and value honest expression, it still feels good to hear something positive to balance the criticism.

In talking more to his Lion, John learned that Natalie sometimes enjoyed making love to ease tension. She wanted to hear more conversation from him and wanted sex to be more exciting. Natalie asked John if they could use a vibrator in bed and he agreed. They also decided to purchase some sex videos to spice up their routine.

Instead of feeling defensive, John started to understand his Lion partner better. He learned that Natalie was easily aroused in the morning, so instead of always making love after *The Late Show,* he started to vary the times he initiated. Instead of blaming himself and feeling like a failure, he worked on listening to Natalie and tried to stretch beyond his own usual security zone. On her birthday, he planned an outlandish escape to a sleazy little motel that had a heart-shaped tub and lights around the bed. This was quite a bit of a stretch for John, and Natalie was delighted.

And what about Natalie? She practiced appreciating John's efforts and learning to take "no" for an answer. She stopped assuming that John's periodic disinterest was a criticism of her and took responsibility for making things more positive in their relationship.

SEX WITH A LION

Although Lions are masterful at taking charge in bed, they also need to know they're desirable. Compliment your Lion, whisper sweet nothings in his or her ear, and they'll follow you anywhere!

Lions love a challenge and enjoy the chase, but they also want to be pursued. The perfect aphrodisiac is an unexpected message proclaiming your love. Whether it's on his or her voice mail, scrawled in lipstick on his

mirror, or jotted on your napkin during lunch, your Lion will appreciate
your romantic efforts.

Lions are very sensual, so remember to indulge *all* of their senses. Spend
time slowly adoring every inch of them and don't jump right into the "main
event." Lions may like an occasional quickie, but it's rarely their preference.

HINTS FOR LIVING WITH A LION

**1. Practice your communication! Nodding in silent agreement
doesn't do it for a Lion. They want to hear you say, "You drive me
wild. I want you now."**

**2. Appearance is important. Don't think you can show up dressed
in any old thing if you're accompanying a Lion. What "everyone else
is wearing" won't matter to them. Lions expect to make an impact
and to stand out from the crowd.**

**3. Lions have an intriguing blend of intensity and sensitivity.
Although they can be powerful, they are also easily hurt. Proceed
cautiously with sarcastic comments. Your jokes may bruise their
delicate skins. Make sure you mean what you say. If your partner is a
Lion, be forewarned—their passion cuts both ways.**

**4. Stand up to your Lion. They will respect you for your efforts.
And don't accumulate your injustices for months before you do.
Lions appreciate immediacy.**

LIFE LESSONS FOR LIONS

When Lions say they're bored, they're usually feeling *unimportant.* Virtually every style has lessons to learn and we can identify the unique lessons
by looking at our choice of partner. Lions usually find themselves with
partners who offer them patience, an understanding ear, a calming influence, nurturance, and an anchor in the storm. They also feel less threatened
when they function as a rescuer, helper, and "mommy" or "daddy" to their
mate.

TRY THESE SUGGESTIONS:

1. To gain more flexibility, learn to listen without interjecting your perspective, control your reactivity and anger, control your tendency toward acting impulsively by counting to ten (or one hundred if necessary), be more affirming with and less critical of your lovers, and increase your tolerance for alternative points of view.

It's not a coincidence that Lions usually wind up with Bear partners who have difficulty asserting themselves. They frequently complain, "He never talks to me or tells me what he's feeling." Lions are initially more comfortable when they are running the show, but this wears thin over time. A part of the Lion would love to share their throne, but another part of their personality fears giving up their power. When their Bear mates finally manage to muster up enough courage to speak up or reach out sexually, Lions may be reluctant to acknowledge their efforts. They may say, "Sure, you asked for sex last night, but you did it because I told you to—it wasn't *your* idea." By discounting their partner's efforts, they don't have to face a change in the balance of power, which would be very threatening to the Lion's self-esteem and usual coping pattern.

2. Instead of accusing your Bear mate of acting like a child, stop acting like a parent. By encouraging and building your partner's self-esteem, you will create a win-win situation for both of you.

3. Recognize that your reality isn't the only reality. Allowing some room for your partner's perspective will go a long way toward fostering his or her self-esteem.

4. Distinguish between assertiveness and aggression and express your opinions less critically. Your all-or-nothing formulations would be better served if you try to find some shades of gray.

5. One important life lesson for a Lion is to tolerate anxiety without having to rush to "fix things." Lions are great enablers who would rather do something themselves, because they know it will be done "right." This is a counterdependent move on your part. As long as others depend on you, you can complain about being overburdened, but never relinquish your throne long enough to share some of the power.

In your relationships, you long for security and stability but fear relying on others to provide it. You protest you want closeness, but make it difficult for your partners to meet your standards. One patient described his Lion wife in this way: "Trying to make love to her is like snuggling up to a porcupine. I have to be careful of her quills!" Showing vulnerability and letting someone see your softness is the most difficult life challenge of all for you. It depends on developing trust and feeling good enough inside. Once a Lion feels secure in their partner's love, they will let him or her find a permanent place in their heart.

YVETTE AND CLIFF: A LION AND AN OTTER

Yvette and Cliff, a Lion and an Otter, had a whirlwind courtship that resulted in marriage after three short months. They were a case of instant compatibility. Each of them played the roles that met the other's expectations—initially.

"Cliff was so different from me," Yvette began in one of our individual sessions. "He was a musician, very laid-back and relaxed, and had a counter-culture vantage point that I found fascinating in an unorthodox way." They met at a local coffeehouse and immediately clicked. "His guitar playing was so wholesome and guileless," Yvette reminisced. "I was immediately captivated by his innocence." Her last boyfriend had been materialistic and not very spiritual. "I was so sick of the stiff corporate types—I wanted more than a suit."

Cliff and Yvette spent hours walking in the woods, reading poetry aloud by a brook, and sharing their hopes and dreams. Yvette admitted that being with Cliff was a stretch for her, but underestimated how much of a stretch it would be. "At first, I didn't realize we had problems because I wanted to please him so much I went along with his fanciful whims." She paused and looked a bit uncomfortable before telling me about some of the "kinky" sex they participated in together. "I hesitate to tell you this, but maybe it's because I've been raised to have such conservative sex. One night he brought home some handcuffs and a blindfold and tied me to the bed! It was something I'd never done before, but I trusted Cliff and went along. By going with the flow, I had the best orgasm of my life. Cliff was good for me in that way. I never considered what would happen when it was time to get serious, put away the toys, and run a real household—I just assumed we'd work it out."

Sixteen months into their marriage, a bomb fell. One evening Cliff announced he felt stifled and couldn't handle the responsibilities of married life—just like that. "He told me he had to be free, like the wind," Yvette announced angrily. "Can you believe that? I thought we had a shared vision of home, family, and outside interests, but I couldn't have been more wrong. Cliff and I had great sex and were terrific playmates, but he wasn't ready to grow up. How could I have been so stupid?"

Unless Lions have a solid dose of Bee in their personalities, they may be led exclusively by their hearts. Yvette's strong attraction to Cliff's wanderlust and her desire to break out of a straitlaced existence obstucted her vision. I'm not suggesting that all Otters are perpetual children who shun responsibility, but some are. It's important not to be so drawn in by their magnetic appeal that you're blinded to the realities.

April and Kent: A Lion and a Bee

Lions and Bees make excellent business partners. The Lion supplies the energy and the Bee provides the action plan. In lovemaking, if the Bee can put down his road map long enough to look at the scenery, they can create exciting moments together. Because Lions and Bees are strong personalities, control can become an area of contention. Bees are excellent partners for Lions who happen to be high in emotionality and limited in rationality. If a Lion is expansive and impressionistic in his or her thinking, the Bee's restrictive factual approach serves as the perfect complement. Each has something of importance to offer the other.

April met Kent while they were in college and she was instantly attracted to his ambition. Kent was a business major who was running his own perfume wholesaling company out of his college dormitory. He developed a catalogue service, an 800 number, and had a staff of five assistants in his junior year. April was impressed, to say the least. She was a fine arts major and Kent loved her enthusiasm and creativity. Together they were an unbeatable team. They planned a storybook wedding and honeymoon in Greece that was sheer perfection. What could possibly go wrong?

April and Kent, a Lion/Bee couple in their late twenties, now share a marriage and a business. Kent provides the business acumen and financial savvy that allows April's creative talents and energy to flourish. Married for six years and the parents of a three-year-old girl, they have all the trappings of a successful marriage. The problem is that Kent has begun to have problems keeping an erection during intercourse.

"Almost immediately I got the sense that Kent was 'doing me' instead of loving me," April complained in one of our meetings. "He would just 'do' too much—I can't really explain it. All I know is that we never laughed or let go in the bedroom, or anywhere else for that matter. I became uncomfortable with the tense deliberate style of lovemaking that seemed as businesslike as our business."

Bees are often driven by a fear of losing control. Their activities function as a glue that cements the cracks created by emotional exposure. Hard-driving Bees are sometimes reluctant to laugh hard or become excited during sex for fear they'll lose their composure. When they *do* let down their containing wall, even for a moment, it's important that the Lion doesn't jump right in. It's tempting to take advantage of the opening, but the Bee needs time to adjust to his vulnerability, so I advise Lions to proceed cautiously.

Kent's Bee personality was driven by "shoulds." He carefully scheduled their sexual rendezvous to produce "maximum enjoyment." If anything didn't go according to plan, especially if he had trouble maintaining his erection, he'd feel the evening had been "wasted." He labored to be efficient, productive, and accurate in his sexual style, but this left April feeling like she was making love to a computer.

It's hard to fault someone for trying too hard, but April felt that Kent was driven to satisfy her perfectly, but that it had nothing to do with her. In fact, she felt almost invisible during lovemaking. If Kent didn't meet his sexual goals, he felt like a failure. Unlike the Bear who reacts to the expectations of others, Bees design their own pressure to please and then try to cope with the strain they produce. When it came to sex, Kent only felt comfortable if he knew what he was supposed to do and how he could do it flawlessly.

The encouraging news is that Kent was aware of his problems and was motivated to make some changes in himself. He compared his existence to that of a locomotive who was running swiftly and efficiently pulling a heavy cargo as long as the track was laid out for him. "I get worried if I don't know what to do and get uncomfortable with a lack of direction," he admitted.

Since April enjoyed giving direction, they fit well until they both realized their restrictive styles were limiting the potential of their sexual passion. As long as Kent had his own little niche of sexual techniques, he was comfortable but knew there had to be more to sex than this.

I suggested that Kent make one important change in his lovemaking. Instead of doing what he felt he "should" do, I asked him to do only what he "wanted" to do. The next time he approached April to make love, he was to invite her only when *he* wanted to, not when he thought the time was right or she'd be most receptive. When he touched her body or kissed her, Kent was to focus on doing whatever brought *him* pleasure and to let go of the "shoulds" and notions of what he thought April might enjoy. I told April not to coach Kent or remind him, but to support him in his experimentations with new behaviors—to make herself available to him according to his own time frame. If anything was uncomfortable for her, she was to tell him, but otherwise she was to trust him and go along for the ride.

The positive results were immediate. After only one session Kent and April came back to describe one of their most pleasurable lovemaking sessions ever. She felt he was making love to *her* and not just to her body parts. "I could tell he was really enjoying me and it really turned me on." Kent had to stop himself from worrying about "shoulds" and remind himself to focus on pleasure, but he noticed the difference from the start. "I felt as though we were sharing something more intimate and more personal. It was wonderful. I got aroused, we had intercourse, and I felt in control in a different way. This time I made sure I did what I wanted to do—not what I thought was expected of me. I know it will take practice, but working hard is easy for me." He laughed.

Not all cases respond so rapidly, but one thing is for sure. If each partner is willing to take a look at their part of the problem, the prognosis is usually excellent.

The secret to enhanced intimacy is in taking responsibility for improving one's own security and stability. By rounding out the rough edges, we're better able to tolerate a wider range of stylistic options and enjoy a more balanced vital connection with our lovers.

The delicious blend of intimacy and passion that I call extraordinary sex emerges out of safety, trust, and vulnerability. Couples who have extraordinary sex tell me that they feel safe and secure with their partners because they feel safe and secure within themselves. In the end, the only lasting security is one you allow yourself to experience.

THE WORST OF LIONS

Each sexual style has its pluses and minuses. At their worst, Lions can lash out at you with the venom of a rattlesnake. When angered, they are masterful at discovering your Achilles' heel. They are king/queen of the jungle and demand respect. To conquer their foe, they are prepared to use whatever is necessary: disarming remarks, sarcasm, shouting, psychological warfare, or whatever else is required to maintain their dominance. They can be egotistical, highly competitive, excitable, and confrontational. They can be so immersed in their own needs that they fail to recognize or accept the limitations of others.

Lions expect their mates' undivided attention. Although they can be amorous and convincingly profess their undying love, they can be fickle and just as easily move on to their next paramour. But a Lion who is content with their partner will stay with their lover for life.

THE BEST OF LIONS

At their best, Lions are Fourth of July every day. They are passionate, peppery, alive, attentive, ambitious, and emphatic. They are energetic and supply the spark necessary to get your project from the drawing board to the assembly line.

They can help you recapture your hidden joy, unleash your sense of humor, and face your fears of spontaneity. Lions are honest, reliable, and caring. They make loyal friends, but fearsome enemies. They are personality personified and your days will never be dull or predictable with a Lion by your side.

CHAPTER 10

WHO ARE THESE BEARS?

Avoiding humiliation is the core of tragedy and comedy.

—JOHN GUARE, LONDON, 1988

ROD AND HOLLY: A BEAR AND HIS LION

Rod, a twenty-eight-year-old data processor Bear, came to see me because his wife "told him to come." Recently married to Holly, a twenty-six-year-old paralegal Lion, Rod has felt insecure about his sexuality for as far back as he can remember and wants to "fix things before they get worse."

Raised in a strict Lutheran home, he describes his father as "a stern man who preached the Gospel but didn't show much affection" and remembers his mother as "always being angry." He recalls hearing, when he was a child, his mother criticize his father for not being around enough to help her with Rod and his three brothers. His father was a minister who devoted the majority of his time to his parishioners. "I didn't know him very well," Rod said. "I don't know why, but I never felt he was very proud of me or that he thought I'd succeed in life."

Although Rod doesn't recall much affection at home, he can vividly call up countless episodes of hostility. "I was yelled at by my mother and she'd take a belt to my backside daily." His parents believed in the axiom "Spare the rod, spoil the child." Home life was often tumultuous, and he'd hear frequent arguments between his mother and father. "Mom couldn't accept that Dad put the family second to his ministry." I'd hear her shouting at my father, "You're so charitable to everyone else, but charity should begin at home!"

"How did you handle all of the conflict?" I asked.

"I guess I used fantasy. I read a lot of C. S. Lewis and science fiction. I've always had a good imagination and did well in creative writing at school. I spent a lot of my free time reading, thinking, and dreaming about the future. When I felt scared or tense, I'd just climb into myself and design a different world where I had loving, supportive parents and lots of friends. I never told anyone about the arguments at home because I was too ashamed. After all, Dad was considered to be a pillar of our community and I felt obliged to maintain that myth. But I could never invite any friends over to the house because I was afraid of an eruption."

Rod had a slight build, but he was tall and long-legged. Although he couldn't compete against the larger guys in contact sports, he excelled as a long-distance runner. But running was a solitary sport and it was never easy for him to feel that he fit in with his peers.

Although it's common for adolescent boys to go through a lanky, awkward period in puberty, it's helpful to have a caring, experienced male around to offer some reassurance. Unfortunately, this was not the case with Rod. Even if his father were home more often, they didn't have *that* kind of relationship. As time went on, Rod became increasingly more self-conscious about his body and uncomfortable taking his clothes off in the locker room. Some of the guys began to taunt him for being "skinny" and he dropped out of the track team.

Fortunately he had one good friend, Jackson Renfrew, who lived next door. They still keep in touch with one another to this day. Jackson was two years younger, but they were soul mates. They played pirates and soldiers together when they were younger, and shared a love for science fiction, spending late hours speculating about what it would be like to live on Mars or Jupiter. Rod was a genuinely sensitive, intelligent, nice guy who merely needed some encouragement when it came to building relationships.

MEETING HOLLY

"When I met Holly in junior high school we were just friends," he said. "We were in the national honor society together and liked math. She was different from the other girls who snubbed me—she was warm and friendly. We went bird-watching, cycling, and hiking. She's the first girl I ever met who liked to play chess. I wasn't sure why Holly liked me, but was really glad that she did.

"After quite some time, our friendship grew into something more. People just assumed we were boyfriend and girlfriend because we were inseparable. We kissed and fooled around a little, but we decided that we wouldn't have intercourse until we were married."

They came to see me because they've been married for five months now but have only had sex four or five times because he feels nervous whenever he does. "Each time I get a little excited, I climax *before* I enter her. It's so embarrassing that we're married but we're still virgins! Holly's really upset. I don't want to lose her."

And what did Holly have to say about all of this? "I'm at the end of my rope," she announced. I wondered out loud to her, "You're at the end of your rope after only five months of marriage?" She laughed. "I guess patience has never been one of my strong points." She continued, "There are so many things I love about Rob—he's really a great guy—I just didn't expect our love life to be this way. I've tried to convince, plead, manipulate, seduce, confront, criticize, argue, and beg Rod to get help. The only reason he came here today is because I've threatened to leave him unless he did. Rod prefers to ignore things and hopes they'll get better on their own, but they're getting worse."

Holly didn't understand that Rod's love for her and fear of losing her was creating the anxiety that triggered his rapid ejaculation. When you review the list of strategies that Holly attempted to employ—pleading, manipulating, etc.—*understanding and support* were not among them.

I encouraged Rod to take a risk and let Holly into his feelings. She couldn't understand him if he was reluctant to share the truth with her. They spent hours talking, using the sexual history tool you'll find on page 245 and building their intimacy. Holly listened in a noncritical way and I suggested she tell Rod some of the many things she loves about him. They explored one another's hopes and fears, sexual preferences and values, and reconnected more deeply than ever before. And what about Rod's rapid ejaculation? All I can say is that according to their last report his timing has become impeccable!

THE BEAR PERSONALITY

I can spot a Bear/Lion duo as soon as they walk through my door. The Lion will generally step forward and shake my hand first, making good eye contact. The Bear will follow suit but in a less demonstrative manner. Bears look well grounded and stand squarely with a comfortable, balanced posture. Eye contact is variable in the Bear. It can be excellent in nonthreatening situations, but inconsistent when the Bear is confronted with a relationship snafu.

Bears aren't always shy or retiring. They'll extend themselves if they feel the mood is right, but will quickly retreat to their den as soon as they sniff out any trouble. They are introspective, contemplative types who appreciate their solitude. They are thinkers who value their conceptual abilities. They are studious observers who attempt to find the "correct" approach by acquiring information. Bears are often bibliophiles who collect books, CDs, and tapes, pursuing their mastery. Although some people may call them quiet, aloof, or arrogant, they prefer to think of themselves as reflective and cautious about what they reveal to others.

In their loving relationships, they appreciate being snuggled up against, but aren't big at initiating the snuggling. But if you need a good listener, and the timing is right—a Bear can be a most appreciative audience.

Bears rarely make the initial contact with me—their Lion, Bee, or Otter mate typically calls for the couple. As their partner describes their unsatisfactory relationship in exquisite detail, the Bear may sit silently without visible emotion as they ponder their response.

An outside observer might assume that the Bear is bored as he listens to a saga he's heard many times before. But that would be an oversimplification. When the Bear is silent, it would be a mistake to jump to the conclusion that he's bored or disinterested; he may just be considering a response that will protect him against undo exposure.

A Bear's circumspect style may be interpreted as inaccessibility by his partner and lead to feelings of helplessness and frustration. Bear partners complain of feeling shut out, confused, and alone. If these dynamics sound familiar, you may be living with a Bear.

QUALITIES OF BEARNESS

The main characteristics of Bear style are solidity and reserved calm. When you're with a Bear, you have the distinct sense of their deep-rooted strength and stability. They provide comfort in a storm, warm arms to protect you, and are excellent mediators. When you're with a Bear, you may feel that you're with a Zen master who can survive on the "bare" necessities (no pun intended)—a good meal, a warm home, and peaceful surroundings.

Bears tend to be private people who are hesitant to disclose personal information. If you want to tell someone a secret with the assurance that it won't go any further, share it with a Bear. They don't like to participate in "locker-room talk" or brag to their buddies about the scoring they did last night. Bears with some Otter or Lion tendencies reveal a bit more, but they usually play their cards close to their vest. Male and female Bears alike aren't much for small talk. They won't run up the telephone bill with idle chatter. The phone is used for conducting business, making reservations, catching up on key details with friends, or discussing an interesting film they've seen, but not for shooting the breeze.

Don't let their implacable exterior fool you, Bears are very concerned with the opinions of others. Their greatest fear is rejection and disappointing people they care about. But when you're with a Bear, it's important to remember that even though they appear to acquiesce to your wishes, you don't necessarily have their full agreement. They dislike being pressured into anything but may reluctantly go along because it's easier than saying "no." Over time, Bears who go along in this way can build up a volcano of resentment that eventually explodes.

Because Bears aren't apt to handle their hostility or annoyance directly, when they finally let loose with their fury it may take them a while to get over it. If you anger your Bear lover, you may find yourself left with an absentminded apology and a forgotten birthday or anniversary. And don't be surprised if it's some time before your next lovemaking session.

Internally, Bears struggle with feeling accepted. They are often attracted to partners who are passionately loving and extremely capable. They are really quite sensitive types and the thickness of their skin is deceiving. Unfortunately, their protective exterior not only keeps them from being hurt; it also blocks them from receiving the intimacy they so desperately desire.

Bears are ambivalent about intimacy and unsure how close they want to get. On the one hand, they long for social acceptance and are confident and secure when discussing some literary topic or world event; on the other hand, they steer clear of settings that demand personal disclosure.

Bears adapt well to living in large cities or small towns. The anonymity of faceless crowds and the stimulation of museums and theaters provide a fitting backdrop for a Bear's inquisitive solitude. They also adjust well to a home in the suburbs or in a rural setting. What matters to the Bear is that they have a safe haven and refuge where their privacy is respected. You won't find a Bear welcoming his new neighbor with a basket of chocolate chip cookies with the message "Drop by any time."

When they're home, you're apt to find them engrossed in some project in a special corner of their home—pruning their bonsai, building a bookcase, working at their computer, or listening to music. They are perfectly content to spend their evenings at home with one special someone and a favorite book, unlike the Otter or Lion, who would much rather be out and about.

Being a Bear is not an exclusively male domain. It's interesting, however, that I've noticed an increasing number of male Bears in my practice over the past ten years who complain of a lack of sexual desire. Whether this is due to sociocultural influences, something biologically hard-wired, or some other combination of variables is uncertain—but as women are more clearly articulating their sexual preferences in a Lionly way, more Bears are reporting that they feel uncomfortable with what they perceive as a frontal assault and consequently retreat deeper into their den.

I'm not suggesting that Lions are responsible for a Bear's lack of sexual enthusiasm, but their influence can't be discounted. There is a subtle dance between the Lion/Energizer, Bear/Stabilizer, Bee/Worker, and Otter/Player that perpetuates and fuels each partner's respective agenda.

BEAR POWER

As you read about the cooperative "peace-loving" stabilizing bears, keep one important fact in mind: *Bears hold the real power in the relationship by not delivering the intimacy that their partners crave.* The passive partner is the one who holds the intimacy card as the active partner, ever hopeful, anxiously awaits the time when it will be played.

But Bears aren't intentionally withholding love. They want approval, not criticism. Although a Bear is slow to anger, if you push, antagonize, or demean a Bear you'll discover their powerful growl. Feeding them some honey to gently coax them out of their hiding place is a better idea than prodding or provocation.

Lions, Otters, and even some Bees complain that Bears aren't romantically demonstrative enough. The power of a Bear is undeniable, because when a Bear limits displays of affection, his partner may begin to question her attractiveness or blame herself in some other way. This power dance usually operates beneath conscious awareness, but can be devastating nonetheless.

Because Bears guard their feelings, their partners can only guess about their emotions. Amanda, a thirty-two-year-old playwright, was upset because her Bear partner seemed to have cooled his ardor. "I assumed he'd lost interest in me because I had put on five or ten pounds, so I joined a health club and got a really buff set of abdominals, but he avoided me even more!" Some frustrated Lions and Otters hire personal trainers, buy how-to sex guides and tapes to spice up their flagging sex life, or order provocative outfits from Frederick's of Hollywood to entice their Bear—all to no avail. It turned out that Amanda's lover was responding to work-related stress. His company had decided to undergo some major downsizing and he feared he'd be laid off. In a typical Bear way, he was trying to handle things on his own, but the stress had diminished his sexual interest. Amanda had obviously misread the *real* problem and jumped to the wrong conclusions.

If a Bear is your lover, you must remember that they want intimacy, too—they're just not sure how to get it. The harder the Lion, Otter, or Bee *pushes* for intimacy, the less likely it is to occur. Both partners become further entrenched in the Bear trap. Unless your Bear's personality is understood, you'll wind up exhausted as you chase your own tail.

As a child, I got a Chinese puzzle in a box of Cracker Jacks. It was tubular and woven out of straw and came with instructions to insert a finger at either end. The goal was to try to remove both fingers. What I discovered is that the more I struggled to pull out my fingers simultaneously, the tighter the tube became. The solution was simple—one of the fingers simply had to stop pulling.

CREATING THE ILLUSION OF INTIMACY

Bears can be confusing to their partners and to themselves. They profess their love, but then seem to do something that frustrates their partners. Bears can be wonderfully charming, witty, and understanding and they can scope out their perfect Lion at a hundred paces. It's hard to dislike them, because they cover their fear of intimacy with a veil of sincere generosity and kindness.

The real hook between a Bear and a Lion is their natural fit around caretaking. Lions are most comfortable caring for others, and Bears are good candidates for mothering. Lions are immensely talented at falling in love with the "potential" in their partners. When I ask an unhappy Lion why she stays in her marriage, she'll reply, "He's so talented, *if only* he would apply himself, or *if only* he would reach out, or *if only* . . ." They are mothers par excellence who will go to the ends of the earth to nurture and protect their cubs. Unfortunately, Lion partners who marry Bear cubs expecting to "grow them up" are often sadly disappointed. Let's keep the dynamics of the Lions in mind. They fear dependency. If a Bear tries to change his approach, unless his partner is ready to examine her motivation for keeping him subjugated, the Bear's efforts will be thwarted. Although Lions insist they want a relationship with a competent, capable adult male, if their Bear does grow up, the basis of their marital contract is altered.

UNDERSTANDING THE BEAR'S AVOIDANCE

When Bears and their partners come to see me for help, they must each be willing to examine how they perpetuate their ongoing problems. As in riding on a seesaw, there's a balance in each relationship that both parties maintain. Before you can focus on being more intimate, it takes time to unearth the layers of hostility and misunderstanding.

It's not unusual for couples to come to see me with a laundry list of complaints that range from minor to monumental. Issues as simple as drinking out of the milk carton or leaving newspapers strewn about the house can escalate to the point of discussing divorce. We all know couples who treat their spouses like children—they don't hesitate to correct one another in public if he or she mispronounces a word or uses the wrong dessert spoon. Is it any wonder that their intimacy suffers?

Bears long for affirmation and support but have trouble asking for these things directly. Instead of confessing their disappointment, it's safer to procrastinate, forget to meet a lover for dinner at the prearranged time, or avoid their partners altogether by working late, playing golf, or staying at the gym. When they behave in an "irresponsible" manner they provoke the wrath that they fear. Bears wind up feeling blamed, belittled, and victimized by the partners who claim they are "only trying to help."

When partners establish these parent-child dynamics, sex often falls by the wayside. After all, who wants to make love to your mother or your son? To get your intimacy back on track, you need to get back on a level playing field.

ASSUMPTIONS ABOUT BEARS

The assumptions we make about our partner affect our tolerance of their behaviors. If you assume your partner is uncaring or unfeeling, instead of recognizing they're also blocked or frightened, you'll be less motivated to find a solution.

If your partner is a Bear, you may wonder why you have to tell him a dozen times how to touch your breasts or genitals and he *still* goes back to his old ways. It's not that your Bear is hearing-impaired, he's just protecting himself from getting too close for his own comfort. One way of protecting himself is to make you furious. Is he aware of all of this? Probably not. Bears aren't malicious types by nature, just frightened of doing it wrong. The irony is that the more frightened a Bear becomes, the more he avoids, obfuscates, and actually creates the problems he fears.

The way to interrupt this self-fulfilling prophecy is by empathizing with your Bear's fear of vulnerability and rejection and cooperating in his efforts to enhance his self-esteem.

Let's look at how some of these difficulties with self-esteem arise.

THE FAMILY OF A BEAR

As is the case in Lion, Otter, and Bee, there isn't one kind of family that produces a Bear. The Bear style emerges in a variety of settings. A large number of Bears, however, tell me that they had parents who were either excessively critical or indifferent.

Jeffrey, a thirty-one-year-old general contractor Bear, said this about his childhood: "My father rarely came to any of my sports events because he was too busy. When he did, he had very little to say. I was a better-than-average swimmer, but never felt encouraged to pursue competitive swimming by either parent. As long as I didn't do anything wrong, I didn't hear much from either of them. I felt invisible."

Bears who have been raised with this kind of message have difficulty feeling adequate. They may suffer from the impostor syndrome and worry that they'll be found out as a fraud. Fearing they're not "good enough," they've learned how to fake their confidence by appearing to be self-assured and well informed in a selected range of subjects. Compensatory strivings may present themselves in the form of the "Renaissance man" who can discuss film, religion, or political trends with sophistication and aplomb but secretly feels like a failure.

At the heart of the Bear's family dynamics is a failure to connect intimately. The Bear is unsure how to establish closeness without jeopardizing his self-esteem. Because they fear rejection, they've learned to suppress their annoyance and adopt a cautionary stance. They make errors of omission, not errors of commission. Unsure of how to please, they wait for the other person to make the move. "Look before you leap" is their motto.

JAY'S SEXUAL SECRET

Like many Bears, Jay had a distant, emotionally unavailable father. His contact with him was sporadic and infrequent. When his father wasn't working, he spent his time staring at the television set and showing little interest in Jay.

His mother was overly critical and impossible to satisfy. If Jay got a B on a report, it should have been an A. No matter how hard he tried, his mom harped on his failings. Jay felt inadequate. Everything was a test, and he was never able to measure up.

During the taking of his individual sex history, Jay disclosed a pivotal sexual event that contributed to his poor self-esteem. "When I was twelve years old, I noticed a swelling and some tenderness in my left testicle," he said with some embarrassment. "It started to ache and turn reddish in color and I got pretty scared. I was afraid I'd injured something by rubbing it. The church had warned of the dangers of masturbation, and I thought I was being punished for sure."

Jay had discovered masturbating by accident when he was ten or eleven. "I was lying on my stomach, bouncing up and down, and then something happened. I thought I'd broken something the first time I came," he said. "It was terrifying. I didn't know all this stuff would come out the tip of my penis and I didn't know who to ask about it, so I didn't tell anyone. I knew that touching myself 'down there' was a sin, but it felt so good that I kept right on doing it."

Jay was perspiring as he continued his story. "I had to tell someone about my testicle because it was getting more and more swollen. When I finally told my mother about it, she looked at me over her glasses. I'll never forget her glare. She didn't say anything and just called the doctor and put an ice pack on my penis.

"I was mortified. It didn't get better, so I had to go to the hospital. They put a needle in my testicle to numb it—I was so scared! The doctor told me he had to cut it open. Even though I couldn't feel his scalpel, it was an unpleasant sensation. Stretching and pressure. As I describe this to you, after all these years, I can feel my testicles retracting and a sick sensation in my gut."

Jay looked pale as he continued. "The local anesthetic wasn't enough to handle the pain, so they decided to put me under. About twenty seconds before they put a mask over my face, a nurse took off my gown and shaved my pubic hair. I remember wishing she'd waited until I was asleep to do that. I felt so exposed. The next thing I remember, I was waking up in the recovery room. My mother was there and she looked uncomfortable about the whole situation. I was lying there with a bandage around my penis and testicle and a big bag of ice on top of all of it.

"Urinating was uncomfortable. It burned. My mother had to change the dressings twice a day. I hated having all of this attention focused on *that* part of my anatomy!"

Jay had pain in the incision area for several weeks. There were several visits to the doctor. "They used a flashlight to look at it and everyone seemed to be coming in to inspect my penis—the doctors, nurses, and even my mother was there. They told me I had something called 'torsion of the testicle' and that somehow my testicle got twisted. I just *knew* I had done it!"

"How do you think this affected you sexually?" I asked.

"Well," he answered, "for one thing, I learned to pay attention to my penis and testicles and worry about them—a lot. People were always asking how *they* were doing—like they were separate from me. And even though I try to tell myself that I wasn't responsible, I still wonder if I didn't create the problem by masturbating too rough, or something.

"I feel silly saying this, but I still feel a little nervous when they're touched, even by the woman I'm engaged to. I have a small scar there and it bothers me to look at it or have anyone else see it. I'm still worried sometimes that if I allow myself to really let go sexually, something bad will happen."

"So your masturbation was pleasurable, but the experience was mixed with shame and worry?" I asked.

"Yes, that's what happened. Another embarrassing incident was when my mother found the towel I used to ejaculate into when I masturbated. She didn't say anything to me, but she left it on my bed with the crusty semen on top and a note asking, 'What's this mess?' "

Throughout these experiences, Jay's father was absent. Working. There was no one to help him sort out his concerns or develop his independence and self-confidence.

Although the doctors told him it shouldn't be a problem, he secretly worried whether the torsion surgery would prevent him from being able to have children someday. "I felt like damaged goods," he said. Jay had questions about the size of his penis, whether he was "normal" sexually, and whether he could ever really satisfy anyone.

The turning point for Jay was sharing this part of his history with me. We spent a number of sessions correcting many of his myths, allowing him to vent, and reassuring him that his past—difficult as it was—was not unique.

Many of us have painful or embarrassing histories and we'd benefit from sharing them with someone we trust. It's impossible to have extraordinary sex unless both parties are willing to risk revealing themselves. Jay's self-disclosure heralded the beginning of other disclosures with his fiancée. As she supported and validated his feelings, a deeper, more satisfying level of intimacy unfolded.

To summarize some of the salient features of a Bear:
Bears are people who:

1. Are strong, stabilizing, patient, and devoted.

2. Have simple tastes—a good meal, comfortable home, and loving life mate are most important to them.

3. Are slow to anger and may smolder quietly for years, but when they erupt—watch out!

4. Deny problems until they become "unbearable."

5. Can be a great supporting cast for a Lion, Otter, or Bee. Are generous, kind, and fiercely protective.

6. Tend to be more reflective and conceptual than emotional.

7. Are not usually the ones to initiate sex.

8. Can be excellent listeners and mediators, but may tune out difficult emotional content.

9. Don't like to be rushed. Their motto is "slow and steady wins the race."

10. Are generally consistent and dependable with few surprises.

11. Are faithful to their mates and not prone to "wandering."

12. Fear rejection and are reluctant to let anyone see their soft underbelly.

13. Participate in errors of omission, rather than errors of commission. They believe if a problem can be sidestepped, why make waves?

14. Enjoy their solitude as much as time with their mate.

15. May say "yes" when they'd rather say "no."

THE ATTRACTION OF A BEAR

What strength, what stability, what comfort your Bear provides! It's easy to see why they're so attractive. They exude power, but do it subtly and with finesse. The body language of a Bear is easy to read. It says "I will protect you if you treat me with respect." Having none of the overt volatility or excess found in the Lion, a Bear communicates his affable nature in a relaxed and easygoing way.

Bears can be extremely generous, nurturing, and supportive. As long as they feel they have something of value to offer you, they'll be happy to provide it. Bears prefer a lack of conflict, so they are more comfortable with partners who share their value system. Unfortunately, they're not very astute in discerning whether their would-be mates are a fit or a nonfit. They are better listeners than talkers and are hesitant to ask personal questions that might be turned back to them for a reply.

If you're attracted to the peacefulness of the woods, walks on the beach, or hiking in the mountains, you'll find an appreciation for all three and more in your accommodating Bear. But he'll also accompany you to a night at the opera as readily as on a weekend kayaking.

When you meet a Bear you will be taken with his comforting presence. No grandstanding here. "A really nice person," you'll think to yourself. If you're a Lion or an Otter trying out your best new jokes, your Bear will laugh appreciatively. If you want to please your Bear, prepare a taste-tempting, sumptuous meal. Being nurtured in a gustatory way is certain to get his attention.

WHAT YOU NEED TO KNOW ABOUT YOURSELF IF YOU'RE ATTRACTED TO A BEAR

If you find yourself attracted to Bears, remember that their thick skin belies their sensitivity. Ask yourself, "What does my Bear do for me that I need to learn to do for myself?" If he anchors you in a storm perhaps it would be important to tone down your emotionality. Maybe you need to be needed. Maybe you admire his patience and his slow simmer. Whatever it is, identify it for yourself and don't forget it.

Couples run into problems when they forget what they love about their partners. Bears can be incredibly stubborn and difficult to budge if you attack them head-on. This is what you're up against if you try to get your Bear partner to change. Nagging your Bear to remember to pick up the towels on the bathroom floor, put down the toilet seat, or exercise more is useless. If you marry a Bear and think, "I can get him to open up or share his feelings with me," think again. If you raise your voice and threaten to leave, they'll tune you out.

The way to change your Bear is change yourself. Instead of accosting them with your litany, focus on what you like about them. The more secure they feel, the more willing they'll be to hear you. Sure, it's annoying to have the toilet seat up and receive an unexpected icy welcome during your midnight wanderings, but is it worth doing battle over?

When you have sex with a Bear, don't spring any surprises on him. He likes to know the game plan in advance—way in advance. *If a Bear says he's "bored," listen up!* He may mean he feels threatened, insecure, criticized, humiliated, fearful, ashamed, or inadequate. Boredom is something your Bear partner thrives on, so it's highly unlikely to hear him complain about it. When he does, it's your job to read between the lines.

When you're partnered with a Bear, you must pick your battles carefully and ask yourself, "Is this the hill I choose to die on?" Use the intensity of the Lion, the logic of the Bee, and the creativity of the Otter to negotiate a solution.

WHAT BEARS WANT FROM RELATIONSHIPS

If your partner is a Bear, here are some things you need to know:

1. Bears have difficulty being criticized and are easily injured. Don't let their "tough" exterior fool you. They want honesty, but not the "whole truth." Bears prefer a "spoonful of sugar" along with their "medicine."

2. Bears hate to be pushed. The direct frontal attack will not work if you're partnered with a Bear. They prefer logical discussions in measured doses and shun emotionality like the plague.

3. Bears need to have their timing respected, and they resent intrusions—especially into their private times. If you're a Lion, Bee, or Otter, your inner clock may be very different than your Bear's. Bears want to be allowed to set their own pace.

4. Bears tend to be generous souls who want their lovers to value their talents. Although they are hesitant to boast or brag about themselves, they appreciate partners who do. If your Bear prepares his "typical" luscious four-star breakfast for you, don't take this display for granted. Make sure to let him (and others) know you're married to a culinary wizard!

5. Don't personalize your Bear's occasional aloofness as disinterest. Bears can appear to be indifferent and need a partner who understands that "You can't always judge a book by its cover." Give your Bear partner the benefit of the doubt. Recognize that showing intimacy may not be their strong suit, but their loyalty and love runs deep.

6. Bears (like the rest of us) want to be nurtured and loved, but they don't know how to ask for your love. Don't assume they don't need affection. Bears want you to understand that they need cuddling, and until they learn how to ask more directly, just give them bunches of it.

SEX WITH A BEAR

The primary complaint I hear about sex with Bears is that they don't reach out. Bears want to be invited, and assure their desirability. It is hard for a Bear to say, "I want to touch you" or "I'd like to make love with you on top." These words cross their minds frequently, but don't make it to their lips.

Bears' sexual partners accuse them of not sharing what they're thinking, feeling, and wanting. Bears make you wonder and, in so doing, retain a great deal of power. Their partners will do their best to get a response or reaction, but it's very rare to hear your Bear squeal with delight.

Some Bears are slow, deliberate lovers who take their time to give you the very best orgasm they can. They'll go down on you for hours and try to please you in any way they know how. Other Bears, who are more insecure about their desirability, will move through sex robotically, have their orgasm, and roll over.

To move beyond mechanical sex with your Bear, you must learn how to make a vital connection between you. This involves establishing a way to communicate safely, intimately, and honestly. Since communication isn't their forte, this is not as easy as it sounds. But don't get discouraged; if a Bear doesn't feel threatened, he can be a very willing participant.

Too many couples wait until their relationship has disintegrated into extramarital affairs, fault-finding, or name-calling before they realize they need help. If you're in love with a Bear, don't try intimidation. It will never work. Make a fresh start, take fifty percent of the responsibility, and suggest you both try a different approach. Remember, it takes two people to maintain a problem, but only one to take the initial step.

HINTS FOR LIVING WITH A BEAR:

1. Be clear and reasonable in your expectations.

2. Don't sweat the small stuff; no one is perfect.

3. Acknowledge your Bear's *positive* efforts.

4. Don't blame—"you always," "you never." If you approach him like a mother, he'll act like a child.

5. Allow him to progress slowly. Don't monitor his progress or pin him down with a specific timeline.

6. Remember that Bears fear rejection and humiliation. Don't feed into their worst fears or you'll undercut their progress.

7. For Bears, sex is about proving their adequacy. Don't demean

their love skills and complain they're the worst lovers on the planet unless you want to erode their self-confidence even more. Look at your own motivation for establishing dominance at their expense. If they feel inferior, they'd rather abstain from sex than face humiliation.

8. Be fair: "We *both* must change." Don't put the responsibility totally on your Bear.

9. If you're insatiable, like his mother, he may not want to even try to make you happy. Notice his effort even if the net result falls short of your ideal. Build his confidence and security. As you continue in this direction, he'll risk a bit more and change will occur.

10. Bears have feelings; it's just hard for them to show them. Their thick skins hide a multitude of fears, including unworthiness and being cast aside.

11. For Bears to want to change, they must feel safe. Don't hit below the belt, use psychological warfare ("You're exactly like your father!"), or belittle them. Enable empathy by using the *stop, look, and listen* format.

12. Intimacy is hard for Bears because of their fear of loss and rejection. They're reluctant to let you in. If you're a Lion, Otter, or Bee, you'll need to give up some control and support your Bear's choices. This will be hard for you, because you'll need to part with some of your control.

13. Pull back. Give him space. Wait him out. Learn patience, and support the development of his powerful identity. You'll both be stronger in the process.

Understanding the fragile alliance between partners will permit you to more properly navigate your part of the journey. Intimacy is a lifelong challenge, but you'll be off to a good start.

IRENE AND NORRIS: TWO BEARS

Irene and Norris, both experimental psychologists, married almost twenty years, are two Bears who have difficulty making decisions. Irene had more Lion tendencies than Norris, so when push came to shove, she'd decide where they went on vacation or what video they rented. Norris never seemed to care.

In their home, Irene made all the decorating decisions. Not only did she decide on the color scheme; she chose how much space Norris would get in the closet and what he could put on the wall. One of Norris' prize possessions is a cuckoo clock given to him by his great-grandmother. Irene hated it and wouldn't let Norris display it. Instead of fighting with Irene, Norris gave in. The same pattern held true with their two daughters, Naomi and Shira. Irene was the more active parent, and Norris capitulated.

One fall weekend, on their annual Vermont foliage trip, Norris was determined to try to change his evasive patterns. It was his fortieth birthday and he was tired of living in Irene's shadow. They had gone to see the road show of *Chicago,* and the lyrics of the song "Mr. Cellophane" had rung uncomfortably true.

On their way home from the show, Irene saw an interesting gift shop and asked Norris to pull over. They usually brought the girls a memento of their trip. The gift shop had a room filled with stuffed animals of every size and variety. Norris was attracted to a bright orange cuddly orangutan that stood about two feet high. He picked it up and purchased it without batting an eye. It was unusual for Norris to make a decision without consulting Irene, but he felt motivated to assert himself and this was as good a time as any to begin. He knew Naomi, his twelve-year-old, would love his selection. "What a great feeling to make a decision for myself," he thought.

Just then, Irene entered the room and glanced at Norris' choice. "What's THAT?" she demanded. "A monkey? Naomi and Shira hate monkeys. There are so many other cute stuffed animals here—look at those adorable dolphins—why did you pick *that* one."

Norris decided it was time to stand up for himself. He kept the monkey, but didn't speak to Irene for the rest of the way home. When he got in the door he went to the closet, got his cuckoo clock, and put it on the wall. "I'm tired of being invisible," he announced.

Although each person is responsible for their own choices, it takes two to support a change of this magnitude. Irene had nagged Norris for years to "stand up and be a man!" She had begged him to be more connected to the girls, but as soon as he tried, she was there to cut him down and reestablish the status quo. Ultimately, although it took some adjustment to make room for Norris' expanding personality, she knew it was the best thing for both of them. Now, instead of waiting for her to make the first move, Norris reached out to Irene and took a more active role in their lovemaking.

Developing individual flexibility is more difficult than it appears. A couple's dynamics resist change. Each partner pulls for the old predictable responses at the same time they complain about wanting something new. Familiarity isn't threatening; change is. Supporting Norris' newly discovered assertiveness required Irene to change. She had to become less self-absorbed and more empathic.

Bears who marry Bears live cautiously. Neither partner is strong in "doing." So when a Bear gathers up enough courage to act on a desire, it's important that his partner is supportive.

TIM AND BRITTANY: A BEAR AND A BEE

A Bear is your shelter in the storm. This was Brittany's feeling when she first met Tim. Engaged for six months, she had never met anyone as thoughtful or kind as Tim. I spoke with her alone for the first half of our initial consultation.

A twenty-four-year-old registered nurse, Brittany has curly dark brown hair and hazel eyes. She is five feet five, has a trim, toned body, and loves to stay active. "I've been in one other serious relationship," she began, "but I never really loved him. I know Tim is the one for me, but there's something missing when we have sex. I'm hoping he'll open up to you so we can figure this thing out."

Brittany, a well-organized Bee, gives the impression of having it "all together." Everything about her, from her carefully pressed white Polo shirt and khaki pants to her matching Coach bag, was neat as a pin. She began to tell her story. "My ex-boyfriend and I were together for almost two years. There were lots of problems in our relationship, but sex was the worst of them all. Lovemaking wasn't on his priority list. When I met Tim, I felt an attraction I hadn't experienced before. I think he's gorgeous! His compact body, sparkling blue eyes, and there's something soothing and exciting about his voice.

"We went out about three times before he tried to kiss me," she said. "I thought this was odd, but assumed he was just being polite. When he finally kissed me, I just melted. He has a great mouth.

"We didn't have sex until the tenth or eleventh date," she continued. "We went back to Tim's apartment, shared a glass of wine, and wound up in his bedroom. Everything was going fine and I was feeling really turned on until I reached for his penis. Tim had an erection, but rolled onto his belly and asked that I massage his shoulders. I didn't think much about this, and intercourse was amazing, so I let it go.

"The next time we made love, he gave me oral sex but didn't want it in return. I've been out with lots of guys who lived to have their penis sucked, so I really thought this was weird. I've asked him if there's a problem, but he's denied having any. I'm hoping you can help."

Tim's Story

Tim is twenty-nine years old, five feet eight, and has the muscular body of an athlete in peak condition. His fair complexion gives him a clean-cut all-American look. His passion is working out in the gym. Tim lifts weights four times a week and competes in bodybuilding contests. During the day he manages a fast-food franchise with hopes of purchasing another soon. As he spoke to me alone, he recalls what he believes is "the problem" by going back more than twenty years.

"My parents were divorced when I was five," he began, "and the custody battle raged on for years." Tim sat seriously on the chair across from me looking nervously at the floor.

"My father told me that my mom cheated on him. I was in court and I remember being pulled from my dad. It was ten years before they would communicate again.

"The memories I have are painful. Dad was verbally abusive to Mom, and she hit him and then he'd hit her back. I wound up in a shelter for two weeks and couldn't see either one of them. He didn't say much to motivate me, but had a lot to say that was denigrating. He called me a 'squirt' and told me to 'be a man.'

"One day, Dad brought home a porno film to show me. I was about twelve years old. All I can remember were these men with huge cocks. It left quite an impression on me.

"When I was with my mother, she was very strict and gave me the physical discipline she said I needed. My dad just wasn't around very much. He died of leukemia when he was thirty-five and I was fourteen. I never really got to know him."

"Tell me about your sexual development," I invited.

"I had a tough time," he said. "I never felt that I measured up to the other guys. I was shorter and smaller. I felt uncomfortable taking group showers because my penis was smaller than everyone else's."

"How did you know?" I asked.

"I looked. All the other guys had bigger ones than me. I tried to skip showering or made sure to face away and keep a towel around me in the locker room.

"The first time a girl actually saw my penis she said, 'Oh, how cute!' I was so humiliated. I was sure she was referring to the size.

"Ever since that time I've been worried that it's too small to satisfy a woman and have been afraid to have women touch it or give me oral sex."

Tim's saga is not atypical. When young boys shower with their dads and find themselves facing their father's mature penis at eye level, it can be a daunting experience. Likewise, when you look at the penis of the guy across the room, it tends to appear much larger than a foreshortened view of one's own penis. Tim's father may have thought he was doing him a favor by showing him a porn flick at the age of twelve—but he was wrong. Penises in adult films are often augmented to give the appearance of super size. When a boy is prepubescent, any adult penis can look overwhelming by comparison.

Tim didn't have a father who could put all of these observations into perspective and allay his son's anxieties. Tim needed a male role model to answer his questions and give him accurate facts. Erections are the great equalizer. The absolute difference between a small penis and a larger penis tends to diminish when they're both erect.

I asked Tim if he'd had a physical exam and what the urologist might have told him about his genitals. "The doctor said it was about average in size," he said. "But I'm still worried about pleasing Brittany."

"Did you know that it's the first two inches or so of the vagina that responds to the pleasurable stimulation of insertion and thrusting?" I asked. Tim's eyes opened wide as he raised his eyebrows in amazement.

"You're kidding," he said.

"No, I'm not," I replied. "The inner part of the vagina and the cervix respond to pressure sensation, so a penis that's two inches long should do the trick."

"Well, mine's much bigger than that." He smiled.

"When you're ready, it's important that you have a personal conversation with Brittany and tell her what's been troubling you," I suggested.

Tim took my advice. He mustered up his courage and told Brittany that he was afraid she'd think his penis was too small or would find it "cute." Brittany was supportive and affirming in her rational Bee style. She said. "Your penis works great and I love it. I've had incredible sex with you. Your penis is only one part of you. It's *you* that I love."

Sawyer and Amy: A Bear and an Otter

Amy is an expressive, inspiring, risk-taking Otter of thirty-two who met Sawyer, thirty-six, on a hiking expedition in the majestic Rockies one clear summer weekend nearly twelve years ago. The chemistry between them was electric. After a picture-perfect courtship, they were married and moved to Ohio to be near Sawyer's family.

This past week they celebrated their tenth anniversary. Sawyer, her intelligent Bear, a professor of cognitive history at the local state university, had always been her best friend and "shelter in the storm," but things have changed. He's still a good listener and "always there" for her, but somehow—Amy doesn't know when or where—they stopped being intimate. "It just happened," she said during one of our sessions, "and I want the magic back.

"Sawyer and I used to share so many interests—an appreciation for nature, raising exotic African violets in our own greenhouse, a passion for Szechwan cooking, and running five-K marathons—that all seems like a hundred years ago," she reported sadly.

Model citizens, Amy and Sawyer live in a family neighborhood of cozy split-level homes on a quiet cul-de-sac. Their two toddlers, Jesse and Tyrone, keep them busy around the clock. When they're not caring for the kids, or the yard, or visiting their family, they're involved in some community responsibility. There's little time or money for romantic trips to the Rockies—or anywhere else.

If you were to ask their neighbors, they'd tell you that Amy and Sawyer have the ideal marriage. But if you look beneath the surface you'll find a sexual relationship that's far from satisfying. Amy has been faking orgasms for more years than she can remember; she is too afraid to ask Sawyer for the kind of sexual touching she needs, because she's sure he'd turn her down.

When Amy and Sawyer were first dating, Amy was a "wild woman" and Sawyer was her sweet "nature boy." They shared countless adventures, including skinny-dipping in the moonlight, making passionate love in the Indiana dunes or in some deserted cabin they discovered while hiking in the woods. Since then, Amy has pulled back and Sawyer hasn't picked up the slack in the relationship. Now, after the kids and all, she felt guilty because she wanted more from Sawyer but was afraid to ask him. "What if Sawyer decides he just can't please me—or worse, what if he decides to leave?" she asked.

For an Otter who loves excitement, their lives had become unbearably dull. She longed for the thrill of the carefree days and resented her antiseptic life.

And what about Sawyer? He wasn't aware there *was* a problem. "After all," he remarked, "after ten years, sex just naturally drops off—doesn't it?"

Amy and Sawyer's marriage is typical of so many marriages that suffer a gradual, almost imperceptible decline in intimacy. Too often, the decrease in excitement and spontaneity gets ignored, pushed aside, or justified as "the natural decline of passion that befalls all marriages."

The good news is that Amy's discontent and Sawyer's acceptance of the status quo *can* be changed.

The first step was for them to face their problem together. Amy expressed her fears openly and told Sawyer, "I'm afraid you might decide to leave me if I'm more direct about what I want sexually, but there are some things I'd like to improve on in our relationship." While there were risks involved in being this open, there were even greater risks in "faking" her pleasure and continuing to ignore the problem.

As soon as Amy took this first step, the next steps became easier. Neither one wanted to end the marriage and each of them vowed to work this out together. Sawyer admitted that he missed his playful Otter and the fun times they used to have, but he had allowed himself to retreat from intimate opportunities. He took responsibility for planning one weekend away each month—it didn't matter where. This was difficult for a Bear who usually waits for his Otter to come up with the agenda. He called his mom and dad, told them that he and Amy had decided to give their marriage some long-overdue TLC, and asked if they'd watch the kids for them. As it turns out, his family was delighted to have more time with their grandsons.

Amy and Sawyer bought some inexpensive camping equipment and ventured back into nature, where they first fell in love. Their plan worked like a charm. The last I heard, sex was hotter than ever.

LIFE LESSONS FOR BEARS

Once you're familiar with your own Bearness, you have some clues about the way you perceive, organize, and respond to certain situations. To create a more flexible sexual style, it's important for you to move past your typical security zone into territory that's less comfortable. By identifying your life lessons and practicing alternative approaches, you'll feel more internally stable and balanced as a lover.

TRY THESE SUGGESTIONS:

1. *Work on understanding your partner's feelings.* Developing empathy is an important life lesson for you. Put yourself in your partner's shoes and see things through her eyes.

2. *Learn to listen to your own feelings.* Touch your lover in ways that feel good to you, not in ways you suspect he or she will like.

3. *Reach out and touch your lover <u>in the moment</u>.* Take a risk and make the first move.

4. *Assert yourself in small ways and then build on it.* Use "I" statements instead of saying, "Let's go to the movies" or "Do you

feel like fooling around?" Using an "I" statement is a much more intimate way of expressing yourself. You must also be willing to face the pain associated with rejection. No one ever died from hearing "no."

5. *Communicate something personal about yourself.* It doesn't have to be some earth-shattering revelation. Tell your partner about any of your hopes, fears, or dreams for the future. Instead of talking about what happened at work or the bills, look at your lover and tell her something you love about her.

6. *Don't ignore your hurts.* Pay attention to them and say "ouch." You've been accustomed to ignoring your pain because it makes you feel more invincible. If your lover says, "I think you need to lose a few pounds," instead of ignoring the statement or laughing it off, say, "Ouch that hurt me."

7. *Do something out of the ordinary.* Get in the car with your lover and decide where to go without asking him or her. Put the music "you" want to hear on the radio. Explore a new restaurant because "you" want to. Decide to make love somewhere else besides the bedroom.

8. *During sex, say something. Anything.* Silence doesn't mean you're a good listener or that you're appreciating the moment—it only means that you're being quiet.

9. *Learn to ask for physical comfort when you feel stressed.* Don't wait for your partner to read your mind.

10. *Learn to say "no" without feeling guilty.* If your partner feels hurt because you don't want a second helping of her special meat loaf recipe, she'll get over it. Don't stuff yourself to please her and then secretly blame her when you put on ten extra pounds.

THE WORST OF BEARS

When Bears finally get angry with you, watch out. Anything goes when a Bear gets mad, and they stay mad for a while. Unlike the Lion, who is a straw fire, the Bear smolders and stews long after you think it should have been over. They can hold on to a grudge for months or even years and you may not even know it. Their timing is slower in every way. It takes longer for them to make a decision, it takes longer for them to follow through, and it may take longer for them to get aroused.

Don't expect your Bear to adjust to your time schedule. If you're a quick-thinking Lion, agile Bee flitting here and there, or an impulsive Otter, you'll be tempted to call your partner a "slug." If you don't accept their pacing, you'll be frustrated and furious and long for someone more fiery, independent, and free-spirited.

THE BEST OF BEARS

Your Bear partner is loyal and devoted to a fault. Leaving is not his style. It has to get pretty bad for a Bear to look for another pair bond or file for divorce. I'm not saying that it never happens—but it's the exception to the rule.

With Bears what you see isn't all there is. Beneath that sometimes gruff stoic exterior beats a heart of genuine compassion, tenderness, and sincerity. The trick is knowing how to access it.

Bears will be your best ally. If anyone tries to harm a Bear's partner, woe be to him! Your Bear will defend you to the bitter end and will pull no punches. Bears are reluctant to defend themselves, but are protective of those they love.

Bears are predictable and love their routine. You don't need to wear yourself out trying new sexual positions. Once you know how he likes to have his penis touched or that he likes sex "doggy style" you can be assured lovemaking won't deviate much. This isn't to suggest that a Bear doesn't like a change now and then, but give him plenty of lead time. Bears aren't big on surprises. They appreciate attention of all kinds, but are just as pleased when they know what's on the agenda.

When your Bear feels secure he can be a teddy bear—accommodating, agreeable, helpful, and cuddly. Bears are wonderful partners to get cozy with in front of the fireplace on a cold winter's night. But when your Bear is threatened, the grizzly may just as easily emerge. You have both in your partner. Don't forget it.

CHAPTER 11

WHO ARE THESE BEES?

Perfection is a trifle dull. It is not the least of life's ironies that this, which we all aim at, is better not quite achieved.

—W. SOMERSET MAUGHAM, 1938

TRAVIS AND NICOLE: TWO PERFECTIONISTIC BEES

Travis, a busy Bee, is driven to neatness. Even when he's running late, he manages to take a few minutes to tidy up his desk and put all of his papers into their appropriate piles. His large, tastefully appointed corner office has become home. Twelve- or fifteen-hour days aren't unusual. When he isn't negotiating a trade or lunching with major clients, he's attending business meetings or drafting a proposal.

"Until tomorrow," he mutters as he picks up his briefcase and switches off the light. The rest of the staff are long gone. It will be close to nine before he gets home.

Trying to squeeze a few extra minutes out of the evening, he hurries to the parking garage. His car is easy to locate; not only is it in his favorite spot—the one protected on both sides by cement barricades—but it gleams with the attention of an owner obsessed with flawlessness.

Travis, like so many worker Bees, is a hard-driving perfectionist. At the age of thirty-nine he has achieved the enviable position of senior fund manager at a prestigious Wall Street firm. He has the respect of his co-workers, an impressive six-figure salary, and all the creature comforts anyone could ask for.

Nicole, his wife of fourteen years, is accustomed to Travis' late nights at the office. It's the exceptional evening when Travis is home early enough to join Nicole and their three children for dinner. Blair, Brianna, and Tyler are all in bed before their father gets home. She pours a glass of wine so it's waiting for Travis as he walks through the door.

Nicole is also a perfectionistic Bee. She balances a busy career as a physician in a local community hospital, managing a household, and looking after her children—all without a hitch. Well, there is one hitch: Travis and Nicole have become used to spending most of their time apart.

When I met the two of them, Nicole had just passed her fortieth birthday and had come to an emotional crossroads. "I just woke one day and realized I needed intimacy from Travis and it was totally absent. Our lives have become all work and no play and I know it's not the way it should be." Nicole also felt that she and her husband have been so driven by the quantity and intensity of their activities that intimacy was afforded no space in their busy lives.

Both Travis and Nicole have exerted continuous pressure on themselves, and have been driven for years. The most prevalent thought of the Worker/Bee is the phrase "I should." The Worker/Bee is always reminding himself of some goal or responsibility that he feels obligated to satisfy.

Thus, Travis' and Nicole's Bee style enabled them to become successful at work, run an impeccable home, dress *à la page,* exercise regularly, and meet a long list of external expectations. Sadly they had failed in one critical area—the quality of their relationship.

Although they complain of a pressured existence, they feel immensely uncomfortable in situations that allow for relaxation. On vacations or holidays, or when regular duties are less compelling, they have difficulty unwinding and usually find some new tasks to fill their "free" time.

When it comes to having sex, Bees search to find the "right" technique or approach. Instead of experimenting with what feels good to them, they think about what they "should do." Over time, the sex life of a Bee goes downhill because it becomes an "ordeal" even for them—they've gotten so involved in evaluating the pros and cons that they'd rather do nothing than do it incorrectly.

For example, Travis would agonize about the right time to make love to Nicole. "Should we make love after the children are asleep, or should I wake Nicole in the morning when she's more refreshed? Perhaps I should just snuggle up to her in the middle of the night for a quickie?" He would labor through all of his options and struggle to find the right decision. Because there obviously isn't any "right" answer, he'd forgo intimacy entirely.

When they would make love, they were each so focused on technical prowess that they missed the sensual substance and meaning of their intimacy. Lying next to one another after having their orgasms, Travis and Nicole felt strangely *alone;* they feared something was very wrong but didn't know what to do.

RECOGNIZING THE WARNING SIGNS AND MOVING AHEAD

Travis and Nicole made an appointment to see me and we spent a number of sessions talking about their Bee-ness. They knew they were exacting but hadn't realized how much their style had blocked their passion. The treatment approach consisted of tuning into their "warning signs" and modifying their focus and pacing.

Their warning signs included: rushing around trying to do more than one thing at a time, greater concern with sexual technique than pleasure, difficulty relaxing and having fun together, needing to control every little detail, and frequently feeling disconnected or inadequate sexually.

Travis and Nicole posted the warning signs on the inside of their bedroom door.

....

I SUGGESTED THEY TRY THE FOLLOWING:

• *Spend one day just slowing down.* **Go to a museum and decide to admire *one* painting—not an entire collection.**
• *Don't set unrealistic deadlines at work.* **Don't take on more than they can comfortably manage.**
• *When they make love, concentrate on enjoying one another's touch*

without thinking about any goal. Using a modified version of the traditional sensate-focus technique, alternate giving and receiving pleasure for pleasure's sake.

• *Instead of always being in control, <u>delegate</u> tasks around the house.* They hired a high school student to give them some help and took the car to be detailed instead of doing it themselves.

• *Practice saying "no."* The next time the company picnic came around, Travis did not volunteer to organize it!

• *Change their attitude from <u>obligation focus to choice focus</u>.* Instead of saying "I should" be a better lover, they said "I could" be a better lover if I choose to be.

• The most important change they made was *to pay attention to <u>living in the here and now</u>.* This meditative way of being has been presented by Zen masters for hundreds of years. Becoming more mindful of one another and looking at your lover as if each time were the first time puts you in touch with your spiritual connection. Being fully present takes practice, but has immensely satisfying rewards.

As Travis and Nicole practiced, their intimacy soared as the quality of loving replaced sheer quantity.

THE BEE PERSONALITY

Practical, ambitious, and image-conscious, Bees attempt to excel at everything they do. Bees make decisions based on facts and process information in a rational analytic way. They're detail-oriented and may miss seeing the bigger picture, especially if some intuition is called for. They labor over projects much longer than is reasonable and have trouble letting go of them until every *t* is crossed and every *i* is dotted.

When I see that a new patient has arrived at my office twenty minutes early, I suspect it's a Bee. They have their checks written *before* the session begins, ask me where I'd like them to sit, and ask me how *I'm* doing. They live by their schedules and usually have one or more personal organizers. Whether it's alphabetizing the spice rack, or making sure the towels are folded neatly in thirds, a Bee is meticulous about order.

Bees will bring predictability, security, and order to your haphazard existence. They are excellent money managers and logicians. If you feel out of control with your body, finances, or home, your Bee partner will shape things up, pronto.

At work, if you want a flowchart designed precisely, ask a Bee to do it. They expect more from themselves than others do, and make excellent team members. Whether they're at work or at home, Bees can be highly critical. They want things done "just so" and tolerate little deviation. One patient complained that her Bee husband threw a fit if all the hangers in the closet weren't pointed in the same direction.

Because they're so detail-focused and fear failure, decision making—even a small matter—can become an enormous task. When Nicole and Travis go out to eat, they spend an inordinate amount of time reading the menu from start to finish. They drive themselves crazy weighing all the pros and cons before making a purchase or planning a vacation. Things that should be relatively easy become major events.

When you meet a Bee, you'll no doubt notice their impeccable grooming. Socially they are polite, poised, and self-confident. You may marvel at their near-flawless presentation. If you're looking for the ideal partner to accompany you to the Governor's Ball, look for a Bee. They're the consummate gentleman or lady and will never cause you any embarrassment.

Pleasing others is what Bees do best. They frequently worry that a job isn't done as well as it could have been and get extremely upset with the slightest criticism. Travis once delivered a paper at a professional meeting. His approval rating was 98 percent but Travis agonized about the 2 percent he missed!

Bees don't allow themselves the most basic opportunities for enjoyment or relaxation. They don't know how to play or have fun if it's not structured. If you're a spontaneous Otter who'd drop everything to camp under the stars with your lover, this will be a difficult stretch for your Bee partner who'd prefer arranging his getaway at a four-star hotel.

Because emotions threaten their self-control and can result in humiliation, they are carefully monitored and are rarely exposed. If they happen to "break through," the Bee finds this unnerving. It will be hard to discover what your Bee lover is *feeling,* but you'll always know what he or she would like to *do.*

Bees expect you to be clean, confident, and under control (at all times). This is difficult to do when you're having an orgasm, but they manage. They're not fond of things that are messy, including slobbery French kisses. If you hear someone screaming "Oh, baby! Yes! Yes! Yes!" in the hotel room next to yours, you can bet a week's salary it's not a Bee.

THE NEED TO CONTROL

Bees are especially sensitive to boundary issues. When they sit in a movie theater or on an airplane, they pay attention to who has which armrest. If you're with a Bee, and put your elbows on the table so that they feel "crowded," they'll tell you that you're in their space.

Bees have a need to control and structure emotional expressions, playfulness, and spontaneous actions. For them there is something unsafe about purposeless activity. By trying to control things around them and within them, they are attempting to ensure security and safety and to minimize the inevitable risks associated with randomness or spontaneity.

Since Bees are sticklers for detail, they can convert a lighthearted impromptu social gathering into an ordeal. Because purely pleasurable experiences can trigger anxiety or a fear of loss of control, Bees are reluctant to open up to the eroticism of the moment and rarely focus on the "now." The embarrassment and fear of allowing impulsive behaviors or wishes to break through their vigilance makes Bees highly structured and controlled in their demeanor.

THE BEE FAMILY

Families who are either intrusive or overly rigid about boundaries, expectations, and performance may find themselves producing Worker/Bees. Although we grow inside the uterus of our mother, from birth we're challenged with how to be a separate person without losing our vital connection. The need/fear dilemma that ensues is evidence of this lifelong struggle. We need to be close, yet fear engulfment and the loss of self, so we pull away and risk the loneliness that accompanies separateness.

Boundaries between ourselves and our parents and lovers define where "we" leave off and "they" begin. If boundaries are too loose or permeable, the result is identity confusion—an uncomfortable merger. I've heard this described as "feeling swallowed up or smothered." Unfortunately, if boundaries are too confining, the death of the organism can result through a restriction of the vital emotions we need to survive.

Children who are raised with unclear boundaries vary in their temperaments and coping strategies: they may back away from conflict (like some Bears), may boldly venture out to establish their own identity (like some Lions), may rebel (like some Otters), or they may carefully define their own rules as a Bee.

Cassidy is a Bee from an intrusive background. Her mother felt entitled to know *everything* about her. It wasn't until she went to college and lived with roommates that she realized it wasn't "normal" to keep the bathroom door wide open while she was sitting on the toilet. You see, in Cassidy's home doors were to be kept open and unlocked at all times. Cassidy's mother couldn't tolerate the smallest amount of separation; she listened in on her phone conversations, read her diary, and searched through her bureau drawers. Even though Cassidy went away to college, her mother called her every day.

Maribeth, also a Bee, came from an entirely different setting. Her mother insisted on being a liberal-minded "pal." Maribeth had no guidelines. At the age of sixteen she could party all night, smoke marijuana, have sex with her boyfriend in their home, and essentially come and go as she pleased. Maribeth's Bee-ness emerged out of her need to bring order to her free-form existence. Bees use structure to manage feelings of loss of control.

Bee families vacillate between being overly judgmental or unconcerned. Children who grow up in Bee families try to perform everything flawlessly to earn their parents' approval and to calm their own anxiety. These children often suffer from unrelenting self-castigation and difficulty enjoying their substantial accomplishments. No matter what they do, it never seems to be perfect enough.

Nan, a thirty-three-year-old probate attorney, remembers a threatening and unpredictably chaotic environment where things could blow at any time. She developed a controlled, compulsive way of handling disarray. The more chaotic things would be, the more orderly she became. "When I was in my teens and felt worried about something, I'd feel better if I bought some pretty floral paper and lined my underwear drawers with it. To this day, straightening things makes me feel calmer."

Children who grow up fearing that their environment is either too rigid or too chaotic come to believe that the best thing to do is depend on yourself. If they create safe rules and regulations to live by, there will be a predictability and certainty to their surroundings.

Everett, a statistics professor at a community college and the married father of two, is a Bee with some Bear features who is said to be standoffish and aloof. He's approximately six feet two inches tall, and although he lives on a teacher's salary, his wardrobe looks like it could be featured in *Gentleman's Quarterly*. Whenever he felt irritated, he didn't hesitate to let people know, but he had a great deal of difficulty being warm or vulnerable.

During one of our individual sessions, I asked him how he'd feel if he let anyone close to him. After a long pause he answered, "If people got to know me, they probably wouldn't like me."

By looking at him no one would have ever guessed how lonely, insecure, and frightened of rejection he was. He'd managed to alienate everyone in his life, including his wife and children.

Everett had come to me because of symptoms of depression. With the exception of his students, nothing seemed to bring him much joy. *"Doing" was a substitute for "being."* The lonelier he felt, the more he tried to accomplish.

Everett's father had wanted him to be a doctor, but his grades weren't good enough. Whenever the holidays would come around and the families were together, his father would make mention of his low-paying career. He might say, "If you'd gone to medical school you'd have enough money for your own home now, or you could afford another baby, or you could take that European vacation . . ." On the surface, it appeared that he wanted Everett to be successful. On closer look, his father felt like a failure and Everett's "success" would point to his own inadequacy.

Many Bees fear that they don't measure up. No matter how hard they try, they don't succeed in pleasing those who are most important to them and their hard work and exacting efforts are aimed at winning that love.

I'm not suggesting that one's childhood is the only variable that shapes a Bee personality. Our environment is the soil that works upon the basic genetic "seed." Many newborns have an affinity for Bee-ness from birth. There are some children who won't tolerate any messiness and complain bitterly the moment their diaper is soiled or their high chair is littered with some leftover Cheerios from breakfast. Compare them with Otter children who like nothing better than squishing their peas and carrots, playing in the mud, or delighting in messy finger paints.

The fastidious Bee is locked inside a prison of his own design. Before you attempt to break him "free," keep in mind that each style serves a particular purpose and will be maintained for as long as that purpose is useful.

THE ATTRACTION OF A BEE

Bees are very attractive to individuals who value stability and predictability. Bees typify the good stable parent who will take care of you and protect you. They make good eye contact and are excellent listeners, as long as you don't overwhelm them with superlatives and excessive emotionality. They may have an abundance of projects going at one time, and you may be impressed at how well they perform their juggling act.

When you meet a Bee you will be taken by their gallantry and faultless manners. They will be charming, thoughtful, soft-spoken, and well informed. They tend not to be overly expansive with gestures and may play things close to the vest. They make superb attorneys, accountants, historians, mathematicians, and engineers. Facts and figures are their forte. They can advise you on your stock portfolio, introduce you to political movers and shakers, and appreciate your taste in high style as well as any Lion.

Touching is not their strong suit. You won't see Bees hugging guests indiscriminately. They are cautious before sharing body space with others. They are excellent people to confide in and they will keep your secret confidential.

Bees will sacrifice virtually everything for their home and family. They put aside their own needs for the greater good of others. If anyone has the "disease to please," it's a Bee. They are great neighbors and always have the right extension cord or power tool readily available in their garage.

Boundaries are their business. They are respectful of other people's space and privacy. You won't find a Bee dropping in on you without a phone call or invitation. They don't just walk into other people's hives and they expect the same from you. Although their product is "honey" and they can be very sweet, watch out for their sting if they're annoyed.

WHAT YOU NEED TO KNOW ABOUT YOURSELF IF YOU'RE ATTRACTED TO A BEE

If you find Bees attractive, no doubt you have need for more order and predictability in your own life. You may know that you bring excitement and passion to relationships but are limited in your linear thinking and factual analysis. Although these traits are not your strong points, you value them nonetheless, and find yourself drawn to partners who can effortlessly sort out "messiness."

Bees bring financial security, dependability, self-reliance, and technical know-how. They will shoulder more than their share of the responsibilities and offer wise counsel. If their "parental" wisdom is appealing to you, it may have been unavailable in your own development. Bees' omniscient approach may seem like arrogance to some, but not to you—you find comfort in their masterful style. If you're someone who longs to be well cared for and protected; you will find yourself with a Bee or Lion every time.

WHAT BEES WANT FROM RELATIONSHIPS

IF YOUR PARTNER IS A BEE, HERE ARE SOME THINGS YOU NEED TO KNOW:

1. Bees appreciate facts, explanations, and rational discussions rather than emotional or intuitive dialogues.

2. They want partners who are patient and allow them time to think about their decisions without pressuring them into a premature conclusion.

3. They value their privacy and have a strong sense of fairness and will feel unsettled if you take the entire armrest in the movie theater or on an airplane.

4. Bees consider themselves to be outstanding lovers and expect

their partners to value and praise their technical expertise. They don't provide loud groans of passion, but assume you know they're "concentrating" on making sex wonderful for you.

5. Bees expect their partners to be reliable. If they schedule sex on Sunday afternoon, unless there's been a mutually agreed-upon modification, your Bee will count on it happening. His word is his bond.

If your Bee is satisfied in this way, he will be more likely to relax his vigilance and let you into the inner sanctum of his heart.

SEX WITH A BEE

Sex with a Bee is a challenge. The joy of sex comes from being in the moment and opening to the surprises and sensations that occur. This is counter to what a Bee finds comfortable. Sex is, by nature, hot, smelly, sweaty, slippery, wet, and even sticky—not favorite experiences for Bees. When Nicole and Travis made love, they made sure they carefully placed a towel beneath them to catch any of the "drippings." Sex was orchestrated so that they remained on the towel at all times. You can see the restrictions built into this approach!

Bees are so focused on what they "should do" sexually that you may feel you're being "done" by your lover. Sex can take on a mechanical work-driven flavor if you're not careful. Bees need to learn that they'll do the best "job" if they pay attention to the moment. Helping them think of pleasure as a "job" will make it more palatable. Redefine work to include play. It takes skill, but I've found it's very successful.

Nicole and Travis felt lonely when they had sex because they weren't being intimate. Intimacy is difficult if both of you are encased in steel. I challenged them by saying, "This will probably be very difficult for you to master, but you need to find a way to let each other inside. It's not enough to spend more time together, although that's a definite plus. You need to open your hearts to each other, not just your legs." This got their attention. Bees never want to be told that they're not doing something right.

Travis and Nicole organized their time to include one hour of touching no less than every forty-eight hours. Before they touched, they spent some relaxing time talking about something personal to each of them. Bees respond well to challenges and prescriptions that include exact times and frequencies. I continued, "To be successful, all you have to do is share some feelings and then touch each other in ways that each of you finds pleasant. This breaks the functional mechanistic pattern of needing to produce an orgasm or an erection each time you make love."

Nicole and Travis came back after one week and (like good Bees) had done their assignment. Bees are excellent at completing their homework. Not only had they talked and touched for one hour, but they did it *every* day. "Do we get extra credit?" Travis smiled. The more they practiced, the more comfortable and less lonely they felt. Soon sex became a regular part of their relationship and they allowed themselves to expand their repertoire. "I can't believe we ignored something that has such benefits to our emotional and physical health," said Nicole. Spoken like a true Bee, I thought.

Initially, the best way to reach your Bee partner is through discussing sexual techniques, *not* feelings. They feel safest when reading a book with you, watching an instructional video on how to give the best oral sex, or having you show them *exactly* how to stroke your clitoris. Feelings will come later.

Bees appreciate gentle coaxing and direction to feel comfortable being more sexual. But don't worry, Bees pride themselves on being excellent learners. Give them the time and structure they need to feel safe and they'll do their best. If they need to do all of the other "tasks" before they can relax, so be it. Don't fight it. Your Bee will never be an Otter, but isn't that why you married him?

And one more point: cleanliness is of primary importance to your Bee mate. If you can afford it, build a *huge* bathroom. Playing in the tub and shower is a great way to introduce some creativity into your sexual routine. I know many Bees who only like oral sex in the bathtub or shower. They discover some very unique positions! If your Bee is sensitive to body odors, they may want you to be squeaky clean. Don't personalize their preferences and feel insulted. After all, you wouldn't get offended if they insisted on putting more salt on their omelet, would you? Find a way to turn their interest into a game. Give them the washcloth, find some wonderfully fragrant shower gel, and have fun!

When Bees say they're sexually "bored" they mean they're confused, goalless, or without direction. To stimulate your Bee's interest, challenge him by suggesting a new game plan complete with objectives and strategies. As long as they know the rules, Bees will be great sports.

It may appear that your Bee is sexless, but this isn't the case. In fact, the reverse is true. The more controlled your Bee appears, the more passion is waiting for you. As long as you add sex and intimacy to their to-do list and approach them in a logical, consistent way, they won't object. Address your Bee slowly and unemotionally. Don't criticize, pressure, or suggest they're sexual failures. Bees have a "sting." Don't dislodge or threaten their orderliness, and you'll soon have great sexual times.

TO SUMMARIZE SOME OF THE SALIENT FEATURES
OF A BEE:
BEES ARE PEOPLE WHO:

1. Are highly ambitious, loyal, and hardworking: they'll give their last breath to defend their home and family.
2. Aim at perfection and try to always give their very best.
3. Have trouble delegating tasks and create an overly scheduled existence because they believe, "If you want it done right, do it yourself!"
4. Are logical, rational, analytical, and detail-oriented.
5. Prefer facts to feelings.
6. Try to be technically flawless in all areas, including sex.
7. Need to feel needed, and live to please others.
8. By focusing on obligations, they limit their pleasure. They are often distracted during sex by thoughts of what they "should" be doing or worries of "not doing it right."
9. Measure themselves by what they "do," not who they "are."
10. Have difficulty relaxing and going with the flow.
11. Are as exacting with others as they are with themselves.

BENJAMIN AND SHARON: A BEE AND A BEAR

After nearly twenty years of marriage, Benjamin and Sharon have decided they'd like to improve their lovemaking. Benjamin, a practicing physician in obstetrics and gynecology, has had problems maintaining his erection for as far back as he can recall. "I was too embarrassed to ask for help," he admitted. "I always thought I should be able to 'doctor' myself."

Sharon, an exceptionally patient Bear, just waited for things to get better. When Benjamin would lose his erection, she tried to say all the "right" things like "It really doesn't matter," or "I'm fine without intercourse." But it really *did* matter to Sharon and it mattered even more to Benjamin.

I asked Benjamin and Sharon to describe their last sexual encounter in detail using the "sportscaster's technique." I wanted to know *who* initiated, *how* they initiated, *where* they were, and *what* they were thinking.

"Well," Benjamin began, "it was last Friday night. We had just gotten home from a movie and I leaned over and gave Sharon an affectionate kiss. She had just poured us both a glass of wine and we walked up to the bedroom."

"That's right," Sharon interjected. "We usually spend some intimate time together on Fridays because the kids sleep over at their friends' house."

As they're telling their story, I've noticed two things: sex is planned and alcohol is part of the formula.

Benjamin continues his story: "We walk into the bedroom and I'm feeling aroused."

I ask, "How do you know?" I'm interested in finding out whether he's scanning his penis for an erection so early in the experience.

"I begin to feel the swelling in my penis," he answers.

"And then what happens?" I ask.

"I continue to kiss Sharon and we take off our clothes and get into bed. Sharon is getting more aroused. I can tell from her body movements and the intensity of her kisses. The more aroused she gets, the more worried I'm becoming that my erection won't last."

"I touch her breasts and give her oral sex, but now I'm noticing that my erection is gone."

"The weird thing is that I have an orgasm almost every time," said

Sharon. "I love Benjamin so much. It really doesn't matter whether we always have intercourse or not."

"Sharon orgasmed," said Benjamin, "but *I was separated from the whole experience.* It reminds me of that Woody Allen picture where Woody's body stands up, leaves the bed where he and Diane Keaton are lying, and comments on what's going on in the bed. Sharon has this passionate experience and I'm sitting across the room somewhere watching her.

"The sense of failure and despair that I feel confirms my inadequacy."

This is a typical example of a Bee who is performance-driven and highly critical of himself. He has a patient, loving partner, but he isn't patient or loving with himself.

The classic spectatoring that Masters and Johnson describe is easy to detect. The treatment is to decrease the attention Benjamin pays to his erection while increasing his focus on pleasure.

I suggested that Benjamin deal with his distractions by not fighting with them. The harder we try not to think of a "pink elephant," the more fixed that image becomes. The best way to deal with distractions is to replace them with something else. It's impossible to think of anxiety and pleasure at the exact same moment.

I suggested that each time Benjamin found his attention wandering to his penis, he announce out loud, "I'm thinking about my erection," and then focus on something he found interesting or arousing in his partner. If the thought about his erection interjected itself a dozen times, then he should comment on it a dozen times—redirecting his attention to pleasure each and every time.

This technique had excellent results. It's no secret that Benjamin monitors his erections and Sharon usually monitors his erection, too. With both of them watching Benjamin's penis it would be a miracle if it *could* stand up—that's a lot of pressure!

Instead of trying to hide his preoccupation with his erection, this technique converts his unconscious intrusive thoughts into something conscious. It brings a degree of control to something that feels out of control.

I also suggested that they eliminate the two glasses of wine for "relaxation," because in some cases it can have an inhibiting effect on physiological arousal.

These very simple suggestions made a world of difference. The more

Benjamin practiced redirecting his attention to arousal, the more pleasure he experienced and the more connected he felt to Sharon during their love-making.

ALEX AND LAURA: A BEE AND A LION

It's hard to imagine a better business partnership than that of a Bee and a Lion. Bees can develop brilliantly accurate business plans and Lions have the drive and energy to carry them to successful completion. Bees and Lions are masters at work as long as they divide the task according to their individual strengths. However, when they crowd one another's turf, they find themselves "locking horns" (metaphorically speaking) around issues of power and control. Unless these problems are faced and resolved, they're usually out in the relationship and in the bedroom.

Alex, thirty-three, and Laura, thirty-two, have been married for eleven years. Together they parlayed a small consulting business into a significant moneymaking enterprise. Laura had a talent for hiring the right staff and convincingly articulating their mission to prospective clients. Alex was the behind-the-scenes genius who engineered the whole thing. They were un-beatable.

When Alex was young, his kindhearted, gentle father took care of him more than his mother did. His mother drifted in and out of his life between hospitalizations for chronic depression. Because of her treatments with elec-troconvulsive shock, her memory was impaired and her moods were unpre-dictable. Although there was no overt abuse, Alex suffered from a profound sense of shame. He used to dream about a home where he could invite his friends—one where there were no piles of dirty dishes in the sink or heaps of unwashed laundry.

Alex devoted his energies to his studies and became an excellent stu-dent. This was something he *could* control. Years later, he applied himself just as diligently to achieving success in his career. He didn't stop long enough to rest or reflect on the emptiness or sadness—his motto was "full speed ahead."

Laura was his childhood sweetheart. She was loving and generous, en-ergetic and ambitious. They married right out of college and established their business soon after.

But their intimacy hadn't fared as well. Laura told me in confidence that she had begun to have thoughts about having an affair with one of their business associates. "I don't want to jeopardize my marriage, but I just don't find Alex sexually exciting." Fortunately, she came to see me before she acted on her impulse. "I need to feel attractive," she continued, "but Alex never seems to notice *me*. I sometimes think that I could substitute someone else in bed with him and he'd never know the difference!" Laura, a sensitive, demanding Lion, was hurt because she wasn't feeling special to her husband.

Laura and Alex had gotten caught in the web of "doing" and had forgotten how to "be" with one another. Doing more doesn't improve intimacy—learning how to *be* differently with one another was their ticket to recapturing romance.

BEES AND OTTERS

Neil Simon's play *The Odd Couple,* with Felix Unger as the obsessive neat freak and Oscar Madison as his sloppy, rough-around-the-edges roommate, presents a well-known example of a Bee/Otter relationship.

Bees and Otters have a polarity that brings a great deal of energy and struggle to their interactions. In an "odd" way, however, the relationship works—Felix needs Oscar's impulsivity and spontaneity to stir his juices, and Oscar would sleep on the same unlaundered sheets for weeks without Felix's organizational acumen. But we also know that their relationship was peppered with daily struggles.

Imagine a husband and wife in the same situation. Esther and Stuart were my real-life Felix and Oscar. I would be hard pressed to come up with two people who were more diametrically opposite in style and approach. Esther, a forty-nine-year-old legal secretary, was the consummate perfectionist. She was immaculate in her appearance, tending toward the more conservative in her dress; Stuart, a fifty-five-year-old recently retired postal worker, preferred to wear sneakers and sweats. Esther liked dining out; he would rather order take-out. But they loved one another and the fit worked "pretty well," according to their own admission, until Stuart's retirement.

"He's always underfoot," Esther remarked during our first meeting. "I used to have some free time to straighten the house because he worked the three-to-eleven shift at the post office. As soon as I put away the magazines, he has them strewn about. We've been arguing more than ever and I'm exhausted!"

And what about our "Oscar Madison"? Stuart was a charmer. He had an easygoing boyishness about him that was captivating. In spite of his "shortcomings" I could see why Esther was attracted to his lighthearted demeanor. "Esther's right," he commented sincerely. "I've never been very good at keeping things tidy. I was fine as a mail sorter, but only because I knew the ropes and would get fired if I screwed up!"

Stuart was unapologetic in his approach and this infuriated Esther even more, "What do I do with a man like this?" After nearly twenty-eight years of marriage, she thought *she* could change *him*. She tried leaving things a mess, but Stuart's tolerance for disorder was much greater than hers.

"How much time do you spend arguing?" I wondered.

"We disagree about a half dozen small things every day," she replied.

"If you didn't argue about the small annoyances, I wonder how you'd spend that precious time?" I asked.

They both were taken aback. I'm not suggesting that living with a sloppy partner isn't annoying, but it's pretty obvious that the constant nagging hadn't changed a thing. The only thing they'd both accomplished was undermining their intimacy.

The question was simple. Were they both prepared to change *their own* styles a bit? Esther was surprised. "Why should I change? I try to do everything right—to keep our home neat and our life on track." She was so accustomed to blaming Stuart that the suggestion she might also have to modify her style seemed absurd. But that was the only way out of their struggle—assuming they were both prepared to try another approach.

After some heated dialogues, they both agreed to try. Esther backed off considerably, and Stuart picked up the ball. The rules were simple: Esther was not to treat him like a child and Stuart was not to act like one. Easier said than done, but no one ever said this was easy.

If the Bee and Otter can come to some fundamental compromises about balancing work and play, and their mutual responsibilities, they can make a lively and highly functional team.

LIFE LESSONS FOR BEES

The ancient sages taught, "Yield and be whole. Bend and overcome. Empty and be full."

Once you're familiar with your own Bee-ness, you have some clues about your need to organize and control situations.

....
TO CREATE A MORE FLEXIBLE STYLE THAT WILL ALLOW INTIMACY AND FUN INTO YOUR OVERLY ORCHESTRATED EXISTENCE, TRY THE FOLLOWING SUGGESTIONS:

1. *Identify feelings and separate them from thoughts.* Make a list of feeling words like *happy, sad, angry, loving, strong, weak, playful, calm, passionate,* etc., and use one feeling word in a sentence each day.

2. *Make time in your schedule for intimacy.* Set aside one evening a week for a "date" evening and take your partner out for dinner and some intimate conversation.

3. *Recognize the positives about your partner and tell him or her in a personal way.*

4. *Share your hopes, dreams, and fears with your lover.* Replace goal-oriented or project-oriented conversation with *feeling-oriented conversation.* Instead of talking about the Dow Jones Average, tell her that her skin is smooth as silk.

5. *Take a walk or a drive with your partner and head for nowhere in particular.*

6. If you think of her during the day, don't wait; pick up the phone to tell her in the moment. *Cultivate spontaneity.* If it feels silly, do it.

7. *Change your "shoulds" to "wants."* Do more things because you want to and fewer because you feel that you should.

8. *Change all-or-nothing thinking.* Look for shades of gray.

9. *Practice settling for less than perfection in yourself and in others.*

10. *On your next trip, <u>don't</u> make an itinerary.*

11. *Surprise her or him.* Bring home a rose, a stuffed animal, a bottle of wine, or a romantic CD—just because. Don't obsess about the "right" thing; anything will be "right."

HINTS FOR LIVING WITH A BEE:

1. Don't personalize your Bee's idiosyncrasies. Their need for structure and order doesn't represent a lack of confidence in you—it's just their preference.

2. Be open about your thoughts or concerns and present them factually. Don't flood your Bee partner with a passionate, tearful entreaty.

3. Don't accumulate a long list of grievances. Share your concerns in a candid but *timely* manner.

4. Remind your Bee of all the things you admire about him. They are desperate to please you and will work their tails off to do so. Let them know how much you appreciate their efforts.

5. Don't forget that feelings don't come easily to them. Empathize with their difficulty and genuinely praise their efforts whenever they try to share their heart with you.

THE WORST OF BEES

Bees will drive you crazy with their compulsivity and need to control. If the kitchen towels aren't folded in thirds or the water drips aren't wiped from the sink, you'll probably hear about it. You may feel as though you can never do things well enough for your Bee mate and feel guilty if you don't share his or her drive for cleanliness and order. Bees rate life in terms of productivity, so your value is based on what you do. If you sit home and watch sitcoms all day, don't expect your Bee to sing your praises. You may resent having to schedule time to talk to your mate and worry that you're way down on his priority list, but this is all part of being a Bee's life partner.

If you long for a free-spirited, childlike nymph who'll drop everything at a moment's notice to make mad passionate love along the side of the road—forget it. But if you're open to taking the time a Bee requires to plan a romantic getaway escape, you can have the best time of your life.

THE BEST OF BEES

Bees are great providers and will give you their last dime. They're caring, highly ambitious, dependable, well-mannered, and socially affable. You'll have a well-padded pension fund, a superb credit rating, and will be considered pillars of the community if your partner is a Bee. A Bee will respect your need for solitude and support your independence, but will expect the same in return. Your Bee partner will provide a comfortable home, a neat closet, and will never reek of body odor. They cultivate a pristine appearance, work at staying fit, and look great on your arm. They never run away from a challenge and will battle to the death to protect their family.

Bees are trustworthy and unwavering in their loyalty. Affairs are too destabilizing and not generally part of their modus operandi. They need their own space, and if you respect their boundaries you will be lavished in finery. Although sexual spontaneity isn't their strong suit, technique is. They will labor to get your sexual preferences right and will care more about *your* sexual pleasure than their own.

CHAPTER 12

WHO ARE THESE OTTERS?

There often seems to be a playfulness to wise people,
as if either their equanimity has as its source this playfulness
or the playfulness flows from equanimity; and they can persuade
other people who are in a state of agitation to calm
down and manage a smile.

—EDWARD HOAGLAND, 1973

MARK AND SANDI: TWO OTTERS IN LOVE

Mark and Sandi met nearly eleven years ago when they were lifeguarding at Cape May, New Jersey. They were inseparable from the beginning—surfing, water skiing, Rollerblading, and rock climbing together. Falling in love was a no-brainer; they were perfect for one another. Or so it appeared.

If it felt good, they did it. This was especially true of sex. Neither one had ever been with a more passionate sex partner. Their orgasms were cataclysmic. Sandi felt comfortable acting out their favorite sexual fantasies with Mark. One fantasy they especially liked was called "the towel boy and the penthouse lady" and they loved the part where the towel boy licked mango sorbet from the penthouse lady's inner thighs!

What could possibly go wrong here? Very little, as long as each day is a fun-filled escapade, but all play and no work makes for a very small bank account. As we remember from the Aesop fable about the Grasshopper and the Ant, if you fiddle away the summer there will be no food in the winter.

Mark and Sandi weren't having sexual problems at first—their problems in the love department came from facing the unavoidable responsibilities of married life. More specifically, when it came to managing a budget, paying the bills, doing necessary home repairs, and weeding the garden—neither was interested. Like two stubborn siblings, each one waited for the other to pick up the slack. Mark tried to find work as a freelance writer, but had difficulty managing his deadlines. Sandy taught preschool, but they had trouble making it on her income alone.

Since Sandi was the more Lionly of the two, she stepped up to the plate and took on the "Lion's share" of the household duties. She got a second job and made sure all the bills were paid on time. Their credit rating improved under her watchful eye, but it wasn't long before she began to feel resentful about Mark's "laziness."

You can predict what happened next. The more Sandi pressured him, the less Mark was at home. He began to spend several evenings out drinking with the guys. As the arguments increased, sex decreased. Even for pleasure experts like these Otters, emotional flexibility and balance are the keys to sustaining satisfying intimacy.

THE OTTER PERSONALITY

At the risk of sounding too New Age, we might say that Otters know that life is about the journey, not the destination. They believe "If it's fun, let's try it—make hay while the sun shines!" Unlike the Bee, the Otter considers neatness inconsequential—why bother making the bed if you're going to get back into it in a few hours?

Otters make charming, lovable, and thoroughly enjoyable playmates. Vacations are their times to shine. There's never a dull moment with an Otter by your side. They can turn a simple trip to the video store or pizza parlor into an adventure. When you're with an Otter, be prepared for anything. They don't need a special occasion to buy you gifts or surprise you with tickets to the Caribbean, so have your bags packed.

Sex with an Otter is like nothing you've ever experienced before. If you're a constricted Bear, your Otter is certain to expand your horizons. A love affair with your precious Otter is like entering a veritable sexual playground. Whatever your fantasy or whim may be, your Otter lover will be game to experience it with you.

Otters love variety. When you hear their résumé, it's not unusual to find that they have sampled numerous professions and have been involved in multiple projects simultaneously. They have little tolerance for sameness and move on to greener pastures at a moment's notice.

Commitment isn't their favorite concept, so don't expect your Otter to want to settle down in that vine-covered cottage. They loathe predictability and routine. Otters need their freedom. They do well with partners who are equally adventuresome, trusting, and can tolerate some boundary ambiguity. Lion partners who are secure in their own career and don't require that their mate be physically bolted to their hip often welcome the freedom an Otter offers.

Jealous, controlling partners are the kiss of death for an Otter. If you try to control them, your relationship will soon be a distant memory, because they will have slipped out in the night.

Otters are generally easygoing and don't harbor resentments. They'll distract you from your problems, and make you forget what you were angry about. They're adaptable, supportive, and accommodating. If you need help with the laundry or another pair of hands to type an overdue report, your Otter will find a way to make the task enjoyable.

When you take your Otter on a date it's best that you don't tell them where you're going. Just tell them how to dress and when to be ready and surprise them with the rest. They'll be grateful for your spontaneity.

Don't expect your Otter to help you organize your affairs. Structure, order, and logic are not their strong points. You'll have to develop these qualities on your own. They're also not paragons of patience. If they get the impulse to try a new restaurant or catch a midnight show, they won't be happy to hear you say, "Maybe next weekend."

When an Otter wants to play, they assume everyone wants to play. It's not as much fun playing alone, so they're seeking perennial playmates. They have little tolerance for lethargy, inertia, or the physically unfit. Otters are forever young, no matter what the calendar says. They appreciate partners who are physically and mentally active and alert and would rather run the Colorado rapids than order room service at the Four Seasons.

And speaking of the Four Seasons, Otters are not very frugal. They spend what they have and don't generally have a lot. Money and other material possessions aren't of primary concern to an Otter. They have a spiritual wealth and worldly abundance that makes them seem anything but impoverished. Otters are magical in their ability to show you the world in a seashell, blade of grass, or raindrop.

THE OTTER FAMILY: DON'T FENCE ME IN

Brenda was my best friend in high school. There was only one problem—I wasn't allowed to phone her. No one could. Brenda wasn't allowed to give *anyone* her phone number. Not girls or guys—so she never had a date.

She and I made a little game out of it. She told me that each year she'd give me one of the last four digits of her phone number, so I would finally be able to call her by senior year. It never happened.

Brenda was almost five feet nine inches tall by freshman year. She used to hunch her shoulders so she wouldn't tower over the guys. Her straight brown hair, with its center part, reached the middle of her back. She wasn't allowed to wear makeup and her skirts were always a little bit longer than everyone else's.

Even though Brenda was such a "plain Jane" I remember her lovely porcelain skin and the way her large brown eyes bashfully peered through her long bangs.

None of the kids understood why Brenda couldn't have a social life. All we knew was that her family, especially her father, was very controlling. It seemed cruel that she could never come to sleepovers or double-date with the rest of us. She missed her junior prom and her senior prom, and couldn't ever have friends over to her house. It was a mystery. But those of us who liked Brenda accepted her rules and socialized with her whenever we could. We sat together in the lunchroom, worked on school projects at the library, and on the weekends when there was a sports event we sat next to one another on the bleachers.

I lost track of Brenda after we graduated. I went to college and assumed she did, too. We were both in the national honor society and Brenda was especially talented in math and science. I always figured she'd become a physicist or mechanical engineer.

One day, many years later, my husband, my young daughter, and I were sitting in an International House of Pancakes ordering breakfast. A waitress with dyed jet-black hair took our order. She looked about my age, but very shopworn and fatigued. Her heavy makeup sat in the deep creases of her forehead. Smudged black mascara and dark eyeliner circled her deep-set eyes. There was something vaguely familiar about her face, and then I noticed her name tag—it was Brenda!

"Brenda?" I asked with what must have been a startled look. "Is it really you?" I felt uncomfortable "discovering" her in this way. How could she have wound up in a diner waiting on tables? She quickly told me her story:

"After high school I just went crazy," she said. "You remember how strict my father was—I wasn't prepared to handle dating, guys, or any freedom at all. I met a married police officer and had an affair. Got pregnant and had twins . . ." I was surprised at how candid she was in revealing this to me, but she hardly took a breath as she continued. "He said he'd leave his wife and marry me, but he never did. Raising two kids with only a high school education hasn't been easy. My parents disowned me and wouldn't pay for college. I'm trying to save some money to go to night school now."

It was hard to hear her story. We talked a few times after that meeting. I discovered she had spent some time in prison for drug dealing. She apparently broke as many rules as she could in those years after high school. She felt she had been imprisoned for a long time by her family, so being in jail came easily to her.

Brenda had become rebellious, nonconforming, and sexually promiscuous. She's had to face poverty, loneliness, and heartbreak. After the police officer, she married an alcoholic who couldn't support her. She divorced him after eight months.

I was troubled by what had happened to my friend. It will take a long time for Brenda to identify what *she* really wants and to stop acting out the anger she still carries from her past.

Otters may be the products of overly permissive or highly restrictive environments. Others are artistic and free-spirited due to a solid spiritual grounding and appreciation for the inner beauty and wonder of nature. There are Otters who are impulse-driven, risk-taking rule breakers, and others who are law-abiding, fun-loving partygoers who simply like to have a good time.

What all Otters share is a reluctance to be fenced in or pinned down. They fear dependency and get claustrophobic when restrictions are placed on their freedom.

When an Otter says they're bored, what they mean is they feel limited *in their expressiveness, creativity, or spontaneity.* Above all, Otters live to play and be happy. Whatever else they do is secondary. Unfortunately there are some Otters, like Brenda, who haven't figured out how to make that happen.

To summarize some of the salient features of an otter:
Otters are people who:

1. Are always turning up with new ideas. You'll never be bored with an Otter as your partner.

2. Seek fun, adventure, and living life to the max.

3. Are risk takers, free spirits, humanitarian, and generous.

4. Are naturally passionate pleasure seekers. They will find joy everywhere.

5. Can be rebellious and may push the envelope legally, morally, ideologically, and religiously. Conservative thinking is anathema to the liberal Otter.

6. Are more concerned with what you're like on the inside than the labels you wear.

7. Are subject to acting on a whim. There is little time between the thought and the action.

8. Are generally positive in their approach and have little interest in those who are not.

9. Enjoy talk about philosophy, travel, adventure, dreams, fantasies, and honest heart-to-heart communication.

10. Are more in touch with their own wishes than other people's feelings.

ATTRACTION OF AN OTTER

Otters are attractive to individuals who crave excitement but are hesitant to provide it for themselves.

If you loathe your humdrum existence and long to explore some fantasies, you can be sure that your adventuresome Otter will be game to experiment with you.

Otters are ever-willing playmates who will beguile you with their charm and penchant for the exotic or obscure. They will show you hidden caverns and cloud formations, know where to find the best fried clams, and arouse erogenous zones you never knew you had!

WHAT YOU NEED TO KNOW ABOUT YOURSELF IF YOU'RE ATTRACTED TO AN OTTER

Kiley, a thirty-two-year-old private secretary to an advertising executive, was raised in Greenwich, Connecticut, by ultraconservative parents who placed the highest value on bloodlines and country club affiliation. Her father told her that she should find a man who was dignified, tasteful, but not flashy. In other words, the nouveau riche need not apply.

Kiley's first boyfriend, Duane, was lead guitarist for a local rock band. His gigs were so infrequent that she covered all their expenses for the entire time they lived together. Her second serious lover, Roberto, was a supremely talented, sexy artist who barely had enough money to rub two paintbrushes together!

Both of these lovers were fun-filled Otters, fabulous in bed, full of sexual surprises, and highly creative. Not a bad match for Kiley, a Bee/Lion who could use some help in the relaxation department. The main reason the relationships failed, however, had to do with *why* she selected them. After a few individual psychotherapy sessions she had an epiphany. "I know why I picked Duane and Roberto," she announced. "They're the complete opposite of what my parents wanted for me!"

Instead of expressing her own rebellion against her parents, Kiley used her Otter lovers to reject the snobbery and materialism she claimed she loathed. After a few years without funds, however, she became critical of both Duane and Roberto. She found herself sounding a lot like her father, saying things to them like "When are you going to get a real job and stop mooching off me?"

I'm pleased to say that Kiley fell in love with her Mr. Right and is now happily married to one of the partners of her advertising firm. Kendell, a Lion/Otter, combines the creative enthusiasm she admires without sacrificing the financial stability that's so important to a security-minded Bee.

If you find yourself attracted to fun-loving impractical Otters, take heed. Are you expressing your rebellious nature through them? Perhaps you're in need of unleashing a bit of your own enthusiasm? Partners who are attracted to Otters have a wild ride, but soon find themselves tiring of the roller-coaster antics unless they learn how to open to the creativity within themselves.

WHAT OTTERS WANT FROM RELATIONSHIPS

Otters look for what is limited in themselves—stability, responsibility, and dependability. Otters expect that their partners will be tolerant, secure, open-minded, and will give them a long leash.

Otters are attracted to partners who can negotiate the hills and valleys of day-to-day existence with style and grace. They admire clear thinking and solid planning in others because they are so short on these qualities themselves.

Above all else, Otters want a lifelong playmate and good parent rolled into one. A person who will do the "adult stuff" joyously and be open to a romp in the hay at a moment's notice.

SEX WITH AN OTTER

No one is a better sex partner than an Otter. Creative, versatile, and spontaneous, they know how to let go. If you want to keep your Otter happy, don't hesitate to try something new. Novelty is crucial. Experiment with toys, games, lotions, costumes, fantasies, and every one of the illustrated positions in *The Joy of Sex* to keep your Otter satisfied.

Otters have sex whenever the spirit moves them, and spirituality is very much a part of sex with an Otter. They can produce altered states of consciousness and transcend physical boundaries by completely absorbing themselves in pleasure. Otters are the consummate pleasure experts. When two Otters make love they describe an ineffable heart connection that lifts them to another galaxy.

To bring your Otter bliss when you make love, focus on your own pleasure and put your worries or concerns out of your mind. Otters aren't interested in finding fault with you, so don't think about your less than flat tummy when you're with your Otter lover. He won't even notice your extra five pounds because he's having so much fun caressing your thighs. As long as you put aside your concerns and critical voices and share his enthusiasm, you'll have a stellar experience.

Otters are masterful at making sex extraordinary. They do all the right things: they let go of hurt and anger, focus on pleasure, intensify their sensuality, and do what they love. They are single-focused and allow nothing to get in the way of their good time. When two Otters make love, "it's the stuff that dreams are made of."

VIVICA AND LEON: A LION AND OTTER EXPERIENCING EXTRAORDINARY SEX

Vivica, forty-two, and Leon, forty-five, have transcendent sex. They own a small photography gallery in Carmel and have been married for nineteen years. Unlike many couples who complain about sex losing its zing, Vivica, an intense verbal Lion, and Leon, a passionate Otter, find that their lovemaking keeps getting better and better.

What's their secret? It's simple. When they make love, they're *nowhere else*. Each of them literally "becomes" their partner's touch, skin, or breath with such intensity that their orgasms feel like "out-of-body experiences." For Vivica and Leon, their sexuality is a vital unifying force that brings them spiritual connection. They drink in opportunities for pleasure—touch slowly, look deeply into each other's eyes, and naturally synchronize their breathing in a "tantric" way.

Although they don't formally practice tantric sex according to traditional Indian teachings, they've learned how to prolong their arousal and enjoy peak sexual experiences that they say are "mind-blowing." "After all," they tell me, "sex is one thing that's free, nonfattening, and fun!" As they approach their twentieth wedding anniversary they say, "We love each other more each day and make certain not to forget to tell one another so."

FRANCINE AND KARL: AN OTTER AND HIS BEAR/BEE

Francine is a thirty-six-year-old Bear/Bee certified public accountant whose middle name is "responsibility." She has a triple-A credit rating, has an impressive portfolio of blue-chip stocks, and owns a home in the suburbs in Massachusetts. The only thing Francine hadn't mastered was how to relax and have fun. That is, before she met Karl.

Karl, thirty-two and self-employed as a freelance journalist, was attracted to Francine's self-confidence and engaging smile the instant he met her. Although she seemed a "bit reserved," there was something intriguing about her. He was sure that beneath her conservative exterior waited the passion of a latent Otter longing to be released.

Francine and Karl were a perfect match. Although she was reluctant to trust Karl at first, he gradually persuaded her to let down her guard and immerse herself in ecstatic sex.

Sex is a playful escape for Francine and Karl. They call each other funny, sexy pet names, create wild sexual scenarios, and release their sexual inhibitions. Francine provides the structure that Karl would rather ignore, and he livens up her previously stultified existence with his Otterly talents. As long as they capitalize on each other's strengths, the relationship is sure to stay a winner.

Francine and Karl practiced what I call "learning from your lover." He helped her extend her playful side, and Karl learned a bit about financial management from Francine. Together, the two of them maximized their potential and increased their flexibility.

STEPHEN AND ROXANNA: AN OTTER AND A BEE

Roxanna, a twenty-nine-year-old Bee and gallery owner, met Stephen, thirty, her dramatic Otter, on a blind date. She was captivated by his charm, conversational ease, and spontaneity. Roxanna wasn't much of a conversationalist, but Stephen carried the ball and time seemed to fly. Stephen told

Roxanna about his idea for a novel he hoped would someday become a screenplay. He rambled on, barely pausing, filling the evening with one interesting tale after another. He was handsome, charming, and funny. Roxanna couldn't help but wonder, "Why isn't this guy married? He's a gem."

As with most Bees, Roxanna's strength is in being well organized, although she is somewhat rigid. Her life is orderly, predictable, and under control. What's missing for her is passion and excitement. She finds herself being attracted to exciting spontaneous Otters or Lions who provide what is lacking. Otters are attracted to Bees because they intuitively know: "Here's someone who will listen to me and help me get things in order." As perfect as this fit sounds, soon the Bee is complaining to the Otter, "Get your act together," and the Otter is saying, "Get off my back!"

Each one saw in the other what they lacked in themselves. In the initial phase of the relationship they were drawn to one another magnetically. But over time, each partner attempted to mold the other into their own image, leading to the near-ruin of their relationship.

PATRICK, GINNY, AND HEATHER: A LOVE TRIANGLE INVOLVING BEE, BEE, AND OTTER

Patrick, a forty-eight-year-old prosperous Bee real estate developer, was married to Ginny, his Bee spouse, for twenty-eight years. They got married right out of high school when they were both barely eighteen.

"Sex was never very good—even early on. I guess I didn't know any better," confessed Patrick apologetically. "We were so young and inexperienced. What does one know about passion at the age of eighteen? We got married because it seemed like the right thing to do at the time. I worked two jobs to have enough money for an apartment, and then the kids were born. Who had time to think about sex?"

Patrick stands just under six feet tall and weighs about 185. Although his hair is streaked with silver, he appears younger than his age. Patrick has a Clint Eastwood appeal with his steel-gray eyes, square jaw, and subtle curl of his lip when he smiles. Dressed in a soft yellow button-down shirt and monogrammed navy pullover sweater, he emanated a distinctly boyish charm.

Ginny is thin, five feet four, with short-cropped hair, and is neatly dressed in a conservative two-piece navy blue pants suit with white piping. She looks like a librarian peering at me from beneath her black-framed glasses. She's also a busy Bee with a full schedule: she co-owns the business with Patrick, looks after their spacious home, and does the majority of the parenting with their four teenage children.

"She's been the ideal partner—hardworking, devoted to our family, and willing to please," said Patrick. "We should have had the perfect marriage. Except for one thing. Ginny never wanted any sex."

Patrick stammered as he struggled to find the right words. He was obviously tense and picked nervously at his fingernails as he spoke. "I just don't think she misses sex," said Patrick. "It's never been anything she seems to enjoy." Ginny sat in silence with her arms folded in front of her. "I don't want to end my marriage," said Patrick, "but I've discovered that there's more to life than earning money and sharing a house together."

"And how did you discover that?" interjected Ginny in an accusatory tone. She turned to Patrick and glared at him. "Did Heather teach you that?"

Heather is a thirty-two-year-old blonde who had worked as Patrick's administrative assistant for the past six years. A lively, high-spirited twice-divorced Otter, she pursued Patrick until she caught him. Sex between them was wild and unbridled. After all, Heather is an Otter and hot sex is her forte. They spent six glorious months "playing house" together in Buenos Aires while Patrick was negotiating a land deal. But Heather wanted more than a casual fling, and Patrick felt an allegiance to Ginny. After a great amount of soul-searching, he broke it off with Heather and decided to make it work with the mother of his children.

Patrick and Ginny were friends, life partners, and parents, and did all three well. Unfortunately, however, they had never learned to be lovers. Ginny's sexual experience was limited, and she had clear boundaries. She had been betrayed and she was justifiably angry and hurt. Opening herself up to passion wasn't first on her list. The affair made her question her faith in a basic sense of morality, her belief in God, and her faith in Patrick. Could she ever trust again?

It's very difficult for anyone to find out their spouse has had an affair. For a Bee, who values control and structure, this fracture of a commitment can be devastating.

Patrick and Ginny had a critically important decision before them. Should they work on regaining lost trust and try to rebuild their intimacy, or end the marriage? Although telling Ginny about the affair was the most difficult thing he'd ever done, he felt relieved. Now they had an opportunity to create the intimacy that has been lacking for years.

It took several sessions with me before Ginny and Patrick were willing to take responsibility for their individual contributions to the erosion of intimacy. Ginny confronted her low self-esteem, problems with intimacy, and fear of letting go. She reflected on some of her early memories—a mother who was a paranoid schizophrenic and would fly into episodic rages, a father who, coincidentally, was away from home a lot on business and who, she suspected, might have had a mistress. There was also an uncle who took advantage of her sexually when she was nine. Patrick's strict Irish Catholic upbringing also colored his ability to feel that sex was an important part of loving.

In some ways they were a perfect "fit" and safe choices for one another—he didn't challenge her defenses and rarely initiated sex; she was a great business partner and a good mom for his kids, and never complained about not having sex. Neither had to face their fears or discomforts about their sexual adequacy. But sometimes, in the still of the night, long before she found out about Heather, Ginny would lie next to Patrick as he slept and wish they shared more tenderness.

This is an example of a couple who were at a crucial crossroads. Fortunately, they decided to take the high road. Together they confronted their past fears and made the difficult choice to reach out to one another.

It was difficult for Ginny to let go of her feelings of betrayal and to trust that Patrick wouldn't deceive her again—but she looked forward to better times. For the first time, Patrick revealed his apprehensions about not being able to please her sexually. She never knew how much he feared failure and genuine intimacy. After some soul-searching, she came to the conclusion that his affair with Heather was just another escape from real intimacy. Her challenge was to forgive and move forward.

Likewise, Patrick discovered the reasons behind Ginny's sexual repression. Once he understood how sex had been associated with hurt, chaos, and abuse, he no longer felt that *he* was unlovable to her.

This case has a positive ending. Patrick and Ginny rewrote their marital contract and broke their "vow of celibacy" with one another. They started slowly, first holding hands, kissing affectionately, and allowing their love and passion to unfold naturally.

By the time they finished therapy, they were making time for loving on a regular basis and having what they both described as "extraordinary sex."

LIFE LESSONS FOR OTTERS

1. *A little structure never hurt anyone.* Open up your own checking account and make sure to keep it balanced every month.

2. *Practice long-range planning.* Establish some goals and make an action plan to meet them.

3. *Delay your impulses and reflect on your choices.* Have some time elapse between thinking and doing. Then, if you still feel like going bungee jumping—Geronimo!

4. *Instead of operating exclusively from your gut, think about your options, consider the facts, and check out your partner's feelings before making your decision.*

5. *Balance practicality with your abundant creativity.* Just because you have the urge to go mountain climbing, don't forget that the bills need to be paid.

6. *Be careful that your rebellious nature doesn't become a prison of your own design.* Responsibility isn't synonymous with the end of passion.

HINTS FOR LIVING WITH AN OTTER:

1. At the risk of introducing yet another animal, don't marry a pig and expect him or her to fly! Otters are by nature playful and fun-loving, so don't bemoan the fact that he's not interested in carrying a briefcase or wearing a gray pin-striped suit.

2. Be prepared for anything and don't expect the obvious.

3. Appreciate his passion and spontaneity and tell him so.

4. Don't become a nagging parent. If he's not going to clean out the gutters, hire someone to do it. It's cheaper than a divorce.

5. See if you can find "fun ways" to do household chores together. Remember how Tom Sawyer interested his gang of friends in whitewashing the fence? I'm not suggesting you be devious, just creative. Instead of asking your Otter to rake the leaves, say, "Let's get the leaves off the lawn so we can have a yummy picnic lunch." Make sure you wink so he knows there will be a special dessert.

6. Remember, in many ways the Otter is a perennial boy or girl who refuses to grow up. This is part of their allure, their uniqueness, and their limitation. Don't try to change it.

THE WORST OF OTTERS

Otters are experts at joy, but they fall short on the practical matters. Unless you expect to spend all of your years in an ashram or commune meditating on nature's magnificence, there comes a time when you have to pay the bills. All play and no work means that certain things don't get attended to. Otters are wonderful playmates, but don't rely on them to do the required "adult stuff." Words like *responsible, reliable, steadfast, disciplined,* or *predictable* don't come to mind in defining an Otter.

Although your Otter's creativity can be a huge draw, it can be overdone. Nose rings, tattoos, angels in the snow, and stargazing can lose their fascination after a while. If you long for a partner who'll be as comfortable in a button-down shirt and pin-striped suit as in a pair of blue jeans, it's unlikely to be an Otter.

Otters are rebels. They march to the beat of a different drummer. The rhythm may be a bit cacophonous, if you're not fully prepared. And don't expect them to feel remorse about their chosen path—even if it includes partying all night. The Otter doesn't take blame for his hedonistic ways; if pinned down he might say jokingly, "The devil made me do it!"

Otters are known to be impulse-driven and spontaneous and their judgment may suffer as a result. Otters who are over forty could be described as perpetual flower children from the sixties, who refuse to be locked into responsibilities. Proverbial kids at heart, like Peter Pan, Otters refuse to grow up. So remember, unless your Otter also has a solid dose of Lion or

Bee, you'd better be prepared to take on the "Lion's share" of the responsibilities.

This isn't to suggest that Otters are unemployed vagabonds whose only interest is to gallivant around town. But enter your whirlwind relationship with your imaginative romantic Otter cautiously. Be cognizant of his free-spirited nature and don't underestimate his need to feel the wind at his heels. He may be here one moment and gone the next.

What appears on the plus side as spontaneity expresses itself on the minus side as limitations in delaying gratification. If your Otter is also short on moral fiber, you may discover they are masters at the con and will say anything to get what they want.

Otters, unlike their polar opposite the Bees, let little time elapse between thinking and doing. Their actions are unplanned and they have difficulty sustaining interest once the fun is over. If they have to choose between immediate gains and long-term rewards, they'll go for the former every time. If you fall in love with an intuitive and charming Otter, keep in mind that empathy isn't their strong suit. They are very connected to pleasure, but it's their own pleasure. If you're a Bee, Bear, or Lion and you want to mature or stabilize your Otter, be forewarned—you may be very disappointed.

THE BEST OF OTTERS

What passion, what enthusiasm, what charisma! There's no creative energy and laughter to equal an Otter's. They are imaginative, energetic, relaxing, entertaining, and carefree. They epitomize what we all wish we had more of in our lives—joy.

Otters exemplify what it means to live fully in each moment. Their motto is "Just do it!" Seeing a rainbow or experiencing a thunderstorm with your Otter lover is like nothing else. They will draw your attention to the subtle nuances of color, shape, texture, and the like that you would have undoubtedly overlooked and will allow their whims to direct them. You will be serenaded with original guitar compositions, lavished with poetry, and given an array of sweet thoughtful gifts that never come in a Tiffany's box.

Otters are charismatic in their appeal. People are drawn to their breezy good-natured charm and easygoing style. In a world so full of worry and pressure, we marvel at the Otter's ability to be "in this world, but not of this world." They seem to have their priorities straight and know that intimacy and sharing love are the most important ingredients in living happily.

Although love is central to an Otter, settling down isn't. If you're looking for a relationship that will give you oodles of space to do your own thing and won't handcuff you to his side—an Otter may be the one for you. But if you value travel, excitement, and making mad passionate love anywhere and everywhere, you've got the right partner. Otters aren't impressed by fancy wine lists or expensive foreign cars. Your Otter won't mind if you drive a Geo and have your credit cards up to the max. Climbing behind your Otter on his Harley-Davidson suits him just fine. Otters aren't concerned with what you *own,* it's who you *are* that interests them.

Your Otter is expansive in his interests and open-minded. He will gladly escort you through a world of gallery hopping, landscape photography, sailing, street mimes, travel, and HIV activism events. He will stretch your consciousness and challenge your ideals and your life will never be humdrum by his side.

CHAPTER 13

BALANCING YOUR SEXUAL STYLES

The strongest principle of growth lies in the human choice.

—GEORGE ELIOT

So you've discovered you're in love with a Lion, Bear, Otter or Bee. At first you found their sexual styles alluring, but now you'd like to tame your Lion, invigorate your Bear, relax your Bee, or mature your Otter just a pinch. Remember, the key to ES is to balance your own style by *learning* from your lover, not by *limiting* your lover.

But first, one cautionary note. None of us is *exclusively* one style. Human behavior is much too complex to be labeled one thing and never another. Whether we happen to demonstrate Lion, Bee, Bear, or Otter tendencies, our preferences will vary over time and in different settings.

Let's assume your profile shows that you're a Lion with some Bee and Otter tendencies. This means you're an intense person who knows how to work and play. On your job you may capitalize on your Bee-ness, but when you're snuggling with your honey, you have the resources on board to let your Otterly qualities flow.

Go back to pages 82–83 and look at how you plotted your score on your graph. The higher the scores, the more well-developed the style. The total number of points of all styles equals 40 and the highest score you can get in any one style is 20. So let's assume you score 14 in Lion, 12 in Bee, 9 in

Otter, and 5 in Bear. This gives you a well-balanced profile with the flexibility to access a wide range of behaviors.

On the other hand, if you scored 19 in Otter, 2 in Bee, 13 in Bear, and 6 in Lion, you're probably a cooperative pleasure seeker out of balance with your organized rational side. Enjoying life to the fullest and dreaming are your strengths, but you may have difficulty achieving your career goals, especially if they involve the attainment of material wealth.

Simply put, flexibility and versatility are key to a balanced emotional portfolio. For example, if your Bear husband forgets to put out the garbage in the morning, a Lion will roar at him, and this might just make your Bear crawl deeper into his den. But a Lion who has a ready blend of other approaches at her fingertips will fare much better. If the Lionly approach has reached its level of benefit, she can draw from her Bee or Otter reserves to come up with a more effective strategy. One approach that a rational Bee might suggest is have him take out the garbage the night before, or pay the next-door neighbor boy to take out the trash, or do it herself. After all, aren't those better solutions than fretting about the trash and making everyone miserable?

As silly as it sounds, it's the petty issues, like taking out the garbage, emptying the dishwasher, drinking milk directly out of the carton, or forgetting to return the toilet seat to it's "original" position, that block sexy feelings. If you're a one-trick pony, your problem-solving approaches will be limited. If all you know how to do is roar louder or more often, you'll probably feel stuck, frustrated, and angry. It's my experience that couples who have cultivated flexibility in their styles are able to handle the gamut of struggles from the most trivial to the more difficult hardships of life.

FRANCINE AND MONTY

Let's look at an example. Francine and Monty, both thirty-nine, have been married for eighteen years. Francine is a Lion with Otter features. Monty is a Bee/Bear. Breast stimulation had always been an important part of their lovemaking, but after Francine's diagnosis of breast cancer and subsequent lumpectomy, she felt less comfortable having her breast touched. Instead of limiting all sexual touching, as some couples might do, Francine used her Lion/Otter talents to initiate a dialogue with Monty about other sexual options. She suggested that Monty stroke her inner thighs, caress her feet, and stimulate the unaffected breast. Monty, a rational, indirect Bee/Bear, would have tended to avoid her breast area entirely if Francine hadn't suggested he do otherwise. After a few weeks, she showed him how to touch the affected breast in gentle ways that were pleasurable to her.

VIVE LA DIFFÉRENCE!

Love isn't static. We grow older, may get ill, and absorb a multitude of lessons that impact on the way we think, feel, and behave. How can we assume that the kind of lovemaking we enjoyed at eighteen or twenty-eight will still turn us on at forty-eight or fifty-eight? That's like believing you'll always crave peanut butter and jelly sandwiches or that a new box of Crayolas or a first driver's license will eternally make your heart skip a beat.

Over time, we all encounter a wide range of sensual and erotic sensations and our preferences shift. For example, you might remember finding a certain cologne appealing, and then one day, for no particular reason, it makes you feel downright ill. Or maybe you always liked the way he nibbled your earlobe or stroked your clitoris until that one evening when you just wanted to scream, "Stop!"

Research has shown that around menopause, sensory alterations frequently occur and pleasurable perceptions shift. What was once felt to be erotic, may no longer be. There may be a change in one's preference for certain sounds, smells, tastes, textures, or temperatures. Instead of buying 100 percent wool sweaters, you find you're now more comfortable in all-cotton or silk.

I don't want you to assume that these variations occur *only* around the middle years. Change is a constant phenomenon and we can differ from moment to moment in what stimulates us. Consider this. What if you were locked into having the same fantasy each time you made love? It would be like having only one book to read or one movie to watch. No matter how much you may love *The Wizard of Oz,* even *it* gets boring the thirtieth time around!

Variety is necessary for sexual fulfillment, but it can be disquieting. To keep sex fresh and beyond the ordinary, we must invite it to emerge without undo fear. But take heart: with practice, the initial anxiety will fade and you'll be rewarded with renewed sexual interest and pleasure.

The kind of connection that Francine and Monty illustrated is crucial to keeping sex extraordinary over the years. Although change *is* difficult, the good news is that we can all learn how to expand our choices. Lovers who experience extraordinary sex have invested in broadening their behavioral repertoire, stretching beyond their security zones, and dramatically increasing their intimacy options.

STRENGTHENING OUR OPTIONS THROUGH OUR PARTNERSHIPS

We usually attract a partner who complements our sexual style. This makes sense. Together you become stronger and more versatile as a team. Of course, there are Lions who marry Lions, and Otters who fall in love with Otters, but this is the exception rather than the rule. If you look a bit closer at these couples, they usually have other secondary styles that are complementary.

Consider the strategy of a basketball coach in selecting a team with a "deep bench." What would be the point of having all members skilled in offensive play but not in defense? The secret to a winning team is depth and breadth of abilities, cooperation, and a shared vision.

The same principles are true in marriage. We're naturally drawn to partners who give the marital team more versatility. In this way it's equipped to handle a broader range of situations.

NO ONE WANTS TO MARRY A CARBON COPY OF THEMSELVES

So, do opposites really attract? This is an age-old question. Few people would say that they'd like to marry carbon copies of themselves. Picking a partner with the right complementary fit is important if you plan to go the distance together. For couples to complement one another, they must share beliefs, interests, and values about the things in life that are important to them both. So even if they behave very differently or have very different sexual styles, they are able to come together around the more meaningful issues.

Everyone thought twenty-eight-year-old Diedre and Tyrone were perfectly matched. Tyrone shared not only her upper-middle-class Jewish background but also her interest in architecture and fashion design. A third-year law student, Tyrone had already selected his area of specialization in the field of labor relations. Diedre looked forward to the traditional trappings of marriage, home, family, and supporting her husband's career.

"I was madly in love with Tyrone and thought I'd found my soul mate," says Diedre. "Not only did we share the same tastes in music, clothing, and foods; he looked like a cross between Sly Stallone and Al Pacino." It wasn't long, however, before they began to realize that although they shared a lot of "surface" issues, they disagreed on the important questions of values and life goals. "I wanted kids, a nice home, and a Volvo station wagon, but Tyrone didn't even know if he wanted kids! I wanted more money than he did and hoped he'd join a large Manhattan firm, but he aspired to a political career as a liberal Democrat!"

Fortunately Tyrone and Diedre were frank enough to admit that their similar backgrounds couldn't carry the entire relationship. Although they loved each other and had "great sex," they were mature enough to admit they'd always be pulling in opposite directions.

DIFFERING STYLES, BUT UNITY OF MIND

Couples can have very different temperaments and styles—one can be intensely emotional, the other more logical—but still feel connected by their common goals.

Cybil, a high school math teacher, liked nothing better than lazy Sunday mornings in bed alternately reading the *New York Times* and engaging in delicious lovemaking. Her partner, Pete, was ready for the lovemaking, but would then bound out of bed to get on with the day. Pete's preference was to not waste a minute of precious time languishing about. He'd fill the entire weekend with tennis, hiking in the woods, or meeting some friends for dinner. At first Cybil pretended to like his hyper existence, but the facade came crashing down one day when she blurted out, "Can't you ever just sit down and relax with me?" Pete was shocked. Cybil had never given him any indication that she was upset with his active nature. They had a fundamental difference in what they valued and since neither was willing to change, it was the beginning of the end.

After the early attraction fades, and we show our true selves to each other, we start to convince our lover to be more like ourselves. If the differences are simply stylistic, and both parties are willing, compromise is possible. But if the problems are structural, it's better to face that fact before the wedding and find a better fit. Luckily, Cybil didn't try an "orthodontic solution" and hope that Pete would "shift a little" once he was wired into place by a wedding band.

The more we push our partners to change their beliefs, attitudes, or values, the less likely change will occur. It's human nature. As we feel ourselves being threatened, we react by doing more of what we've been doing. Even when we *know* that what we're doing isn't helpful, it's difficult to stop or try something new.

ELLEN AND OLIVER

I'm reminded of Ellen and Oliver, who had been struggling over their differing political views for years. Ellen was a staunch pro-choice feminist and first selectman for her town. Oliver was a dyed-in-the-wool retired pro-life Republican who was the prototypical conservative Yankee. Although they were in their late fifties and had been seeing each other for eight years, they couldn't reconcile their diverse ideologies. The sparks would fly over topics like abortion or the EPA and romance would go out the window. Something kept them together—maybe the thrill of battle—but they were reluctant to compromise and were equally reluctant to make a formal commitment to each other.

Years later Ellen called me to tell me of an upcoming election of hers. "I've broken up with Ollie," she announced. "He finally revealed a secret he had hidden from me all this time. His first wife didn't die of cancer, as he had led me to believe; she left him for another man. Ollie was crushed and never fully recovered. Our political differences were real, but they were magnified because Ollie was afraid to commit to another woman who could hurt him." Ellen suggested Ollie get some therapy to work out his fears and then call her. "If he couldn't trust me after almost ten years, how much longer was I supposed to wait?" she asked. "Apparently only one of us was open to compromise."

THINGS TO KEEP IN MIND ABOUT SEXUAL STYLES

1. IT'S IMPORTANT TO STEP BACK FROM YOUR STYLE

I'm reminded of a story of the little starfish who asked, "Mommy, where's the ocean? I've heard that it's a big place with lots of water and huge waves that make a crashing sound."

The mother starfish smiled. "You're in the ocean, my little one. It's all around us."

"But I can't see the ocean, Mommy," the little starfish continued. "How can I see it?"

"That's easy," said the mother. "All you have to do is swim until you see the sandy beach, hop onto the sand, and you'll see the ocean."

Each of us is an expert in our *partner's* style. We say, "I know him or her like a book." But to enhance the intimacy in your relationship you must become experts in *your own* style.

2. IT'S DIFFICULT, BUT NOT IMPOSSIBLE TO MODIFY YOUR STYLE

What you'll discover is that your style has evolved over a lifetime and is resistant to change. Resistant, but *not* impossible to change. We tend to want to keep what's familiar, even when it has outlasted its usefulness. If you have a style that avoids conflict, it will be difficult to confront your feelings. Be patient. With the right motivation and persistence, change is possible.

3. STYLES ARE DESCRIPTIONS OF TENDENCIES, NOT REALITIES

Whatever you do, don't use your style as an excuse. Don't say to your partner, "I can't be spontaneous when we make love. After all, I'm a Worker/Bee!" Sexual styles are preferences, not fixed realities. Styles describe typical behaviors or patterns, but aren't absolutes like eye color or height. Don't use them to justify your inertia or defend your stance. If you do, they will prevent you from learning about yourself and your lover.

4. EACH STRENGTH CAN BECOME A LIMITATION, AND EACH LIMITATION CAN BECOME A STRENGTH

This is probably the most important point about styles. There is no perfect style. Lions, Bears, Otters, and Bees have their strengths and limitations. If any of their unique qualities are exaggerated, they become limitations. The extremes of any style limit your ability to switch perspectives when it is necessary. The closer you are to incorporating a variety of vantage points, the more valuable you become to your team, your partner, and yourself.

PART 3

MAKING IT EXTRAORDINARY

....

"If I were to wish for anything, I should not wish for wealth and power, but for the passionate sense of the potential, for the eye which, ever young and ardent, sees the possible."

—SØREN KIERKEGAARD

CHAPTER 14

EXTRAORDINARY SEX: AN INTRICATE BLEND OF SEXUAL STYLES

*Our memory is like a shop in the window of which
is exposed now one, now another photograph of the same person.
And as a rule the most recent exhibit remains for some time
the only one to be seen.*

—MARCEL PROUST, 1924

EXPLORING YOUR SEXUAL STYLES

The development and modification of sexual styles is a complex process. As we've learned, memory, sensory, and other perceptual apparatus are operative from birth. Neonates move from relatively helpless states to being able to control and regulate their comfort. It's not entirely clear how we select one sexual style over another and why one is more comfortable for us. But over time, through trial and error, we choose characteristic modes of functioning that bring the desired results.

Each style, whether it is Lion, Bear, Otter, Bee, or some combination, responds differently when threatened or anxious. When Bees feel threatened, they become more cautious. A Bee examines the ground before he takes a step to see if it's solid. Lions are naturally more surefooted and self-confident, but continue to pay attention to their surroundings. Bears are less apt to venture forth, and respond to threat by withdrawing; their security comes from cautious deliberation. The Otter ventures forward eagerly and impulsively without considering the safety of his underpinnings.

To review, if you're interested in "speaking" Lion, present information clearly, directly, with feeling and passion; if you're interested in speaking Bear, be less confrontational, present your comments in small, manageable doses, don't criticize in front of others, and use a judicious amount of praise to counterbalance your negative comments; when speaking Bee, use precise words, draw maps if needed, don't rely on emotional persuasion, and keep your conversation logical and fact-focused; finally, when speaking Otter, don't plan your approach, speak spontaneously, rely on your enthusiasm, passion, and speak from your heart.

All four styles and combinations of styles evolve through a host of familial and cultural factors that construct the environment in which our styles develop and evolve. When a child's security feels challenged, they learn to defend themselves in a way that feels most comfortable to them. If a style seems to "work" to eliminate or modify the threat, it is practiced again and again until it becomes a stable operating mechanism. Unless the style is sufficiently flexible, however, it will limit you from reaching your maximum potential.

The same is true in your intimate relationships. One's sexual style is comfortable, predictable, and familiar. It works to control anxiety and make it more manageable. Unfortunately, unless you venture beyond your old security zone, it's unlikely that your relationship will reach its potential for extraordinary sex and intimacy.

The downside of stability and comfort is sexual atrophy. Shrinkage. In the same way our muscles waste away through disuse, our intimacy does the same. It becomes dusty, dry, and lackluster.

The key to extraordinary sex is challenging your security zone by building the flexibility that will make you maximally adaptive and open to a variety of opportunities for passion.

Each style, Lion, Bear, Otter, and Bee, has specific strengths and growing edges and each responds to passionate opportunities in characteristic ways. Lions must learn to share center stage, focus on cooperation, and listen to other people's perspectives; Bears must address their hesitancy to confront, their "selective" listening, and passivity; Bees must develop their emotionality and allow for more permeability by letting down restrictive boundaries and balance play with work; and Otters must learn to live within the "real" world by taking some things seriously, balancing responsibility with play, and shouldering some of the workload.

As you allow yourself to experiment with alternative styles and perspectives, a range of unforeseen options will emerge for you and your partner.

STYLES AT A GLANCE

The following table gives you a quick overview of your sexual styles. Notice once again that each style has strengths and growing edges. What you'll also see is that what we "need" is diametrically opposed to what we "fear."

To establish rewarding, lasting sexual intimacy through a vital connection, it's important to recognize how *both* sides of this dialectic operate in yourself and in your partner.

SEXUAL STYLE SUMMARY

STYLES	LION	BEAR	BEE	OTTER
Major Strength:	Energize	Support	Organize	Create
Major Weakness:	Dominance	Avoidance	Rigidity	Immaturity
What they Need:	Attention	Approval	Order	Freedom
What they Fear:	Abandonment	Rejection	Chaos	Restriction
What they really mean when they say they're bored:	"I feel unimportant"	"I feel threatened"	"I am confused"	"I feel trapped"
Sexually they Need:	Variety and display	Security and direction	Rules and explanation	Play and spontaneity
Appeal to their:	Emotions	Thoughts	Actions	Instincts
Life lessons for them:	To hear	To initiate	To trust	To limit

Sex Advice for Lions, Bears, Bees, and Otters

Directions: Locate your dominant sexual style along the top row of the following table and your partner's preferred sexual style along the side. At the intersection of the two points you'll find some key advice for negotiating sex with your special someone.

IF YOU ARE A(N) . . .

		LION	BEAR	BEE	OTTER
AND YOUR PARTNER IS A(N) . . .	**LION**	· Be careful of competiton—sex isn't about winning · It's not about whose is bigger or better, it's the pleasure that counts	· Talk more during sex—say something, anything · Instead of just following, take the lead every so often	· Analyze less and experience more · Challenge yourself to replace logic with emotions	· Lavish your partner with surprises and attention · Your combined energy and passion can take you to extraordinary heights
	BEAR	· Suggest instead of criticize · Try an indirect approach instead of your typical frontal attack	· Don't just sit there, *do* something · Assert your preferences using "I" statements—don't wait to have your mind read	· Relax your control and be supportive of your partner's efforts · Just once, put away your day planner and let the spirit move you	· Share your fantasies, but temper your expectations · Remember that your desire for the ultimate sexual experience can threaten—so go slowly

IF YOU ARE A(N) . . .

		LION	BEAR	BEE	OTTER
AND YOUR PARTNER IS A(N) . . .	**BEE**	· Make plans for great sex and explain your interests in detail	· Initiate some scheduled time for sex	· Take time for play in your busy day	· Schedule sexy fun times together
		· Respect their need for order and predictability—surprises don't turn them on	· Overcome your inertia and put sex and intimacy higher on your priority lists	· All work and no play leads to a passionless existence	· Don't expect your partner to jump on the back of the motorcycle with you without a road map
	OTTER	· Be sensual and spontaneous	· Let yourself go with the flow more often	· Decide to allow more spontaneity into your plans	· Enjoy the passion—the two of you have the winning combination for living in the moment (but don't forget to pay the bills once in a while!)
		· The wilder the better—get out the flavored lotions, vibrators, sexy videos, and let your imagination lead you	· Let your Otter teach you how to take risks	· Let your Otter teach you how to relax and let go	

SELECTING THE "RIGHT" SEXY APPROACH

Selecting the right "sexy" approach with your mate isn't a sure thing. Remember that although you and your partner have a preferred sexual style of Lion, Bear, Bee, or Otter, you probably have secondary tendencies that emerge depending upon the particular context, your mood, and a number of other variables.

Too many lovers assume that *their* way of creating romance is the right way or the only way. After all, who wouldn't find it romantic to slather a lover with whipped cream or eat rocky road ice cream out of her navel? I have a news flash for you—lots of people.

We're not robots, thank heavens, and there's no magic formula for turning him or her on *every* time. Too many people wish there were an owner's manual of sorts that would give us fail-safe instructions for making erections as hard as steel or orgasms that will last for hours. I don't know about you, but I'm delighted that humans aren't as predictable as carefully programmed computers.

You've no doubt noticed that sometimes your partner moans with delight when you run your tongue across the tip of his penis, and other times he'll tell you that it feels a bit too sensitive. You may appreciate a partner who takes his or her time touching you, the slower the better, and then suddenly click into a mode where you crave some toe-curling intensity.

When it comes to sex, we paint ourselves into a corner when we look for THE approach, or THE spot, or THE aphrodisiac that will do it for us every time. What's a turn-on for one person can be a definite turn-off for another. To complicate things even more, what is a turn-on for one person *one moment* can be a turn-off the next. So when you find yourself thinking, "Doesn't *everyone* love to have candles lit when they make love?"or "Wouldn't *everyone* want to have their partner talk sexy to them or have daring sex in an unusual setting?" proceed with caution. The answer is: not necessarily.

There are no "surefire ways" to be romantic every time. If you bring your lover a dozen red roses every evening, it won't be long before the gesture loses its impact.

The following chart isn't meant to be carved in stone, because there are exceptions to every rule. Some Bees enjoy fantasy and some Otters are agreeable to scheduling sex. Whatever you do, don't think of it as a way to read your partner's mind or make assumptions about what they'd like without asking!

The following suggestions are what a "typical" Lion, Bear, Bee, or Otter might prefer given their personality style. But remember, your partner isn't typical, he or she is unique.

Use the list on the left side of the chart as an exercise to guide you on your exploration of your partner's sexual preferences. Remember that a lot of this will vary, but don't let that stop you. And even if you think you know your partner's sexual style, before assuming that any of the items on the chart hold true, be sure to check it out with them.

Go down the list of questions with your Lion, Bear, Bee, or Otter and see how they respond to the various approaches listed. When you're done, reverse your roles.

If YOUR partner is a . . .	LION	BEAR	BEE	OTTER
Is he/she open to quickies?	Rarely—they prefer the longer version.	Agreeable to follow your lead.	Yes—if *they* suggest it.	Sure—anytime and anywhere.
Do they prefer to initiate lovemaking?	Yes. Enjoy taking the lead.	Would rather that you set the pace.	Yes. Bees like to be in charge—if they know the rules.	Will go either way. They're happy to lead or follow.
Should you share a sexy fantasy?	Sure, as long as they have a starring role.	They're open to hearing yours, but are reluctant to reveal theirs.	They'll listen, but probably won't "act" it out.	Absolutely, and they'll share lots of their own.

If YOUR partner is a . . .	LION	BEAR	BEE	OTTER
Will they talk sexy to you?	Anytime. Words are one of their prime assets.	No. But they won't mind if you talk sexy to them.	Yes, but only if they know the script ahead of time.	Anytime. They'll dazzle you with their sultry prose.
Will they appreciate a "sexy surprise"?	Absolutely. They love surprises.	Only if they're in the mood.	No—will rock their sense of "order." Better warn them.	Definitely! The less expected, the better.
Should you schedule intimate time?	Prefer impromptu encounters, but will go along.	Yes. They're happiest when they're rested and ready.	Yes. They do their best "work" that way.	Better not. It will dampen their spirits.
Will they watch explicit videos?	Yes. Especially if they're tasteful high-end productions.	Start slowly. They're more comfortable viewing them alone.	Yes. They go for instructional videos, books, and tapes.	Definitely. The more variety, the better.
Will they discuss sexual techniques?	They're happy to discuss until your heart's content.	Open to hearing your preferences, but are reluctant to share theirs.	Yes—the more specific the guidelines, the better.	Prefer "doing" to discussing, but are open to hearing your preferences.

If YOUR partner is a . . .	LION	BEAR	BEE	OTTER
Do they like to receive oral sex?	Yes— especially when they're in the mood.	Yes—if they're sure you like giving it so they can sit back and enjoy!	If they're "ready" for it and everyone has showered.	Love it!
Do they like to give oral sex?	If they're feeling generous.	If they know you won't turn them down.	If you show them how to do it "properly."	Giving or receiving— they're in heaven. The more creative, the better.
How important is setting a sexy mood (candles, music, and so on)?	Definitely. Very important.	Props aren't necessary to their enjoyment.	As long as it's part of the established routine.	Mood is important, so bring out the rose petals and whipped cream!
How important is appearance?	Very important. They admire a "well turned out" look	Not essential. They're very tolerant lovers.	Very important, especially cleanliness.	The more varied and provocative, the better.
Would they go for outrageous sex (elevator, airplane bathroom, and so on)?	They're game if you're confident in your approach.	Probably not. Risky behavior isn't their forte.	No— dangerous liaisons disturb their sense of order.	Yes—and the wilder, the better!

If YOUR partner is a . . .	LION	BEAR	BEE	OTTER
How important is a good meal before sex?	Would love you to feed them.	Absolutely. A good meal will put them in an amorous mood.	Yes. Prefer a well-orchestrated evening from beginning to end.	Not necessary, but when they indulge, they can enjoy a picnic as much as fine dining.
How can you interest them?	Be classically romantic. Flowers, wine, and poetry are sure things.	Compliment their abilities and strengths. Don't threaten their safety.	Don't be overly emotional. Impress them with your mind.	Free your creative child and have fun. Laughter, play, and passion are key.

I've treated couples who have been married for years who were amazed to hear their partner's responses to these questions.

By opening a forum for intimate discussion, you'll jump-start your sexual intimacy and be on the road to extraordinary sex.

∿

CHAPTER 15

CHALLENGING YOUR SECURITY ZONE

The lust for comfort, that stealthy thing that enters the house a guest, and then becomes a host, and then a master.

—KAHLIL GIBRAN, 1923

Each of us has a security zone—a comfortable way of behaving that we're used to. Although our styles reflect preferred patterns or redundancies in feeling, thinking, and behavior, over time we begin to believe that we *are* our styles and have no choice but to acquiesce in them. They take on a life force of their own.

Nathan, a forty-eight-year-old married insurance underwriter, was late for our session once again. I could predict his pattern by now. His car would roar into the parking lot and I'd hear the squeal of his tires and the car door slam about a minute before he ran up the flight of stairs to my office. Out of breath he'd apologize, "I got caught in traffic," or "I had a last-minute meeting at work." The last time Nathan ran in breathless, I smiled and asked, "Have you noticed a pattern here, Nathan?" "Oh, you know me," he'd reply. "That's just the way I am—always late."

When your spouse asks, "Why are you chronically late?" or "Why do you get so angry over minor things?" is your answer "Because that's just how I am, you know me"? That answer is a cop-out. It only serves to fortify the status quo and suggests that we don't have the ability to choose another action.

GET OFF THE OLD MERRY-GO-ROUND: MAKE THE UNCONSCIOUS CONSCIOUS

When you *do* anything over and over again, it becomes a practiced form of behavior. Patterns are performed automatically, without thinking, and that can be deadly when it comes to keeping sex vital. And as anxiety and frustration increase, so does patterned behavior. They are part of a reactive response style or defensive armament that's activated in the face of fatigue, impatience, annoyance, or threat.

Patterns include certain words or phrases, a look or gesture, a tone in your voice, or a repetitive response. There are patterns that get triggered in a variety of settings, including those that accompany or lead to sex. One way to stop this merry-go-round is to make your *unconscious* patterns *conscious*.

IDENTIFY YOUR SEXUAL ROUTINE

Think of the last time you had sex. Try to bring back the entire episode as vividly as you can. Then answer the following questions:

1. Who initiated?
2. How did the person being invited show they accepted?
3. Who led and who followed?
4. Where did you make love and who decided?
5. What did you touch and what did he or she touch?
6. Who moved things along?
7. Who set the pacing?
8. How much give-and-take occurred?
9. Assuming you had intercourse, who decided it was "time."
10. How was the position for intercourse decided?
11. Assuming there was orgasm or ejaculation, who came first?
12. How did things "end"?
13. How satisfied were you with the experience?

Now that you have ONE experience firmly mapped out in your mind, answer the following twelve questions about your USUAL sexual routine:

1. Who *usually* initiates lovemaking?
2. How do you usually signal that *you're* interested in sex?
3. How does your partner usually signal that *he/she* is interested in sex?
4. What do you usually *think* when your lover approaches you (or you approach him/her)? What thoughts go through your mind?
5. What do you usually *do* when your lover approaches you?
6. Where do you usually make love? What's the typical lighting, music, setting?
7. When do you usually make love?
8. What do you usually wear when you make love?
9. What usually happens nonverbally (gestures, eye contact, posture) leading up to and during sex?
10. What is the *routine* during sex?
11. How do you usually know when it's "over"?
12. What do you usually do *after* lovemaking?

Changing the answers to any of the twelve questions—the way you think, feel, or act—will set a different pattern in motion.

BARRY AND ELISE

Barry, a forty-one-year-old mental health counselor, and Elise, a thirty-eight-year-old reporter for a local newspaper, were approaching their tenth wedding anniversary. Both of them had been married before and they were thinking about having a party to renew their vows. Elise, a hardworking Bee, toils from seven in the morning until eight or nine each evening, always bringing work home. She even goes to the office on weekends to finish a story or do some research. She leaves little time for play, but says, "I wish there was more romance in our life."

Barry, the Otter in this couple, has no trouble being playful and romantic; it's just that Elise is "never around." As with many couples, when they do get some time together, Elise feels awkward getting started. There are times when she admits to me that she'd like a "quickie" but is too embarrassed to say so.

When I ask Barry how he likes to have sex, he says, "In the dark, in the light, under the stars, in the afternoon, with or without wine." For Barry, sex can be hot, cool, serious, playful or spiritual.

Elise has a wonderful live-in teacher in Barry. Lovers aren't always on the same erotic wavelength, but Elise doesn't even have her transmitter turned on.

By suggesting they renew their vows, she was designing a structure, in her Bee-like way, that would bring intimacy back into their marriage. They each shared their prospective vows:

"I, Elise, promise to love you, Barry, and to show you that love each and every day. I promise to never place work above our marriage and to remember why I married you. You are my favorite playmate, my joy, and my best friend. I promise to play more, work less, and celebrate our blessed union."

Barry replied, "I, Barry, promise to love you, Elise, with all of my heart. I thank you for teaching me discipline and for tolerating my childishness. You are my rock and my strength, my lover and best friend, my soul mate into eternity."

CHANGING PATTERNS

I was recently given a tip by a successful marketing consultant. He makes a point of noticing the color of his client's eyes when he shakes hands. In this way he says that he's sure to "make contact" with each person. Try this yourself. The next time you kiss your lover, look into his eyes as if it were the first time. Notice the eyelashes, the texture of the eyebrows. Take a mental photograph. Now you're making contact. Kissing without contact isn't very sexy. Watch the really talented romantic film idols practice their craft. They always begin making love through their eyes.

IT DOESN'T MATTER WHERE YOU START OR WHAT YOU CHANGE—ONLY THAT YOU DO

Remember, patterns are made up of characteristic ways of thinking, feeling, and acting. Each of these can be changed. As you change your thinking, you feel and act differently. As you change your feelings, your thinking and behaviors change, and as you change your behaviors, you'll begin to feel and think differently. The first step is to catch yourself in the act of being yourself and then make a conscious decision to modify something. Ask yourself: what would I like to be doing? Go back to your usual sexual routine and change something—anything at all. It's like throwing a pebble into a pond—the ripples will be far-reaching.

CONSIDER THE FOLLOWING SUGGESTIONS TO BREAK OUT OF OLD PATTERNS

Linger at the doorway for an extra one or two seconds (are you really that busy?) instead of giving an automatic peck goodbye or hello. Kiss as if you mean it. Too many couples engage in ritualized kissing. A peck hello or good night. This is an easy pattern to change.

Recently I tried something different with my husband. When he came home from work, instead of beginning our usual catch-up-on-the-day chatter, when he walked through the door I just looked at him, smiled, and said "Hi!" He returned the smile and walked over and gave me a warm kiss. I'll leave the rest to your imagination.

Once in a while my husband and I go to the airport and spend some time kissing "goodbye." It's lots of fun. Especially when neither one of us is going anywhere.

Challenge yourself to find something new. Anything. A new little laugh line, an interesting curve. Explore it . . . gently or warmly depending on your mood. By looking for something fresh in the familiar you'll open yourself to a whole range of possibilities and increase your sense of wonder.

SIX AREAS YOU CAN CHANGE

1. CHANGE HOW YOU **FEEL**

If you're feeling down, take a warm bath, slip into something comfortable, lift your spirits on your own before making love. If you feel frustrated, rejected, or negative, choose to put your anger aside. You'll be more receptive to a positive experience if you feel better about yourself. At the very least, if you can't get to a neutral feeling it's better to postpone lovemaking until you do.

2. CHANGE NEGATIVE THOUGHTS

Don't approach lovemaking with a mind full of unfinished errands or worries. Stop. Make a conscious transition. Talk to yourself and prepare yourself for a special moment. The way we think affects how we feel and how we behave. During sex, telling yourself, "Hurry up, have an orgasm before he gets bored or loses his erection," is a sure way to dampen your arousal.

3. CHANGE THE WAY YOU TUNE INTO SENSATIONS

Remove criticism, but preserve and heighten awareness. The way you focus on your senses actually increases arousal and pleasure. Experiment by changing how you hear or feel something. Concentrate on giving pleasure, then on receiving. You can influence your enjoyment much more than you think.

4. CHANGE YOUR IMAGES

The fleeting images or full-length movies that cross through your mind can be harnessed and savored. Watch something erotic and focus on it during lovemaking or just let your mind wander to pleasant fantasies and enjoy!

5. CHANGE YOUR RELATIONSHIP IN A POSITIVE WAY

Remember why you chose to share your life with this special person? Like Barry and Elise, if you were going to rewrite your wedding vows, what would *you* say? Take a moment to actually write your vows and read them to your lover at a special time, and be sure to practice what you preach. I guarantee this will change your relationship.

Extraordinary sex is so much more than perfecting positions or increasing the intensity of orgasms. Although you can have very satisfying orgasms with masturbation, there is a richness in making an intimate heart connection with your lover that transcends any technique.

6. Change your PREREQUISITES for sex

Everyone has a list of prerequisites for sex. Here are some examples:

- I must be rested
- I can't have my period
- I can't feel fat or "bloated"
- The children must be asleep
- I can't have an important meeting early in the morning
- I have to be freshly shaved, showered, buffed, lotioned, or whatever
- I must have at least an hour of uninterrupted time
- I must be ready for a sexual marathon
- I must be "in the mood"
- The relationship must feel positive
- I must want intercourse . . . oral sex . . . etc.
- I must want an orgasm or multiple orgasms

A list like this can be overwhelming and stop anyone in their tracks. What are *your* prerequisites for sex? Challenge your assumptions, and a range of options for sexual closeness emerges. First of all, *sex* is not equal to intercourse and each loving encounter doesn't have to end with penetration. When couples understand that every tender touch does not have to lead to a sexual marathon, they're more likely to indulge in sexual pleasures regularly.

Erotic touching can be wonderfully satisfying by itself. Just because he gets an erection doesn't mean you have to use it. Erections come and go and come back again. The same is true for vaginal wetness. When sensual touching is enjoyed apart from intercourse, you might feel differently about being close during the time of your period, or at other times when you might be uninterested in having genital sex.

Sex is not an all-or-none proposition. You can sign on for a part of the lovemaking and not feel pressured to go the limit. I tell my couples to touch often—the location is unimportant.

You don't have to feel *entirely* positive about yourself, your body, or your relationship to have intimate touching. Waiting for perfection or for uncontrollable horniness is like eating only when you feel ravenous! We need to fuel our bodies and our relationships on a regular basis. Sexual episodes become less and less frequent as the list of prerequisites grows. Reexamine and modify your list of essentials and you'll discover ways to sneak in some unexpected passion.

SMALL CHANGES, HUGE RESULTS

Extraordinary sex doesn't take great effort. Small changes in any of these areas produce huge results. I hope I've persuaded you that change is critical to keeping things fresh and we're never exactly the same from one moment to the next.

Think about food cravings. You may want something salty one minute and then desire something sweet. When I was a child I hated olives and now I love them. It's the quixotic nature of human beings that makes it impossible to predict the success of a sensual encounter before it happens.

Change occurs at various levels—from the cellular to the interaction between individuals. We fluctuate hormonally, chemically, psychologically, and in many other ways. But without change we'd fail to adapt to our surroundings and we'd die.

Even though we have characteristic styles, we also have choice and free will. Learning to increase our adaptability, versatility, and coping repertoire is essential to happiness, sexual and otherwise. Flexibility involves developing a multifaceted approach to situations and offers a variety of options to deal with the inevitable twists and turns in the road of life. The more balanced and flexible we are, the more able we are to take things in stride.

Let's assume you have passed your thirtieth birthday. Perhaps you have even passed your fortieth or your fiftieth. In what ways have your preferences changed over the years? Do you remember how you used to like to make love in the back seat of your boyfriend's red Mustang convertible? Do you still like to make love that way or would you prefer a comfortable suite at the Ritz-Carlton? I remember when the most exciting thing I could do was to take my dollar allowance and buy an ice-cream cone and two comic books. Needless to say, I have changed. The more convinced we are that we finally know exactly how to do it to make ourselves happy forever, the more we set ourselves up for failure. There just isn't any such thing.

As time passes, everything changes. That's a simple fact. If you're wedded to the idea that we must maintain the perfect size-eight body to enjoy sex or your partner has to have a full head of black curly hair, it's only a matter of time before you'll face a challenge. The challenge is to stretch beyond your typical security zone or to watch sex fade like the dried prom corsage pressed in your high school yearbook.

So what if things aren't the same. Did you ever think they could get better? Passion has no limits or age restrictions. Instead of bemoaning the fact that sex isn't like it was in the "old days," take an opportunity to get on a sexual fitness program and try something new.

THE FITNESS METAPHOR

We're all so health-conscious these days that I've found my couples easily relate to fitness metaphors. In attempting to modify your sexual styles, try using the following well-known principles:

1. IDENTIFY YOUR GOALS

Do you think you want to do some "spot" toning or tone all over? We all know that spot toning or reducing doesn't work. You may say you just want to improve your sex life, but we all know that sex is one part of the total relationship. It's the rare couple who has great sex but doesn't communicate outside of the bedroom. Communication, trust, and intimacy are just one aspect of "overall sexual fitness."

2. FIND YOUR SECURITY ZONE AND STRETCH BEYOND IT WITHOUT INJURY

If you're comfortable when your partner initiates sex and you passively "go along," that's your security zone. Make a plan to stretch beyond it but start slowly. As with all good programs, if you go too fast you'll risk trauma and quit. If you have problems initiating sex, start by asking your lover to massage your back or make you a cup of tea. Ask for something that challenges without overwhelming.

3. ALWAYS BEGIN WITH SOME "AEROBIC ACTIVITY"

Warm up the apparatus and get the blood flowing. After all, that's what arousal is—blood flow and imagination! Start your foreplay early in the day with a letter in her briefcase or a call to his voice mail. Prepare a romantic dinner. Buy yourself some beautiful flowers—you deserve it. Put yourself into a relaxed mood so that the warmth of the evening unfolds naturally. When you begin to make love, take time to allow the heat to develop.

4. VISUALIZE YOUR PLEASURE IN THE SAME WAY AN ATHLETE VISUALIZES A PERFECT GOLF OR TENNIS SWING

Remember that the mind is where extraordinary sex really happens. Allow your fantasies and images to take you to places that you love.

5. SCHEDULE REGULAR SEX "WORKOUTS"

Making love once or twice a month isn't enough to maintain momentum. Regular sexual touching times at least every forty-eight hours are crucial to stretching your comfort zone.

6. VARY YOUR TECHNIQUES

As with any program, we get tired with the same exercises each time. Find other ways to say I love you. One of my patients left a rose on the kitchen table with a note that said, "Until tonight . . ." You don't have to write pages of poetry or spend hours dreaming up an original song. Don't make sex an ordeal. It's simpler than you think to have the kind of results you're looking for.

7. BALANCE YOUR APPROACH

Remember that there are four dimensions to sexual style: an active or energizing dimension, a passive or stabilizing dimension, an organized, logical work-oriented dimension, and an intuitive, creative play-oriented dimension. All four of these attributes are important in a well-balanced relationship. When you make sex extraordinary, your heart, mind, body, spirit, and imagination are all involved. Incorporate all of these areas into your lovemaking and be prepared for something wonderful to happen.

MAKING IT HAPPEN

It's a snowy day in December. From my office window on the second floor I listen as a driver attempts to free herself from her snowbound parking space. As she presses on the accelerator, the wheels make that familiar whine, first softly, then louder and louder. It's nearly dinnertime and there's little daylight remaining. With each depression of the gas pedal, her tires become more deeply entrenched.

I identify with the driver's mounting frustration. Having grown up in New England, I'm used to getting stuck in snowdrifts. As our tensions mount, reason seems to fly out the window. Even though we know we're making matters worse, there's an irrational voice that says, "I know that there's pavement under here somewhere and I'm going to burn my way through to hell if that's what it takes to find it!"

There's something about the sound of the spinning wheels and the embarrassment of having gotten stuck that blocks our saner self. Release eventually comes in the form of surrender. Admitting that we won't tunnel out of this one alone, we get some help. Giving up the futile behavior is freeing in and of itself. Soon our reason returns and we remember that the formula for getting unstuck is *counterintuitive.* Instead of continuing to press wildly on the accelerator, we need to go against our nature by gently pressing the pedal to create a slow and intermittent rocking motion. Getting unstuck may also require a little push from a friend.

Relationships are no different. We try the same old behaviors with more and more conviction, but notice that we're getting stuck more deeply in our self-imposed ruts. As we recognize the depth of the rut, anxiety increases along with embarrassment and self-blame. We second-guess ourselves: "Maybe I married too early? Maybe I'm just too old, too fat, not sexy enough? Maybe she's having an affair?" The wheels continue to spin, and the relationship feels doomed. To get out of this negative chasm, you just need the right push and a subtle but critical shift in your approach.

BEHAVIOR IS MEANINGFUL

Although Annie Harris was only five feet two she was an imposing woman with broad shoulders and penetrating eyes. According to rumor, her signature hairdo (a tight black bun perched high on her head) had remained unchanged over more than four decades of teaching at Boston University. As Annie sat in a circle with her twelve would-be therapists, arms stretching across her ample breasts, we struggled to deflect her all-knowing gaze.

Annie was no ordinary woman. She was the first female allowed to conduct group therapy sessions in maximum-security male prisons. Her thick Boston accent and no-nonsense approach had earned her the reputation of being one tough lady. No one doubted her ability to handle any situation. Annie commanded respect.

At the age of eighteen, the psychiatric seminar felt like a huge waste of time to me. Freshmen in college welcome opportunities to become distracted from study, especially in a city as interesting as Boston. I was no exception. How could I be blamed for missing one of Annie's classes? All we did was talk about our "feelings." It seemed infinitely more important to go to the rock concert I was lucky enough to get tickets for. The only downside was that I had to pull an all-nighter to prepare for a biology midterm the next day. In my humble opinion, I needed to catch up on my sleep more than instruction in group therapy.

Now Annie was staring at me. "So, missy" (she called me "missy" when she was annoyed), "way-uh were you yesterday?" Her thick Boston accent broke through my reverie.

"Well . . . uh . . . you see . . . I needed to study for a midterm and I overslept." I conveniently omitted the part about the concert.

"Oh, so you *chose* to disappoint your fellow group members and not come to class."

"No," I protested, knowing full well she was right. "I just slept through my alarm. I *wanted* to come to class." Now I had *everyone's* eyes on me. I heard my hollow words echo through the room.

"You know, missy, we all *want* things. We want to be rich, or successful or loved. We want to be educated and to be good therapists. But wanting isn't enough. It's not the words you say that make people believe you, it's what you DO that really counts. If you want to be a good therapist, you need to make responsible choices, and most of all . . . you need to show me some behavior. *Behavior* is meaningful!"

I am eternally grateful to Annie. Hardly a day goes by without recalling her sage advice. "Show me some behavior," I say to couples who say they "want" a better sex life or "want" to feel more passion. Challenge your security zone! If you keep doing what you've done, you'll get what you've gotten. Taking that first action step is the toughest.

CHAPTER 16

SEX IS EASY, INTIMACY IS DIFFICULT

It takes two to see one.

—C. S. LEWIS

It's a cool, crisp Sunday morning in September at a bistro in Manhattan. Rhonda sits on the patio at a table for one idly sipping her double espresso. Fall always brings back memories of hopeful beginnings. She recalls the excitement of being a student and starting classes with her textbooks piled precariously in her backpack, and the promise of new love around any corner. Life seemed so simple then. But that was so long ago, before the complications of ex-spouses and joint custody.

It is her birthday. Thirty-eight, single, and alone. A sobering thought that startles her from her reverie. She searches the *New York Times* best-seller list for a title that might entertain her through the rest of the day. The restaurant is filled with couples. The sounds of their laughter and conversation make her miss Paul even more. They used to sit at a window table and people-watch for hours. It had been nearly a year since their breakup, but the pain hadn't subsided very much.

She imagines him with his new lover and gets a sinking feeling. She still had trouble believing he would leave her for a younger woman. It was so clichéd. Like a soap opera. Why does she continue to torture herself? Roller-bladers, bikers, and people hurry by, reminding her that the rest of the world has a purpose. Unlike her. What to do? Maybe she should just call

Paul on some pretense? Letting go and conceding defeat had never been one of her strengths. But no, it's time to move on . . . to develop other interests. She considers the Annie Leibovitz exhibit at the International Center for Photography, but fears the photos will only bring her down even more. Perhaps the Metropolitan . . . Her thoughts are interrupted by a voice.

"Can I bring you your check?" he asks. "Yes, I may as well be going . . . although I'm not sure where . . ." Her confession surprised her . . . and to a waiter! There was something about his welcoming dark brown eyes and easy smile that caught her off guard. The next thing she knows, they are making plans for after he gets off from work. She accepts before she has a chance to evaluate the wisdom of her decision.

The autumn leaves in Central Park sparkle in the late afternoon sunlight as she and Peter walk arm in arm. It feels good being part of a couple again. He's tall and solidly built, a little young for her, but definitely attractive in a rugged sort of way. The fact that he's a stranger suddenly doesn't seem to matter. After all, romance strikes in the most unexpected ways. "Let's go up to my place so I can change," he offers with a squeeze. Was she really that naive? He might as well have asked her to "see his etchings"! In a matter of minutes she finds herself on Peter's futon struggling against his advances. "What did you think I wanted, honey, a bigger tip?" he shouted as she ran from his apartment. Humiliated and shaken, Rhonda wonders if she'll ever find a satisfying intimate relationship.

Sex is easy. Intimacy is difficult. The truth is that finding an intimate, trusting relationship is one of life's most difficult challenges. As with Rhonda, intimacy often eludes us. It requires being fully known by another person. It's not a process that happens quickly, like instant oatmeal. What is even more baffling is that once you think that you've found that special person and make a lifelong commitment, intimacy can appear to mysteriously evaporate, leaving you with good-enough sex.

Intimacy is a rare treasure, an oyster that has a shell to protect its pearl from harm and only reluctantly reveals its gift of the sea. Ask yourself this question: How many people have I allowed to know me? Not the *me* that I pretend to be sometimes, in the role of mother, business executive, or confident tennis player, but the *me* inside that hurts, fears, hopes, dreams, worries, plans, or wonders, "Is this all there is?"

If you're like many people, your list of trusted intimates may not be very long. Real intimacy is difficult to develop and maintain because it demands a significant self-investment. Think about how difficult it is to nurture genuine friendships. Not acquaintances, but people with whom you can be *yourself*. Special friendships require tender loving care, time, and disclosure to flourish. Intimacy demands the kind of vulnerability that coaxes us to let go of ourselves long enough to join with another human being. Once tasted, the intimacy shared with a soul mate fills us like nothing else imaginable.

The Need-Fear Dilemma

So why don't we enter into deeply satisfying intimate connections more often? The answer lies in the risk of abandonment. There can be no attachment without the possibility of loss. Eventually all things come to a physical end. After a bitter divorce, or the death of a beloved spouse, or an unexpected betrayal, it is not unusual to wonder "whether it is better to have loved and lost, or never to have loved at all." This is the need-fear dilemma: the need to be fully connected at the heart, and the fear of lost love.

The wish to be completely known and the fear of not being accepted are at the center of the intimacy struggle. Each of us needs intimacy to survive, while we studiously avoid it. It's not easy being truly intimate—sometimes it's easier to avoid it altogether by not making time for one another or putting our lovers at the bottom of the "to do" list. By making love in familiar ways, we minimize the self-disclosure and personal risk necessary for true intimacy to emerge. By the choices we make from moment to moment, we create the watered-down intimacy that robs sexuality of its meaning. Familiar sexual routines protect us from exposure and vulnerability. To ignite your lover's passion, you need some passion of your own. You can't turn on without taking things in—senses, thoughts, images, and fantasies. In opening we risk abandonment. In staying closed we risk loneliness. These are our choices.

We can pretend that hiding our wishes, feelings, hopes, and dreams will protect against rejection and the pain of lost love, but within the safety of our false self-sufficiency, we curse the loneliness that is self-created. Loneliness is, after all, about losing contact with yourself. The first vital connection that must be made is the one inside ourselves. Once that has happened, the connection between you and your lover can realistically occur.

Jennifer, twenty-three, has been married for a year. She met Scott in high school and they have been sweethearts since their teens. She came to see me because she felt "something was missing." "We share a house, and little Katy, but sex is just sex." She knew it was time to see me when she found herself crying silently the last time they had sex. "It was so impersonal." Tears filled her eyes as she spoke. "I felt invisible . . . like I could have been anyone."

Scott's matter-of-fact approach to lovemaking left Jennifer unfulfilled. What she didn't understand was his difficulty with and fear of intimacy. When I spoke with Scott alone, he told me about his history. His mother died of cancer when he was eight. The disease spread rapidly and he was unaware how serious it really was. In an effort to protect him, the truth was masked. One day she was gone. From that point on, Scott was cautious about getting close to females. He developed a superficial charm and effervescence that made him very attractive to women, but he kept his distance emotionally. As I pointed out this pattern to Scott, he became silent. After a few minutes he spoke. "I guess I've been afraid of getting close to anyone. Jennifer is the person I want to be close to, but I don't know how. I guess I'm afraid of needing her . . . of needing anyone." Fortunately Scott was willing to learn and to grow.

MARTHA'S CHOICE

When I was in graduate school, I worked as a student therapist on a back ward of a psychiatric unit of a local hospital. In those days back wards of state hospitals were reserved for the most chronically ill patients. It wasn't unusual to hear them shouting from the many seclusion rooms that were used to control their violent outbursts. One day, as I looked through the small window of one of the seclusion rooms, I saw a naked woman sitting crouched in a corner, an image that continues to haunt me. Her torn institutional clothing lay on the floor next to her smeared excrement. Martha was probably in her mid-thirties and had been in and out of hospitals since she was fourteen. My assignment was to get to know this woman and begin the process of "building trust."

In the course of normal psychological development a child moves through attachment and healthy dependence on a loving caregiver to a state of separateness and mature psychological integration. Theoretically, over time, the child develops security and the ability to trust in their own independent thoughts, feelings, and actions separate from merely accommodating to the wishes of their caregiver.

For a host of reasons that go well beyond the scope of this book, Martha had failed to develop a secure, healthy self-integration. Among other things, her psychotic behaviors reflected her profound fear, vulnerability, and impaired trust. One way she dealt with these feelings was by escaping into her own reality. Tennessee Williams said, "We are all sentenced to solitary confinement inside our own skins for life." Martha detached from outside contact and communicated only with the projections of her own mind.

I began my awesome task by sitting in silence in the opposite corner of the room. One day, after more than three months, Martha looked up and her eyes met mine—just for an instant. She looked away quickly. When one's sense of self is so poorly defined, there is a fear of being merged or swallowed up by the other. Even a gaze can be threatening. Closeness is especially risky for someone who feels they have no "self." Over the next six months, Martha tested me in many ways. When she discovered that I would respect her boundaries and not push beyond her comfort level, she made a life-changing decision—slowly she reached through her barrier of self-imposed isolation and connected with another human being.

I use this extreme example to illustrate the need for intimacy as a central driving force in all of us. Martha's choice was whether or not to face the need-fear dilemma. She could remain in her fantasy world, safe but profoundly alone. Or she could reach out, once again, and risk annihilation.

The truth is that we must all make this choice, at different times in our lives and in different ways. We are born alone, die alone, and in the middle of it all search for genuine heartfelt intimacy. Like other animals, we find support and survival in the herd. Periodic episodes of isolation and solitude provide space for needed reflection, but we simultaneously crave the contact of intimate attachments. If this were not the case, Martha would have probably chosen to stay locked in her emotional prison forever.

Intimacy challenges us to move from parental love to the development of a separate identity, to fulfilling interdependence with a lover. The risks are never-ending, but the rewards are abundant.

Most of the couples I treat want better sex, more closeness, and more passion. When I see how they live their lives, it's apparent that they're continually making choices that separate them from their vital connection.

If we acknowledge the fact that intimacy is difficult and even scary, we'll be prepared to face the challenges of sexual closeness with less self-recrimination. Showing your deepest self to someone can be daunting. "What if I'm not good enough?" "What if I'm a fraud and the real me isn't acceptable?" But it is only by confronting the voice of our inner critic that extraordinary passion can unfold.

However, before we can achieve intimacy that's extraordinary, we must first be prepared to let go of the ordinary.

WHY WE SETTLE FOR "ORDINARY" SEX

You might remember when sex between you and your lover was exciting, freeing, and fulfilling for your body and your soul. The almost-anything-goes kind of sex and almost anywhere! Then you settled into a pattern that was "ordinary" and uneventful. If everyone knows that ordinary sex kills great sex, then why do we stay with the boring variety?

Virtually every sex book tells of dozens of ways to spice up a stale relationship. It's not that we don't know that it's important not to get trapped in a rut; we all know that monotony kills passion. But if something "new" can be reenergizing—a new set of silky sheets, a new fragrance, or an unexpected getaway to a romantic retreat—then why is ordinary sex the norm?

1. ORDINARY SEX IS COMFORTABLE AND SAFE

Since it involves mind reading, you don't have to ask for what you want or expose your intimate wishes. You just lie there and hope he or she will hit the right spot.

Downside:
Hoping is not a very effective strategy for getting what you want. Asking for what you want greatly increases the possibility you'll receive it.

Mind reading restricts our flexibility. What if you don't feel like having your breasts rubbed three times counterclockwise tonight but that's part of the *usual* routine? You better clue your partner into the simple fact that you're not always in the same mood. Of course, it will take more work, but it will be well worth the effort.

2. Ordinary sex doesn't involve much risk

Since you're doing it the same way each time, there's little risk. If no one asks for a different kind of touch or reveals a special wished-for fantasy, there's little risk of emotional exposure, rejection, or embarrassment.

Downside:

Without emotional exposure, there's little emotional connection. Without risks and requests, intimacy fades.

3. Ordinary sex is easy, effortless, mindless, and sweat-free

Fondly referred to as a "quickie," it serves the same purpose as a fast-food restaurant. It fills a need with little expenditure of resources.

Downside:

Quickies are fine for an occasional release, but when they become a steady diet, couples soon complain to me that their relationship suffers from a lack of substance.

Mindless (and sometimes heartless) sex, where everything is turned off except your genitals, can be fun on occasion. But because quickies are automatic and involve a formula approach to sex, I caution you that a steady diet of this can make you feel emotionally undernourished and resentful.

4. ORDINARY SEX DOESN'T NECESSITATE IMAGINATION OR CREATIVITY

Since you "perform" it the same way, it takes little planning or thought. You both know the well-worn routine. It's just like brushing your teeth—you do it without thinking.

Downside:

When you're served leftovers from the fridge night after night, you begin to feel unimportant—not special. Automatic, unimaginative sex seems easy in the moment, but there are losses to the relationship that accumulate over time.

You begin to feel cheated out of the real thing.

If you keep doing what you've always done, you'll keep getting what you've always gotten. Ordinary sex actually blocks extraordinary sex from emerging. Once you're ready to face the challenge, start by reading the following sexual viewpoints exercise. It will focus the areas you'd like to change. Then select one of the exercises in the back of the book and you'll be on your way.

SEXUAL VIEWPOINTS INVENTORY

The following inventory is designed to help you identify and share your sexual preferences. There are no right or wrong answers. This format is intended to stimulate intimate discussions and to help you share information about your own and your partner's sexual viewpoints. Right now, you may feel uncomfortable revealing some of your personal preferences to your partner. That's not unusual. This inventory will help you develop more comfort and honesty discussing sex-related topics.

Start with the questions that are easier for you. Take turns answering each question. Try not to be critical of each other's responses and listen attentively.

Instructions:

- Complete the following items individually, not as a couple.
- Don't feel pushed to finish the entire inventory at one time.

• Allow enough time to share your responses using the "Stop, Look, and Listen" guidelines on page 255.

A. *Setting the Mood:*

1. For me, it's important that sex (is/is not) part of a general feeling of closeness outside the bedroom.

2. When I feel angry, I (do/do not) usually feel like making love.

3. Doing something enjoyable (but nonsexual) together first (does/does not) put me in the mood for sex.

4. Going out to dinner (does/does not) increase my romantic mood.

5. Taking a shower with my partner (does/does not) relax me.

6. I prefer (candlelight, daylight, or no light) as the most romantic for me.

7. Reading erotica or watching explicit videotapes (does/does not) turn me on.

8. Starting with a sensual but not explicitly sexual body massage (is/is not) pleasant for me.

9. What puts me in a loving mood most is .... •

B. *Touching and Being Touched:*

1. I prefer (spontaneous/scheduled) touching.

2. I am more comfortable (giving/receiving) touch.

3. When I'm being touched I (do/do not) let you know if something is uncomfortable.

4. When I'm being touched I (do/do not) let you know if something is especially erotic.

5. Although this varies, I generally (like sex to begin slowly and then get passionate/like it slow all the way through/or like it passionate from the outset).

6. The parts of my body that I typically like having touched are my .... •

7. The parts of my body that I typically don't like being touched are my .... •

8. The parts of your body that I love to touch are your ....

9. I like having my breasts/genitals touched (early/later) in lovemaking.

10. I feel (comfortable/less comfortable) when my naked body is seen during lovemaking.

C. *Feelings About Masturbation:*

1. I am (comfortable/uncomfortable) masturbating.

2. If I knew you masturbated, it (would/would not) bother me.

3. I (would/would not) feel comfortable masturbating in front of you.

4. I (would/would not) like to see you masturbate in front of me.

5. Using sex toys for sexual variety is a (turn-off/turn-on) for me.

D. *Sexual Response:*

1. I (do/do not) worry about maintaining an erection.

2. I (do/do not) feel pressure to keep my erection longer.

3. I (sometimes/always/never) have pain with penetration.

4. I (sometimes/always/never) have problems getting as wet as I'd like to be.

5. If I have a problem with my erection, I (do/do not) try to hide it from you.

6. If I have a problem getting wet, I (do/do not) try to hide it from you.

7. If I have a problem with my erection, what I would like you to do is ....

8. If I have a problem with wetness and getting aroused, what I would like you to do is ....

9. Having an orgasm each time we make love (is/is not) important to me.

10. Having an ejaculation each time we make love (is/is not) important to me.

11. When it comes to sexual positions for intercourse, I (would/ would not) like more variety.

12. I would like sexual intercourse (more often/less often/at the same frequency).

13. When it comes to initiating lovemaking, I'd like you to be (more/less assertive).

14. When it comes to making love, I'd like you to be (more active/more passive).

15. Hearing sexy talk during lovemaking is a (turn-on/turn-off) for me.

E. *Sexual Fears, Obstacles, and Secret Wishes:*

1. The things that block me from feeling sexy are ....

2. Sometimes I'm afraid that you might ....

3. One thing I'd love to try that you might not know is ....

4. One thing that you/we used to do that I'd like to do again

is ....

Now that you've identified your preferences, try something new. Anything unknown can stimulate renewed excitement. Select something from the "mood" or "touching" section and alter your usual behavior. If you're accustomed to making love in daylight, touch by candlelight or moonlight. If your lover enjoys sunrise sex but you've preferred an afternoon matinee, forget breakfast one day and indulge in some early moments of pleasure *before* going to the office.

A change in setting can stir the embers of love. Touching on a blanket on the family-room rug (once the kids are safely in bed) can ignite your passion. Try making love to music. Some couples find the rhythm of music can trigger erotic response—remember Ravel's Bolero in the movie *10?*

Suzie and Tyler are two Otters who say that the more risky sex is, the better they like it. A bit of danger acts as an aphrodisiac for them. If there is a possibility of being caught, it stimulates their arousal. Like teenagers making out under a blanket at a concert, risky sex can remind us of those lusty days.

Suzie and Tyler's favorite scenario is to pick one another up in a dating club or neck in one of their parked cars. If there's a chance that they'll be interrupted by the police, so much the better. The fact that anyone might discover them and witness their lovemaking fuels their excitement. Sex that's spiced with the possibility of being discovered isn't for everyone, but it's just what they need to get their juices flowing.

Use your responses to the sexual viewpoints inventory to construct your own personal program for stretching past your security zone. Remember, there isn't one path to exquisite sexual arousal. Experiment and let the spirit move you.

CHAPTER 17

TAKING THE FEAR OUT
OF SEX

Keep not your roses for my dead cold brow.
The way is lonely, let me feel them now.

—ARABELLA SMITH

So many couples say they want more frequent, more pleasurable sex but it's not happening. Why not? There's a wide range of *excuses,* including no time, no privacy, no energy, and so on. I say that these are excuses, because when we're first bitten by the love bug, none of these reasons stop us from making love. Remember those heavenly thirty-minute "lunch breaks" in the back seat of your car? Neither time nor privacy constrained your passion in the old days.

Compared with other time-consuming activities, like standing in line at the post office or department of motor vehicles, we spend relatively little time making love. If you're like most people, after an especially satisfying sexual episode you might wonder, "Why don't we do this more often?" Even if you're having sex for a full hour three times a week, that still amounts to only one week in an entire year. Isn't it curious that something that's free, not fattening, and fun (once you get into it) happens so infrequently?

As surprising as it sounds, most couples aren't having sex more often because they're *afraid.* **Let's take an honest look at the six most common fears that affect sexual enjoyment:**

- The Fear of Change
- The Fear of the Uncomfortable
- The Fear of Responsibility
- The Fear of the Unknown
- The Fear of Disapproval
- The Fear of Vulnerability

1. FACING CHANGES IN SEXUAL DESIRE AND AROUSAL

Many couples become anxious and afraid when they notice that their ardor has taken an unexpected dip. After all, if you're in love, shouldn't you always be interested in sex—or at the very least want sex on a fairly regular basis? Movies that feature lusty sex scenes with voracious partners humping against the kitchen counter or in elevators fuel our mythology and sense of inadequacy. We think back to those distant sizzles with longing and sadness. "How come everyone else is having all the fun?" we wonder. "What happened to our passion?" Desperately we search for a glimmer of those old feelings—the hunger for seeing our lover, tasting their lips, or feeling their naked body next to ours. But alas, the memories are barely accessible. All that remains is a lingering recollection or hint of a time in the past.

Does a change in desire and arousal herald disaster? Is this shift inevitable and unavoidable? Should lovemaking stay constant or should it decline until it is barely recognizable? And what can we do to get back on track?

BEYOND MONKEY SEX

The kind of sex we saw in the movie *Fatal Attraction* is what I call "monkey sex." Intense pheromone-driven sexual activity that has little or nothing to do with real intimacy. It is the way monkeys or other mammals have sex. After a ritualized "foreplay" consisting of a chase, sniffing under each other's tails, and a mating dance, the male mounts the female, thrusts a few times—ee-ee-ee, and it's over.

Monkey sex is natural, release-driven, and situation-specific. It doesn't take any particular talent or skill to put column A into slot B under the right conditions. It is usually mechanical, functional, and goal-directed.

Monkey sex gets triggered in a variety of circumstances: when something or someone is new or forbidden, when your inhibitions are released by alcohol or drugs, when you feel desired by a new "mate," or when you feel the challenge of conquering *someone else*'s mate. The sexual excitement of a clandestine affair or one with a new partner is biologically driven, time-limited, and fall under the category of monkey sex.

When couples complain that their burning passion has dwindled, they are usually referring to the decrease in their monkey-sex urge. I'm not here to condemn monkey sex or to suggest that it be eliminated from your sexual repertoire. But if monkey sex is your sole way of connecting, your passion will soon fade into oblivion.

THE A-Z PHENOMENON

Arousal normally fluctuates along a continuum vacillating from absent to extreme. When the biology doesn't happen to be in high gear, some couples become concerned that their passion has died. Because these couples are programmed to make love only when they feel horny or turned on, they find themselves making love less and less often. As the distance between them and their worry that something is wrong increase, their intimacy decreases.

The problem with dips in libido is that some partners stop touching completely. Couples who have problems with intercourse due to pain, erectile problems, illness, or some other reason may avoid intimacy altogether. They think, "why bother getting all hot and steamy if we're not going to have 'sex'?" If A naturally leads to B and then to C but we can't do Z, why do anything? This all-or-none definition of sex illustrates the kind of thinking that leads to disuse and disaster. Couples trapped in the A-Z phenomenon may even stop sleeping in the same bed or in the same room!

If this is your problem, begin with A and enjoy it for what it is, not for where it might lead. It doesn't take a wet vagina or an erect penis to caress your lover or reach out and hold their hand. And when you do, you'll remember how good it feels to touch.

There's an unforgettable thrill of new love that we mourn. The touch of a new lover that burns through your skin. But it's only after the initial lust passes and the glow recedes that we can take on the real challenge of forming a lifelong connection. Human beings differ from other mammals in their ability to reflect on their choices in ways that enrich their lives and deepen intimacy. When we work to combine sexual urgency with intimacy, the extraordinary passion that emerges is boundless and forever new.

GINA AND JUAN

Gina and Juan, both thirty-one, have been married nearly five years. Like most of us, during their courtship they couldn't get enough of one another sexually. Juan would call Gina at lunch, whisper sweet nothings, and they'd slip away for a torrid interlude. They were so physically attracted to each other that they couldn't imagine it would ever change. "We thought the lusty feelings would last forever, but now we have sex about once a month—in a good month!" Gina lamented. "Can you please help us?"

Although most people would say they want thrilling sex, what are they willing to do to get it? *Wanting* is easy. We want a lot of things. Perhaps you want to be rich or famous. Or maybe you want to be an excellent parent. But what are you willing to sacrifice to get it? Yes—sacrifice. A willingness to give up something to gain something. Sacrifice may seem like an odd word for a book about sex, but I don't believe you can have extraordinary sex without some sacrifice.

2. FACING THE UNCOMFORTABLE

Gina and Juan had become afraid to bring up the subject of sex. "What's the point? What good would it do?" Gina asked. By shutting off communication, they had become even more cut off from each other. Unprepared for the ebb and flow of their desire, they panicked when the "rip his clothes off" intensity disappeared. Instead of facing their concerns, they avoided sex, which further decreased their intimacy. Soon they were on the slippery slope of diminishing returns.

Changes in desire can represent a normal fluctuation or may indicate a problem of more seriousness. Discussing the fact that your interest has waned can be a threatening subject. Instead of facing the uncomfortable, many couples try to pretend all is well by filling their days with other activities. It's as if they hope the other one won't notice that they're making love once or twice a month. But couples *do* notice.

There are reasons for diminished desire and they deserve appropriate attention. Begin to solve this dilemma by stepping up to the plate and facing your uncomfortable feelings. When you find yourself less interested in reaching out, ask: "Is there something I'm anxious, angry, or hurt about?" "When did my feelings change?" "How have I dealt with the change in my feelings?" "If ignoring things and waiting to feel turned on hasn't helped, what else can I do?" If you're feeling more lukewarm about sex than you once did, do you *really* think this will come as a revelation to your lover? Don't you think he or she already knows? Unless you have the courage and willingness to face the truth together, you'll continue to collude in silence.

TOUCH REGULARLY

Like many couples, Gina and Juan revealed that they made love only when they both felt turned on, and it was hard to get on the same wavelength. When Juan was interested, Gina was "not in the mood" and vice versa. Both of them thought something was "wrong" because they weren't on the same page more often, but neither wanted to admit it.

Waiting to feel "lusty" before you touch is like eating only when you're famished. We all know it's important to regularly fuel our bodies by eating three balanced meals a day. Even when you have the flu or aren't particularly hungry, you make sure to take in *some* nourishment.

Research in the field of neonatology shows that newborns fail to thrive when they aren't touched. These babies have difficulty putting on weight and many of them have compromised immune systems. In the same way, holding, touching, and caressing are essential for intimacy and the overall well-being of a relationship.

Because Gina and Juan touched so infrequently, they felt awkward and uncomfortable when they did try to make love. Juan described the process perfectly when he said, "I felt like I was starting a cold engine." His efforts to turn Gina on led to an ejaculatory problem. Instead of being able to enjoy penetration, he found himself climaxing within a minute. The harder he worked to please Gina, the quicker he ejaculated. Gina felt she didn't have enough time to orgasm through intercourse and felt too shy to ask for oral sex or other kinds of pleasuring. After Juan ejaculated, he'd sometimes ask, "Is there anything else I can do for you?" Gina would usually say, "No, I'm fine. Let's just go to sleep."

Both Gina and Juan "hoped" things would get better on their own, but they didn't. Sex became more discouraging and soon Gina and Juan had gotten out of the *habit* of touching. The less they touched, the more uncomfortable things became. Both made excuses that they were too tired or too busy. Juan was frustrated, Gina felt unloved and confused.

Contrary to what you might think, some habits can be good things. When you forget to touch one day, and then the next day, soon you may find you've gone an entire month or longer without any meaningful physical closeness.

TREAT ONE ANOTHER LOVINGLY AND YOU'LL FEEL LOVE

The philosopher William James said if you behave a certain way for a long enough time it becomes you. There are so many couples who are waiting for love to return on its own, as if love is an inexplicable weather pattern that descends upon us like morning mist and leaves just as suddenly. Jaclyn, a thirty-eight-year-old unmarried elementary school teacher, once described to me one of the saddest moments in her life. She was walking along a path in Central Park and she saw him. Sitting on a park bench directly across from her was Eric. In his dark green corduroy jacket, white oxford cloth shirt, khaki slacks, and cordovan penny loafers, he looked just as she remembered him. On his lap was a little girl with long blond hair calling him Daddy and snuggled against his shoulder was his wife.

They looked so happy and connected. "What an idiot I was," Jaclyn thought. "I should be with him and I'm not." After a two-year relationship, the flames of passion had seemed to be dying out and she thought she'd fallen out of love with Eric. What upset her so much about this event wasn't her jealousy or envy; it was her regret. "I gave up on something that was special because I was too young to understand that love doesn't just happen, we *make* it happen."

All relationships have their ups and downs. There are times when the fires of love burn brightly and other times when the embers are more faint.

There is an ebb and flow to intimacy, with peaks and valleys that can leave us breathless and uncertain. Our challenge lies in how we cope with that uncertainty.

If you believe that you "fall" into love or out of love, you'll feel helpless when you look at your partner on the other side of your king-size bed and wonder, "Where did the love go?" You'll remember how comfortable you once felt wrapped in his arms in your single bed. When you're in love, no bed is too small. When you're not in love, no bed is big enough.

But neither love nor sexual passion is a constant. If you grew up without appropriate role models for intimacy and affection, it may be difficult to hang in there during the lean times. Some couples make the mistake of running to a divorce lawyer at the first hint that love has faded instead of understanding that there are phases in love's evolution. As with all phases, there are growth spurts and lag times.

When your intimacy has dipped, it's time to refocus on what you love about your partner. Go ahead and bring out the old photo albums. Remember the qualities that first attracted you to one another. I have no doubt that they are still there, waiting to be appreciated. Take the giant step of reinstating loving gestures *before* you feel them one hundred percent. It's an investment worth making. You may not be in the mood to touch, but once you begin to reach out in loving ways, you'll surprise yourself by actually *feeling* more loving toward your partner.

TOUCH WHEN YOU FEEL NEUTRAL

Another problem is that too many couples wait for some kind of burning desire before they think of making love. Masters and Johnson recommended that couples "touch when they feel neutral or positive, but not when they feel negative." I've been passing on their sage advice to couples for more than twenty years. Neutral means "I can take it or leave it." There's nothing wrong with touching when you feel neutral. It's certainly preferable to not touching at all, isn't it?

Gina and Juan were locked into a pattern of abstinence. Because they were waiting to feel passion before they reached out, their romance was dying a slow death. I suggested they agree to take a few moments several times a day to ask themselves, "Do I feel either neutral or positive about touching my lover right now?" If their answer was "yes," that would be a green light to touch. If they felt negatively, that would be a "no."

If the answer is "yes," the next step is to *tell* their partner they're thinking of touching them as soon as they can. Gina tried this approach and found that she thought of Juan quite often, but he never knew this. She started calling him and leaving voice-mail and E-mail messages telling him he was on her mind. Juan felt great knowing that Gina was thinking about him. He had begun to wonder if there was another man. Her loving calls reminded him of the old days when they first met. He found himself writing her little notes during the day and bringing home flowers for no particular occasion. Gina and Juan were working on bringing their love back. I also told them to spend some time using sensate focus—"just touching" without rushing into penetration.

It wasn't long before Gina and Juan were touching often. The more they touched, the more they wanted to touch and the better things became. They were encouraged by their progress and looked forward to being together. Relaxed, enjoyable lovemaking led to a freshness in their passion that they feared had been lost.

After a few months Juan noticed that his ejaculations had slowed down and Gina had begun to trust him again. As she felt more safe and secure, she relaxed enough to focus on *her* pleasure. The more she immersed herself in pleasure, the more aroused she became. Soon she was having deeply satisfying orgasms again.

More complicated cases of rapid ejaculation or problems with orgasm may require additional treatment approaches. But for Gina and Juan, these problems were simply related to their anxiety about touching and reversed themselves as quickly as they had occurred.

Gina and Juan were relieved that their sexual heat and enthusiasm hadn't evaporated. They found sex was different from the early days but equally memorable. At the end of our last therapy session Juan was convinced that sexual desire doesn't just mysteriously leave a marriage. "You know, you're right," he said. "The passion doesn't leave us. *We* leave the passion!"

3. FACING YOUR RESPONSIBILITY

Do you believe that no one can make you feel good about yourself except you? The fact is, the person we love can't bear all the responsibility for making us feel smarter, more desirable, or more beautiful. Remember the last time you gained ten pounds? You looked in the mirror in the department store fitting room and sucked in your gut as you asked the salesperson, "Does this make me look fat?" As you listened to her predictable response, "Oh no, dear, it's fabulous. So slimming, youthful, and chic—it's really you," for a moment you may even have believed her, but an entire Greek chorus couldn't change the truth—you'd gained ten pounds and it was all around your middle.

Of course the truth hurts. It's comforting to have your lover temporarily nurse your wounds of insecurity as he supports you through a premenstrual or perimenopausal moment of irrationality. But in the end, each of us must face the responsibility for our own self-worth and our own sexual arousal.

When you consistently put your partner's needs first, you're fostering a breeding ground for resentment. While it's fine to touch him in ways that *he* loves, you have to also touch him in ways that *you* love. *You are responsible for your own pleasure.* "But isn't that selfish," people ask, "thinking of yourself during sex?" I usually reply, "Yes, it is." Loving fully involves losing yourself in the joy so deeply that the other person can temporarily cease to exist. Hundreds of women described such blissfully transcendent orgasms in my book *Ordinary Women, Extraordinary Sex.*

When lovers realize that their own ability to absorb themselves in passion is responsible for their arousal, they sometimes have a rude awakening. After all, isn't the purpose of sex the connection between two hearts? There's no doubt that our longings for skin against skin, for sounds and smells, and for excitement intertwined with intimacy motivate our urge to merge. However, until we discover how to leave our lover momentarily, just long enough to create our own passion, our ecstasy will likely be a shadow of what it might be.

WHO'S RESPONSIBLE FOR YOUR ORGASM?

While attending a comedy club in Boston one evening, I noticed three serious-looking men sitting in the front row. As they sat there, stone-faced, arms crossed in front of them, they seemed to be saying, "Make me laugh, I dare you." Throughout the three sets, I noticed that they rarely laughed, or even smiled. I also became aware that I was focusing more on them than on the show.

Later that evening, while sharing an after-dinner drink with my husband, Rob, I asked his impressions of the rude men at the comedy club. But Rob had been so engrossed in the comedy routines, and laughing so hard, he hadn't even noticed the men in the front row. Rob had a terrific time, but I allowed myself to be distracted.

Let's look at another example. George, a typical Otter with Lion tendencies, and Nancy, his Bear/Bee wife, are invited to a black-tie party. The best food, wine, and music have been selected by the hosts along with an impressive guest list to make this a gala occasion. No expense is spared but Nancy has a horrible time. Why? Ever since her senior prom date stood her up twenty years ago, she has shunned formal affairs. She refers to them as "stiff and pretentious," avoiding them like the plague. Her preferred venue is a small comfortable gathering with a few good friends sharing a pepperoni pizza. Because this is an important business event for George, Nancy had agreed to accompany him, but then proceeded to make herself miserable. How did she spend her time? She did what she always does at these parties—found a quiet corner and nursed two or three glasses of wine all evening. George, on the other hand, had a stellar evening.

And what do you think typically happens when George and Nancy have sex? The same thing. George manages to enjoy himself no matter what, but Nancy allows herself to have fun only if things go according to her plan. She has a well-practiced routine in bed, and although she has begun to feel that sex is no longer exciting (surprise, surprise), she's reluctant to try anything new.

This leads me to ask you an important question. Who's responsible for *your* good time? Whether it's the enjoyment of a play, concert, party, or mind-blowing orgasm. Who are you counting on to make it fun for you? During a potentially romantic moment when your lover runs his hands over your body, are you thinking, "I hope he doesn't find those extra five pounds I've put on my thighs!" Instead of melting into his touch, do you hold back and wonder, "I hope he isn't going to want oral sex tonight, because I haven't showered." Or maybe you take responsibility for his or her orgasm by asking, "How was it for you?" When you really want to know, "How was I?"

Whether you're sexually turned on or turned off is *not* your partner's responsibility. Of course your lover's technique has something to do with your pleasure, but that's only half of the story. The real source of your passion is within you. If you lie there, distracted, uninterested, and uninvolved, you're not going to feel very much pleasure. But if you make your own good time in bed by letting your passion lead you into erotic adventures and sensory delights, your experience can be ecstatic.

It's human nature to go on a fault-finding mission when there's no orgasm or erection—and it spells disaster in the bedroom. It's very empowering to discover that the secret to extraordinary sex is within our reach.

THE SECRET INGREDIENT

When I was a young girl, Sabbath preparations were always special times. Mom began cooking at sunup. The aromas of freshly baked challah, homemade chicken soup, and potatoes roasted in paprika and garlic filled the apartment. Dad would say proudly (and only half in jest), "Your mom cooks enough for the whole Russian army." It was true that there was always enough food for anyone who happened to stop by. As my brother Stephan and I eagerly waited for supper, Dad would come into the kitchen to taste the chef's creations and give my mother a hug and a helping hand.

Precisely at sundown, Mom would light the Sabbath candles as Stephan and I watched. There was something magical about the ritual candle-lighting ceremony as Mom whispered the prayer, circled her hands over the flames, and then pressed them to her face. Later, while we were all seated for dinner, Dad would recite the blessings over the bread and wine. It was a simple life. Family togetherness, singing and praying around the kitchen table, and delicacies created with abundant love. These were the cornerstones of my childhood.

My mom was an iron woman whose strength belied her five-foot-two-inch frame. She worked a full-time job outside of the home and was the consummate housekeeper. The bathrooms always sparkled and I often wondered why there were never any water droplets on the porcelain sinks. In spite of her full schedule, she never seemed to tire, always making time for enveloping hugs, encouraging words, and periodic tastes of the kitchen's wonders from her magical soup ladle. It was amazing to me that she didn't use any recipes—just a *feeling* of what was needed. A pinch of this and a dash of that, and oh, the tastes! No one can replicate the symphony of spices and flavors emerging from my mom's kitchen.

As she cooked, my dad might sing a melody of old favorites like "That's Amore," "Autumn Leaves," or "Yes Sir, That's My Baby." Every so often he'd sweep her into his arms and spin her around the kitchen floor for a quick dance. Dad loved to sing. For years he'd entertain at weddings or bat mitzvahs. His most prized gift was a karaoke player we gave him for his birthday. Whenever there was a spotlight, you could be sure that Dad would be in it, and Mom (his most ardent fan) would be applauding from the sidelines.

But Mom and Dad had more than their share of tragedy in their fifty years of marriage. Both of them are Holocaust survivors and lost nearly their entire family in the war. As if that were not enough, their only son, my brother Stephan, died of testicular cancer when he was thirty-seven, leaving his wife and a two-year-old son. Instead of cultivating bitterness, my parents taught me to appreciate life, seize the moment, and find any excuse for celebration, laughter, and love. As I watched my parents dance and sing together, I learned the recipe for keeping joy and romance alive.

I recently had a phone conversation with my parents, who are now in their seventies. They are fortunately still very healthy, vibrant, and passionate about each other. Mom described returning from a New Year's Eve party and her surprise that so many younger couples sat around the table looking bored. "You know," she said with that wonderful lilt in her voice, "your dad and I didn't miss one dance!" *"Life flies by, honey, you have to make your own good time. No one will make it for you."*

These words of wisdom guide me more than any academic training or degree. When couples come to my office bemoaning the fact that their sex life has gotten boring and romance has left their relationship, I gratefully remember the secret ingredients of lasting love, and I smile.

SECRETS OF SELF-SEDUCTION

Since we're talking about extraordinary sex, what is it that makes a person really "sexy"? Have you ever seen a person who isn't especially handsome or beautiful but you find them sexy anyway? They have that *je ne sais quoi*—that "I don't know what." They have "it"!

Think of the people you find sexy. What qualities do they have in common? Do you think you're sexy? Is your partner sexy? Were you sexy once? If not, what's missing and where did it go?

As I approach my middle years, I'm especially curious about mature women who continue to exude sexiness beyond the fifth and sixth decades. During a recent trip to St. Bart's in the French West Indies, I marveled at how sexy the French women looked as they sauntered along the nude beaches and boardwalks. These women have an ageless appeal that defies explanation.

I remember one woman in particular who must have been in her mid-sixties; her long hair streaked with silver and full bare breasts, she walked with a confident swing to her hips. Despite the effects of gravity and the passing years, there was something about her that transcended the physical and communicated a timeless, unmistakable sex appeal.

Although most self-help sex manuals promise surefire ways to turn a partner on, I feel they overlook a critical point—turning yourself on. To have extraordinary sex, you have to know how to *enjoy yourself.* Sex appeal involves cultivating a feeling of confidence and comfort that's undeniable. If you don't feel sexy in thong underwear, don't wear it! Try it once to see how you feel, but if you feel awkward and uncomfortable, why put yourself through the torture? Dress in an outfit that flatters the parts of your body that you love. If you feel a bit thick around the middle, but love your legs, feature them. Put on those fabulous black fishnets or thigh-highs and strut your stuff.

Practice self-seduction. Give yourself the experience you wish he or she would give you. Take a relaxing bath or shower. Light your scented candles. Put on your most delicious cologne. Play your favorite mood music. Let your imagination go as you put yourself in a wonderfully receptive mood. After all, if you're in a sexy mood, won't you be more likely to enjoy sex? Smooth lotion on your body as you imagine the pleasures that await you.

Foreplay begins within your own mind. Don't expect your partner to do *all* the work—to make you feel attractive, desirable, aroused, and orgasmic. There's nothing sexy about making love to someone who's lying there waiting to be done—like a turkey waiting to be basted! Whether you become distracted or wildly enthusiastic during sex is a reflection of the conscious and unconscious choices we make.

4. FACING YOUR FEAR OF THE UNKNOWN

Have you ever gone to the hairdresser wanting a new look and then proceeded to tell him not to cut off very much? I have. With the patience of a saint my hairdresser asks, "So let's see if I've got this right. You'd like a new look, but you're not sure you want to change your old look. Is that right?" "That's it," I said, "you've got it!"

Everyone wants a sure thing, an unconditional money-back guarantee. We want something refreshingly different, but are reluctant to let go of the familiar. Even though you've read about a thousand new ways to please your lover, for some reason you stay with the old "fail-safe" approach.

I'm reminded of a forty-three-year-old accountant who came to see me because he had begun to have problems maintaining his erection. Thomas, an industrious Bee type, had been married for almost twenty-five years and he thought they had "pretty good" sex. Allison, his cooperative Bear wife, was afraid to complain. After all, Thomas was a good dad to their three sons, an above-average provider, and could fix anything that needed repairing around the house. She didn't want to break the news to him that sex could be more exciting if he'd just "let loose a bit."

To begin with, I suggested that Thomas touch Allison at a different time and in a different location. His usual approach was to ask, "Do you feel like fooling around?" It would be Friday evening at nine o'clock and Allison could set her watch by it. Instead of touching in the "old way," I told Thomas, he was to touch all of Allison's body and see what he could discover.

The next time they came to my office, I asked how the session went. "It was fine," he replied. "I started at the top of her head and I touched, touched, touched all down her front side and then I flipped her over" (like a flapjack) "and touched, touched, touched all down her back side. Then I was done." Allison looked exasperated as Thomas described his touching. "Isn't that what I was supposed to do?" he questioned. Thomas was a person who needed to play by the rules. He was uncomfortable with the unknown. It was precisely this quality that was deadening his arousal and interfering with his erection. His lovemaking consisted of doing what was familiar.

Next I recommended that Thomas spend time touching *one* part of Allison's body, but to use all of his senses in doing so. To look at her, touch, taste, smell, and absorb her into himself. To touch with his eyes closed as well as open, to use his tongue, the tip of his nose, and to have fun. This was an unusual request for Thomas, but he was open to trying.

He was amazed with the results. He told me that he found an especially intriguing place behind Allison's knees and decided to spend time licking, stroking, and enjoying her smooth skin. He spent the rest of his time appreciating the backs of her legs and the curves of her calves. What was even more incredible to him was how much he enjoyed touching her and how firm his erection became! The lovemaking that followed was more passionate than it had been in years.

Too many couples explore "what if" in their minds, but are afraid to deviate from what they know will work. They think to themselves, "What if I wanted to use a vibrator on her while we have intercourse?" or "What if I wanted to watch a sexy video before we make love?" but don't act on these thoughts.

Instead of playing "what if," take the chance and suggest it. Don't be discouraged if he or she says "no," they may say "yes" the next time. Letting go of the familiar road map, the "right" techniques, and the perfect mechanics frees you to explore anew.

FINDING THE FRESH IN THE FAMILIAR

At my last Extraordinary Sex workshop I gave a red apple to each of the hundred and fifty people in the auditorium. I asked those in attendance to take as much time as they needed to "get to know their apple" and to use as many senses as they wished in the process.

Although this seemed like a silly request, the couples were willing to give it a try. I watched as they carefully examined the color, shape, stem, leaves, and unusual markings of their apples. Some people felt their apple with their cheeks, smelled it, and looked at it from every angle.

They were then instructed to put all of their apples into a pile and turn around as I mixed them up. A few people seemed reluctant to part with their apple, but eventually did. I then asked everyone to find their apple. In less than fifteen seconds, everyone found their own apple. When I asked if they'd be willing to exchange their apple for their neighbor's apple, many were reluctant to do so. After all, they had discovered a uniqueness in their apple that made it special to them. People were surprised. How could one hundred and fifty red apples be so different?

The rapt attention that made each apple so unique is what separates "ordinary" from "extraordinary." Extraordinary sex—a potential brimming with possibilities—is only limited by our imagination and energy. Intimacy is a lifelong challenge. If we live within the realm of certainty, possibilities diminish. Each sexual experience is different. You only have to look for the uniqueness. It's there, waiting to be found.

5. FACING YOUR FEAR OF DISAPPROVAL

Another fear that blocks extraordinary passion is the fear of disapproval. So many of us seek approval for so many things, from living in the "right" neighborhood to being seen driving the most prestigious car. These are the same people who seek approval from their lovers for being the "best" in that area, too.

Hank, thirty-eight, came to therapy four months after he divorced Lydia. He had married her right out of high school and she had been his only sex partner. "I know it may sound silly, but Lydia pressured me so much for sex that I started to lose my interest in it." Hank felt controlled and smothered by Lydia's frequent sexual demands. Although he knew a lot of men who might envy him, he had trouble standing up to her pushiness.

The more Lydia pushed, the more he avoided. Hank was a Bear by nature and disliked confrontation. Lydia's insatiable, intense Lionness contributed to his feelings of inadequacy and shame.

Hank started spending more time with his friends but when he'd come home she'd be there—pressuring him into making love. Whenever he walked by or stepped out of the shower she'd begin to stimulate him until he became aroused and "gave in" to making love. Before long Lydia became angry at Hank's avoidance and started to accuse him of having an affair. She felt unattractive and neglected. During one nasty argument, she told him she thought he must be gay and lashed out saying, "Who'd want that little penis anyway!"

Hank, whose self-confidence hadn't been great to begin with, started doubting himself even more. He began to wonder if there *was* something wrong with him. The more he wondered, the less he felt like making love. Instead of facing up to his hurt and anger, he filed for divorce.

In therapy, Hank learned that his fear of disapproval had robbed him of his own self-esteem and his marriage. He had allowed one woman's sexual interests and hurtfulness to cause him to question his sex appeal and seriously damage his overall self-confidence. It was unfortunate that Hank ran from his marriage, because the enemy he feared was himself. In one illuminating session, he remembered how his intrusive mother had shamed him when she discovered a *Playboy* magazine under his mattress and asked him what he was doing with that trash.

Over the next six months, Hank's treatment included facing the negative messages he had about himself, recognizing the emotions that blocked his intimacy, overcoming his shame about being a sexual person, and learning to assert his feelings clearly and more confidently.

The best part of this story is the end. Hank sent me a note last month saying, "I'm in love with another Lion woman, but this time the Bear has learned how to be energized by *his own* emotions!"

6. FACING YOUR FEAR OF VULNERABILITY

Bruce's mother was hospitalized for a suicide attempt on his fourth birthday. He says he'll never forget that day. "I was trying out my new shiny red two-wheeler bicycle with training wheels and going to get an ice cream from the ice-cream truck, when a car came out of nowhere, drove up onto the curb, and put me in the hospital for three months in a full body cast. I had twelve broken bones. Mom said she blamed herself for the accident and that's why she tried to kill herself. Dad handled all of this by drinking himself into a stupor.

I don't remember seeing much of Mom and Dad during my childhood.

She was in and out of psychiatric hospitals and was usually strung out on medication. We had a housekeeper, Loretta, but I don't remember much about her either."

Bruce remembers lying in his crib in the hospital in a full plaster body cast, spread-eagled, with his genital area exposed. One night a man in a white uniform came into his room and sexually molested him. The orderly inserted an object into Bruce's anus while he performed oral sex on him. Bruce cried and screamed, but no one came to help. Immobile, frightened, dependent, and unable to trust his caregivers, he withdrew and became mute for nearly a year. Several years of psychotherapy and physical rehabilitation followed.

This wasn't the end of Bruce's trauma. At the age of eight, while roughhousing with his fourteen-year-old brother, he fell through a plate-glass window and severely lacerated his face and neck. He bled for nearly an hour before a neighbor took him to the hospital for emergency treatment and stitches.

In school, the kids made fun of his scarred face. "I had no friends and hated everyone. It wasn't until I joined a local gang when I was thirteen that I finally felt like I belonged. They were my family and were always there for me." By the time Bruce was eighteen he had become addicted to alcohol, smoked crack, and had been arrested eight times. His father always paid for the best lawyers to get him off without any jail time.

Bruce came to see me many years later. He was forty years old and was afraid of intimacy. Thanks to a twelve-step program and his perseverance, he had been dry and sober for ten years, but he never faced his fear of attachment. He had succeeded in creating a secure haven by not allowing anyone to get close. He went through life wearing a mask that protected him from pain, but it also blocked pleasure. Using this strategy, he survived.

The problem was that Bruce was lonely. He ached for love, but it terrified him. He had dated several women, but broke up with them before they had a chance to walk out on him. And what kind of women did Bruce find himself attracted to? Unavailable, unpredictable women, like his mom. He'd find them challenging and intriguing, until he realized he was replicating the old patterns from his childhood.

Bruce worked hard in therapy. He confronted his childhood ghosts of not being loved or adequately protected, the guilt and responsibility for his mother's depression, his dad's alcoholism, and the rage at his molestation by an alleged caregiver. He began to realize that his decision not to let anyone close had left him feeling sad and unlovable.

Therapy was a slow process. It was not easy to connect with Bruce. I had to tread lightly while making sure to respect his boundaries. After some time, Bruce decided to try again. He realized that he could protect himself more *selectively* by allowing certain people access to the "real" Bruce. It did not have to be an all-or-nothing proposition. Although he was terrified of making the wrong choice, I reminded him that he was a survivor and was no longer that fragile four-year-old boy in a body cast.

By getting in touch with his vulnerability and his strengths he gained a deeper understanding of what he needed in a real partner and became ready to face that challenge.

Taking off your clothes and letting someone inside your body or inserting part of your body into someone else is only one part of sex. Intimacy involves opening in a more profound way—dealing with fears of merger, dependency, self-disclosure, and self-revelation. The capacity for uniting body and soul, sharing our adequacies and our inadequacies, being honest, clear, and comfortable with our partners, and establishing appropriate boundaries are at the center of the intimacy struggle.

Mature love depends upon a balance between merger and separation. Too much distance and we have isolation; too much merger and we have lost ourselves.

Boundaries that protect one's vulnerability can fool you into thinking you're invincible. But isolation often accompanies safety. There can be no love without facing your fear of dependency and the risk of abandonment. It's all part of the process.

In the next chapter you'll have an opportunity to take a good honest look at your own sexual history to discover the origins of your own sexual feelings and preferences. As you face your past vulnerability, it becomes easier to leave behind your anxiety and make more satisfying, enriching choices.

CHAPTER 18

HOW YOUR PAST
AFFECTS YOUR SEXUALITY
TODAY

The Past—the dark unfathom'd retrospect!
The teeming gulf—the sleepers and the shadows!
The past! the infinite greatness of the past!
For what is the present after all but a growth out of the past?

—WALT WHITMAN, "PASSAGE TO INDIA"

There's no such thing as a natural-born lover. Most people hope they'll "just know" how to please each other sexually when the time is right. Unfortunately this is often not the case. The way you feel about sexuality and intimacy today reflects lessons from the past. Sexual "facts of life" are not actually facts per se, but information filtered through our recollections and colored by our imaginations. They are given shape, texture, and meaning in the context of life experience.

In 1902, the British playwright J. M. Barrie wrote, "A safe but sometimes chilly way of recalling the past is to force open a crammed drawer. If you are searching for anything in particular you don't find it, but sometimes something falls out at the back that is often more interesting."

Megan, a dynamic twenty-six-year-old woman of French Canadian descent, came to my office because she was having difficulty relaxing and enjoying sex with her longtime lover, Antoine. While I was taking her sex history, she shared the following story with me that she had never before revealed to anyone.

"I always liked to be nearby when my mom and dad did their spring cleaning. Six-year-olds love to play dress-up and I was no exception. So many treasures would appear from an attic or closet—a fancy red velvet hat with a feather or a string of Grandma's antique crystal beads.

I can still recall the dining room in our Victorian home. The high ceilings bordered with pink flowers and the periwinkle-blue corner cupboard filled with untouchables.

As I sat watching intently, Mom and Dad sorted through years of accumulation. Then a strange thing happened. Mom found a small package tucked behind a pile of old greeting cards and memorabilia. She looked alarmed, said something to Dad in French (they spoke French when they wanted to speak privately), and returned the package to the top shelf.

"What's that, what's that?" I asked insistently. I can remember the shocked looks on their faces and my mother's words as clearly today as I did twenty years ago. "It's not for you, it's for grown-ups," she said, "It will only give you nightmares."

Her admonitions fueled my curiosity even more. The first chance I had to hunt for the forbidden box was the next afternoon. I didn't really know what I was searching for, but I knew it was a small package and that it was somewhere in that cupboard. My excitement grew as I carefully moved the stepladder from the kitchen into the dining room. "What could possibly give me nightmares?" I wondered as I excitedly searched the top shelf.

Behind some china and old letters, I found it. A small package wrapped in yellowing newsprint. It looked as if it had been there for years. I knew I didn't have much time and didn't want to get caught. My heart was pounding loudly. With trembling hands, I carefully unwrapped the box to discover a deck of cards. But as I inspected them more closely I discovered this was no ordinary deck. On the back of each card was a black-and-white photo of naked women and men—and they were doing things to each other's private parts! I can still remember the funny feeling in my belly and a weird stirring in my genitals. There was something disgusting but intriguing about these photos. "Is this what my parents do together?" I wondered. "And why would they *have* these pictures?" I never told my parents that I found those cards.

For years after that, Megan would sneak into the dining-room cupboard, remove the "forbidden" playing cards, and masturbate to the images. As she got older, she would hold those images in her mind when she made love with a boyfriend. But as she began to date, she discovered that she couldn't feel sexually turned on without also feeling anxious and guilty about her arousal.

Until she shared this story with me, she had never made the connection between her early history and her current problem.

FAMILY LOVE SCRIPTS

Where did *you* learn about affection, tenderness, respect, and your own sexuality? Were loving gestures between parents or significant others locked behind closed doors and criticism aired publicly? Did you think that sex was something your parents did "once" to have you and never again? We learn about sex and intimacy from what is said and not said. From what we hear, and see, and feel in the world around us.

The following section will give you a format to explore your family love scripts and offer some guidelines for sharing your awareness with your lover.

YOUR OWN SEXUAL AWAKENING

What do you remember about your own sexual awakening? If you grew up feeling confused or humiliated about sexuality or nudity, those feelings will probably be reflected in some way today.

Gabrielle shared with me some sentiments about her first impressions of nudity. "When I was seven or eight years old, I inadvertently walked in on my father as he was getting dressed. He yelled and turned around. I remember apologizing and feeling that I had done something terribly wrong. I remember his large dark penis and how scary it was to me. For a long time I couldn't look at my father without remembering that image.

"Years later—I must have been nine or ten—I caught a glimpse of my mother changing into her swimsuit. Her large pendulous breasts hung on her abdomen. Her pubic hair was graying and sparse. She saw me standing at the bathroom door and quickly reached for a towel. I hoped and prayed that my body wouldn't look like hers.

"It wasn't until I was in my teens that I discovered that bodies came in all shapes and sizes. I know it sounds silly, but I assumed that breasts and penises came in one size and shape. Then I began to take small parts in community theater productions and got to see male and female dancers changing costumes backstage. I saw breasts in all shapes, pubic hair in a variety of colors, and penises of all sizes! Of course, I thought, we each have different faces, noses, and the like. It's the same for our genitals. What a relief!"

As I have taken sex histories from literally thousands of couples, I have become more impressed with the importance of clients' early childhood sexual recollections. Memories of friends comparing prepubescent bodies, admiring their reflections in the mirror and commenting, "Your butt is a lot rounder" or "Your arms are so much longer than mine," may seem insignificant at the time. But whether you grow up feeling adequate or insecure about your body image and about sexuality in general has a great deal to do with how well you sorted out the experiences and impressions from the past.

WHEN SEX HURTS

Marietta, a twenty-seven-year-old Bear/Bee and engaged copy editor, sat in my office pulling one Kleenex after another out of the box. Red-faced and hesitating, she began to tell her story. "I really don't know how to say this but I just hate sex!" Marietta had never uttered those words out loud. "I've pretended to like it for years," she continued, "but I've just been going through the motions." She rubbed her eyes with the tissues and had difficulty speaking through her sobs. "Now I really love Alan and want to enjoy sex with him. Can you please help me?"

Marietta grew up in the north end of Boston in a traditional Italian family. She knew her parents had sex, because she had eight siblings, but there was certainly never any talk of it in the home. "When I was almost ten, I found a crumpled brown paper bag on the bathroom floor next to the wastebasket. I peeked inside and discovered something bloody inside on some fluffy white pads. Frightened, I took the bag to my mother to show her." I remember the surprised look on her face. "Your dad cut himself while he was shaving, it's nothing."

When I finally learned about periods from Mrs. Peterman, my fifth-grade health teacher, my mother was enraged. She stormed into the classroom and blasted my teacher for giving me this information. "I'll tell Marietta what she needs to know when the time is right," she protested. "Apparently the time was never right, because I heard nothing more about sex after that day.

"My best friend, Tina, had a very different experience. She got her period when she was only ten, but was well prepared for it. Her mother gave her a box of her own Modess pads and a little belt to hold them up." Tina proudly shared what her mother said. "When your body starts to menstruate it means you've become a healthy young lady and everything is working according to God's design."

"I remember feeling so jealous of Tina and wishing I had her mother. This incident affected me more than I knew. Whenever I had my period I had a mixed feeling of revulsion, shame, and disgust that I couldn't figure out. Even though I knew it was supposed to be natural, I hated it and I know it affected the way I feel about being a woman."

This one incident isn't enough to poison one's attitude toward oneself and one's sexuality. However, childhood experiences have more impact than we acknowledge.

I can remember my own experience using tampons the first time. I carefully unrolled the directions in the bathroom and was greeted with a diagram of a uterus in *cross section!* How would a teenage girl know what a uterus *was*, much less what it would look like sliced in half? Most young girls aren't even sure where their vagina is located, let alone what angle to use when inserting a tampon. Questions like "What if it gets lost in my body and never comes out?" or "Will it hurt?" or "Will this mean I'm not a virgin anymore?" are all common and often unspoken.

Many girls worry about the smell of their menses, the messiness, and being "discovered" having their period, as if there's something shameful about the whole thing. Comments like "I have the curse" or "She's on the rag" unfortunately still prevail. Many years later, I hear stories from women who are embarrassed about their natural body functions and trace it to some misinformation from their youth.

Marietta had had a frightening experience when she first tried to insert a tampon. "I put it in and it got stuck halfway. It really hurt! I couldn't put it in and I couldn't pull it out. I was terrified that I'd have to go to the emergency room. Eventually I pulled it out and there was a gush of blood. About two days later I started to have some burning in my genitals when I urinated. The doctor said he thought I had a urinary tract infection, but to be certain he had to put a thin tube inside my bladder to get a sterile urine specimen." Marietta's entire vulval area hurt and burned for days after that.

Marietta was thirteen when she learned about sexual intercourse from another friend, Loretta Morretti. "Loretta knew everything about sex. She said that a boy puts his penis into a girl's hole and then something sticky comes out and that's how babies are made. It really sounded disgusting to me."

Years later, after her sweet-sixteen party, she was making out with Billy Tyler in his father's white Ford station wagon when she felt a sharp pain between her legs. "Billy had tried to put his finger inside my vagina. I didn't tell him it hurt, because I didn't want to lose him as a boyfriend—he was the most popular boy in our class. I remember thinking to myself, 'If a finger hurts so badly I'll never be able to have a penis inside of me.' "

From the time she discovered her mother's Modess pads, each subsequent experience reinforced the notion that sex was something shameful and that genitals *hurt*. Is it any wonder that she comes into my office, saying, "I hate sex"?

I explained this pattern to Marietta in detail and described why it would make sense that she would feel pain in her genitals. Beginning with her tampon experience, which may have torn a hymenal strand, and the catheterization that followed, she learned to experience her genitals as *a place that hurts*.

I asked her whether she ever feels pleasure when she's with her partner. "Oh yes," she answered. "I love it when Antoine kisses me and touches my breasts. I begin to feel warm and my heart starts to beat more rapidly. I know I'm sexually attracted to him. It's only when he moves to my genitals that I get scared."

"And then what happens?" I ask.

"I usually let him enter me because I'm afraid of frustrating him, but it hurts."

"So you don't hate sex," I said. "You hate pain!"

"I've never thought of it that way before," she said, looking a bit startled. "That makes a lot of sense."

"You enjoy sexual closeness, but are understandably uncomfortable about having your genitals touched. You enjoy sex, but don't want to feel discomfort."

Marietta felt better instantly. It was as if a light had gone on. She accepted the fact that she was a healthy sexual woman who was understandably afraid of feeling pain.

TREATING VAGINISMUS

Over the next few months we worked together to treat her vaginismus. Marietta had developed an involuntary contraction in the outer one-third of her vagina when she anticipated penetration of any kind. In its mildest form, vaginismus can make the insertion of a tampon or finger or intercourse uncomfortable, and in its extreme form, makes penetration impossible.

Antoine joined us for a number of sessions and he was understanding and supportive. The key element in reversing Marietta's vaginismus was for her not to allow anything uncomfortable to happen to her body. Instead of denying her discomfort, Marietta learned how to take control of her body, protect it from pain, and discover what she liked sexually.

At a time that was appropriate, I gave her a set of graduated vaginal dilators with instructions for inserting them. I told her to find a time when she was alone and relaxed. She was to select the smallest dilator, make sure it was well lubricated, and touch the tip of it to the outside of her vagina. If anything felt uncomfortable she was to pause until the discomfort passed. Without rushing, she was to insert the dilator very slowly and gently into her vagina, with a turning motion, as she breathed comfortably. Once the dilator was inserted, she was to keep it in place for five to ten minutes while she read a book or just relaxed. I also suggested that she practice Kegel's exercises and tighten and relax her circumvaginal muscles with the dilator inserted. After only two months, she was able to insert the largest dilator comfortably and to enjoy intercourse without discomfort.

A Picture Is Worth Ten Thousand Words . . .

Ari and Ruth, recently married, are both twenty-three. They are an Orthodox Jewish couple who want to have children. There's only one problem: Ari can't ejaculate inside his partner and Ruth is "afraid" of sexual intercourse. He's puzzled because he can ejaculate during genital touching or if he pulls out of Ruth during intercourse, but not inside of her.

As a boy, Ari grew up in Brooklyn and led a sheltered life. His parents sent him to parochial school from kindergarten through the eighth grade. He wasn't exposed to people of different religions or racial backgrounds. He only knew of others like himself—Orthodox Jews.

"My parents never explained anything about sex. The subject was taboo in our house," said Ari. "I never knew one swear word until I was almost twelve years old and that was the year my parents decided to send me to summer camp. There I learned an assortment of swear words from my less sheltered bunkmates."

"What I'll never forget was the day I learned about sex. It was in social studies class and my teacher showed us a film about a woman giving birth. It shattered all of my myths about the beauty of childbirth. To say that I was shocked would be an incredible understatement. All I could remember was this gigantic head coming out of this woman's body and blood gushing out. I had nightmares about that image for weeks. I was so thankful I hadn't been born a woman and never wanted to make one pregnant."

Ruth was also raised in a traditional Jewish home and was the only daughter. Her father was a physician, and sex was explained in medical terms, utilizing a biology book.

She was an early bloomer and wore a size 34B bra by the time she was nine years old. One event, at the age of ten, set the stage for her later fear of sexual intercourse:

"My mother dropped me off at Hebrew School and didn't realize the school was closed. I waited outside for a while but didn't know what to do. I didn't have any money to make a phone call. After about a half hour a middle-aged man came over and spoke to me and started telling me about 'love.' I was so naive and inexperienced I didn't understand what he was about to do. He took me to the bottom of the stairs which led to the entrance of the synagogue and pulled down my pants. Everything happened so quickly. Before I knew what was going on he pulled out his penis and tried to stick it inside of me. It hurt so badly. I don't think he got it in all the way. I didn't understand what happened until years later. I never told anyone about the event because I felt so guilty."

Ari and Ruth had tried to forget these memories and never disclosed them to one another. The film of childbirth had left an indelible impression on Ari, and although he was intellectually "ready" to have children, his body wasn't cooperating. Ruth carried with her the fear that penetration would be as uncomfortable as when she was ten years old.

When these incidents were explored and the myths of childbirth and intercourse corrected, their symptoms gradually subsided. As they understood one another's histories, they stopped blaming themselves and their sexual comfort skyrocketed. Six months ago I received in the mail a photo of their eight-pound-four-ounce son, Jacob, and a note saying they've never been happier.

Is it possible to overcome unpleasant elements of our early sexual shaping and relearn ways to love more comfortably or completely? Absolutely. With the right motivation, direction, and practice you can create rewarding and satisfying sexual outcomes.

Use the following sexual history exercise as a guide to help you and your partner communicate about early antecedents to your sexual attitudes, values, beliefs, and preferences.

SEXUAL HISTORY EXERCISE

One way to develop closeness with your lover is by sharing sexual memories. Sometimes it's easier when you have some guidelines. The following tool is designed to enhance self-disclosure and self-reflection about your individual sexual histories.

GUIDELINES

1. Select a time when neither of you feels rushed or preoccupied with other things. Begin by saying, "I'd like us to exchange some personal infor-

mation with one another. Is now a good time for you?" *Don't skip this step.*
Too many well-intentioned spouses spring a conversation on their mates and
wonder why they don't seem enthusiastic or motivated to participate. If he's
watching his favorite Celtics game, he may not be in the mood to interrupt
what he's doing just then.

2. If your partner says "yes," then go to the next step. Sit comfortably
facing each other and ask the questions in the sexual history tool. This tool
is meant only as a guide, so feel free to modify it in any way you like. You'll
need at least an hour for each of you to give and receive sexual memories.
You may find that your conversation goes on for much longer.

3. As you listen, be attentive and noncritical. Take turns answering the
questions. Don't be so interested in what you're going to say next that you
don't fully listen to what your lover is saying. Remember, this is very personal information.

4. Don't worry if there's an imbalance in the amount you each share.
This isn't a competition. Quantity isn't important; the act of sharing personal feelings about yourself is. Some of this material may be difficult to talk
about for a variety of reasons. No doubt, one of you may have an easier time
talking than the other.

5. Be prepared to have powerful feelings stirred. Don't feel that you
have to answer every question in detail. But try to be honest and not "make
up" information that you think will be more palatable than the naked truth.

6. Being honest doesn't mean that you need to reveal *everything.* You
can "pass" on questions you'd rather not discuss, but pay attention to which
issues make you feel anxious or uncomfortable.

7. It is important that *any* information shared between you be kept
private. You shouldn't divulge any of it even to best friends or parents.

Many couples who have been married for years tell me that this exercise
helped them make new discoveries and intensified their intimacy and trust.

Questions:

1. *What do you remember about being a boy or girl as you were
growing up? How did you feel about children of the opposite sex* (envy/
dislike/affection)? If you had siblings, did your parents expect
different things from you than from your sisters/brothers? If so, how
did you feel about that?

2. *What was the emotional climate in your home when it came to sex or nudity?* Was affection openly expressed? Was anger openly shown? Between your parents? Between parents and children? How were disagreements handled?

3. *Did you have any privacy as a child?* Were boundaries (like diaries or locked doors to the bedroom or bathroom) respected?

4. *What did you learn about the role of women and men and about the "ideal" marriage from your family, school, and peers?* Have you changed your views?

5. *What, when, and how did you learn about sex?* What did you learn from your parents, peers of the same sex, peers of the opposite sex? What feelings do you have about these events or information now?

6. *What memories do you have of sex play as a child?* How old were you when you first discovered the pleasure in your genitals? If you masturbated, did your parents know? What do you think their reactions would be if they knew? How did you masturbate? Did you masturbate to any erotica? If you ejaculated, what did you do with the ejaculate? How did you feel after you masturbated?

7. *What memories do you have about same-sex exploration in your childhood or adolescence?* What feelings did you have about those experiences? How do you feel about them now?

8. *What do you remember about puberty?* Were you prepared for your first period or first ejaculation, wet dreams, breast development/ body development (or lack of it)?

How did you compare with your peers? Were you a late bloomer or early out of the starting gate? Were you ever bullied or teased? How did you cope with the teasing?

9. *What are your memories of the first time you were kissed or touched in a sexual way?* First love? First sexual involvement? Assuming you've had sexual intercourse, did you feel emotionally ready?

10. *If you were ever touched against your will or molested, what feelings remain of those incidents?*

11. *Did you have any sexual fantasies you'd like to share with me?*

12. *How do you think your personal history relates to the way you feel about sex today?*

You may not have time to complete all of these questions in one sitting. Don't feel compelled to do so. One question usually stimulates a number of responses. As with other exercises, make sure to take your time during this experience. End the exercise with a statement of appreciation and a warm hug.

HOW TO USE THIS INFORMATION

No doubt the sexual history exercise raised a number of feelings for you and your lover. If your household was filled with animosity or open seductiveness, your role modeling for intimacy may contain some of these features. It's fascinating to recognize how much of our present style reflects what we were taught twenty or more years ago.

Even if we promised ourselves, "I'll never treat my husband that way," or "I'll never say those cruel things to my child," when you least expect it you find yourself becoming your mother or father! It's a sobering experience, but not one to be feared. Once you face your history and share the salient issues with your partner, you have given yourself another opportunity to empathize with the one you love.

The sexual history exercise is not easy to do, but it has far-reaching effects in opening up communication. *If you're going to have extraordinary sex, it has to begin with extraordinary communication.* After all, isn't that the purpose of sex—exchanging parts of ourselves with one another? You may have never dared to even think about your early and later sexual development, and would certainly never tell anyone about such personal memories, thoughts, and feelings. By completing this exercise you've taken a bold new step.

Although it may not be easy to open up to your lover in this way, I strongly recommend you give it a try. If you can manage only one or two questions, that's fine. Keep trying. One of you may feel more comfortable communicating than the other. When you're done with the exercise, ask your lover, "How are you feeling right now and what would feel good to you?" Perhaps your partner will ask you to lie next to him quietly, or maybe she'll want to celebrate the moment with a glass of wine. Be open to listening to what he or she would like.

Many couples find that sharing their early sexual histories is a milestone for them. Remember that these words were shared in safety and trust and are *not* to be abused. Don't play psychological mind games by throwing up some secret the next time you have an argument. A partner who says, "No wonder your father never loved you, you're so stubborn," may feel like he's firing torpedoes at his wife, but they'll explode in his own face. The information your lover has entrusted to you is sacred. Make sure you treat it that way.

By discussing your histories and sharing your hurts, hopes, and dreams, you've begun to allow yourself to be vulnerable with your lover. This process builds safety and security, helps you feel more connected and understood, and gives each of you an opportunity to embrace parts of your own past that you may have chosen to suppress or ignore. Accepting your own shame, fear, or confusion is an important first step in being able to love someone else.

Don't be surprised if sharing your sexual history stimulates feelings of warmth, closeness, or a desire to be physically intimate. Other couples have described wanting to have some time alone. Whatever happens, allow the feelings to emerge and respect them without censure.

The German critic Walter Benjamin wrote about self-knowledge in this way:

He who seeks to approach his own buried past must conduct himself like a man digging . . . He must not be afraid to return again and again to the same matter; to scatter it as one scatters earth, to turn it over as one turns over soil. For the matter itself is only a deposit, a stratum, which yields only to the most meticulous examination what constitutes the real treasure hidden within the earth: the images, severed from all earlier associations, that stand—like precious fragments or torsos in a collector's gallery—in the prosaic rooms of our later understanding.

CHAPTER 19

UNDERSTANDING AND OVERCOMING BOREDOM

Man finds nothing so intolerable as to be in a state of complete rest, without passions, without occupation, without diversion, without effort. Then he feels his nullity, loneliness, inadequacy, dependence, helplessness, emptiness.

—BLAISE PASCAL (1623–62), PENSÉES

AFTER THE STORM

When Peter, a Lion with Otter tendencies, and Susan, a Bee with a bit of Lion, were married six years, their four-year-old son, Anthony, was diagnosed with osteosarcoma, an aggressive form of bone cancer. Thus began a five-year battle for Tony's survival that filled Peter's and Susan's every waking moment. Peter, a pro golfer with a great deal of promise, and Susan, a freelance writer, put their careers on hold and filled their days with visits to oncologists, surgeons, psychologists, family therapists, herbalists, and acupuncturists. They explored traditional and alternative approaches, including biofeedback for pain management, hypnosis for healing and relaxation, and macrobiotic cooking. No stone was left unturned or avenue uninvestigated.

To outsiders it looked like Susan and Peter were the perfect couple—devoted, loving, and united in their determination to help their son. In fact, they weathered the storm of Tony's illness very well. The good news is that after several rounds of chemotherapy, radiation therapy, and multiple surgeries, Tony's cancer went into remission. As he approaches his eleventh birthday, he has been disease-free for nearly two years. The bad news is that now that the tempest is over, Peter and Susan's thirteen-year marriage is coming apart at the seams. Like so many other couples I have treated, they maintained their parental relationship at the expense of their spousal relationship. After years of being parents, they had forgotten how to be lovers.

Seeking Therapy

"Sex is so boring," Peter complained when he first called me for an appointment. "If things don't change soon, I'm going to talk to a lawyer." Because of the urgency in Peter's voice, I scheduled an appointment for the next day.

Peter and Susan sat down next to one another on the couch, but looked miles apart. "It feels like Susan and I are strangers going through the motions," he began. "She's a great mom, and I know I try to be a good dad, but we stopped being lovers when Tony got ill—that was *seven* years ago." Susan's face flushed and her eyes welled up as Peter spoke. "There's got to be more to marriage than this," he continued. "Now that Tony's over the worst of it, we don't seem to have anything in common." His voice trembled. "I wish I knew where the love went and how to get it back."

Susan spoke through her tears. "For years, all of our love and attention went to Anthony," she said, trying not to be defensive. "He was such a sick little boy and we came so close to losing him. I didn't realize that we were ignoring our marriage. With all the running around, I was too tired for sex." Peter interrupted her; he had an edge of hostility to his voice. "You know, Dr. Scantling, we fought so hard to save Tony's life, but we forgot about us. If I learned anything from Tony's illness, it's that life's just too damn precious to waste. I'm sorry to say this, but I'd rather have no marriage than the empty, boring existence we have now."

As I listened to them lament about their lost love, I wondered about their good times together. They had two years together before Anthony was born and four years before he became ill. Were they ever satisfied with their intimacy? What kind of love and passion had they enjoyed together?

Peter, a demanding risk taker, enjoyed living on the edge. His Otter spontaneity and Lionly assertiveness combined to make him a scratch golfer and dynamic personality. Susan's Bee-ness showed itself in her organizational wizardry. She balanced the family finances, household chores, social responsibilities, and her writing with ease.

When it came to sex, Peter loved surprises and Susan planned them beautifully. She'd orchestrated many a sexy evening starting with a sumptuous meal or sensual shower that led to a finale of passionate lovemaking. Susan loved Peter's touch and was easily orgasmic in the heat of passion, but spontaneity is less important for her; she'd rather know what's coming next. It's probably for this reason that Peter found their sex life getting boring long before she knew anything was wrong.

SEX AFTER THE BABY ARRIVES

As soon as a baby enters a household, things change out of necessity. Couples need to accommodate the new demands placed on their time and shift their priorities. Sometimes intimacy gets relegated to the bottom of the priority list.

One immediate change following the birth of a child is that you become parents. The word "parents" may be enough to dampen your enthusiasm. No longer are your wife's lovely breasts just for you. Now you have to share them. You also have to share each other with a helpless being who seems insatiable. Life and love as you knew it has changed forever. Instead of running out the door to grab a pizza and a quick movie, there needs to be careful planning, sitters called, and phone numbers of the police and fire department carefully placed next to the phone.

Peter was surprised at his response to having a child. He thought he'd be delighted—and he was, but he had mixed emotions. He was happy to have a son, but resented the intrusion. He knew he was being immature, but he missed having Susan all to himself. At first Peter tried to hide his resentment, but it expressed itself when his sexual interest took a nosedive.

WHAT COUPLES MEAN WHEN THEY SAY THEY'RE "BORED"

Of course, there are the *usual* reasons for boredom: lack of imagination and creativity, spending more time on your career than on your relationship, forgetting to make time for loving moments, not communicating sexually, turning sex into an arena for performance instead of an opportunity for pleasure, getting stuck in mechanical patterns or approaches that "get the job done," and taking each other for granted. *But the primary reason people feel bored is a lack of connection.* Instead of feeling that warm spark between the two of you, you're left feeling unsatisfied and lonely.

When partners like Peter and Susan offer "boredom" as their primary problem, it rarely is. In addition to the factors I mentioned above, I've discovered it's the feelings that lurk beneath the boredom that destroy sexual vitality.

The French word *ennui* actually means "annoyance." Although we've learned to think of boredom as a lack of variety or sameness, I've found that it is usually a cover for emotions that are difficult to express—feelings of anger, hurt, disappointment, fear, or resentment. Boredom signals the presence of something, not the absence of something.

In 1880, the German philosopher Friedrich Nietzsche wrote of ennui in this way: "He who completely entrenches himself against boredom also entrenches himself against himself: he will never get to drink the strongest refreshing draught from his own innermost fountain."

When I hear couples say that "boredom has set in" or "the romance has left our marriage," I don't rush to prescribe a sexy new negligee or massage lotion; rather, I listen closely to their underlying concerns.

Candice and Isaac thought their lovemaking would stay steamy forever, but after eight years of marriage they felt bored. They were puzzled. "I don't know what it is," said Candice. "We've tried a variety of things, but something's missing." It wasn't unusual for Isaac to bring home an erotic videotape for them to watch together, or for Candice to reach into her bag of toys during sex and come up with a new vibrator or some peppermint-flavored massage lotion. "But lighting the candles and putting on the mood music just isn't doing it for us anymore," said Isaac.

"What *are* you feeling during lovemaking?" I asked.

"Sometimes I feel nothing," said Candice. "Oh sure, my body still feels good when Isaac touches me, but I feel something missing inside. It's like we're miles away from each other. What I feel most of the time is *alone.*"

Isaac looked amazed. "I knew something was wrong, honey, but I didn't know you felt this bad," he said, turning to Candice.

"I was afraid to tell you," she replied tearfully. Isaac listened as Candice described what she wanted during lovemaking. "You try so hard to make each time wonderful, but I'd like you to just pay attention to *me,* and not to *sex.* Does that make sense to you?" Candice continued, "I'd really like to put away the silk scarves and other props and just have you hold me."

This was one of my easiest sessions and most rapid successes because Candice and Isaac were ready to share their honest feelings with one another. They learned that even though they had done all the "right things" to have sexual variety, they had forgotten the main ingredient of great sex— making the heart connection. By revealing their vulnerability to one another, they recaptured the real novelty that made sex exciting again.

BELIEVING IN FAIRY TALES

I tell the couples in my practice: *When expectations we set conflict with expectations unmet, the result is dissatisfaction.*

Sigmund Freud said, "The time comes when each of us has to give up as illusions the expectations which in our youth we pinned upon our fellow men" (1930). When reality belies our expectations the result is anger, hurt, fear, sadness, and disappointment.

Our wish to meet Prince or Princess Charming and live happily ever after with the one person destined to be our "soul mate" does not evaporate in childhood. Although the mature part of our psyche may not believe in fairy tales, the child inside each of us hopes we are mistaken. Partners come to marriage with a long list of expectations, some realistic and some based on myth, misinformation, and fantasy. Dealing with unmet expectations is no small task.

UNMASKING EXPECTATIONS

Like fairy tales, expectations are not truths. The truth of expectations lies in the truth of our beliefs. When it comes to sex, there are countless myths and misconceptions that define what we expect from great sex. When expectations are unrealistic, they create a set of conditions that lead to disappointment, hurt, frustration, and complaints of "boring" sex.

In the years Susan and Peter had been married, they'd never talked about their expectations or how they might have changed. Expectations can shift over time, and they can shift unilaterally. You've heard the expression "I outgrew him." This often happens when one person is in therapy and the other isn't. Unless there are provisions to keep each other informed, the marriage can break down.

Over the years, Peter's expectations hadn't changed, but Susan's had. Simply stated, their initial contract consisted of Susan giving and Peter receiving. In exchange for Susan's attention, Peter provided intensity. But Tony's illness had put so many demands on Susan that her resources were rapidly depleted. In order to stay physically and emotionally healthy, she had to find a way to replenish herself. Unfortunately, Peter expected her to be the same person he married. As she spent more time on herself, Peter became resentful and less interested in being sexual.

When one partner matures, it's inevitable that the other is affected. We all know couples who made a great team in their twenties, but not in their thirties. Maybe they loved to party, but didn't do the parent thing very well. Or were terrific business partners in their thirties, but didn't learn how to relax together in their later years.

Problems ensue when we cling to outmoded expectations in the same way a hermit crab resists finding a more suitable shell. Familiarity is comforting, but restricts growth. Peter and Susan's relationship had been challenged. However, by using the "Stop, Look, and Listen" format they found a way to reconnect and overcome the obstacles in their way.

STOP, LOOK, AND LISTEN

In the late fifties, Carl Rogers, a well-known psychologist, wrote about three essential attitudes in therapeutic listening: "empathic understanding," "unconditional positive regard," and "genuineness." This active listening approach is the centerpiece of the "Stop, Look, and Listen" exercise and has been used by countless therapists for years. It has been referred to as "reflective listening," "mirroring," "intentional listening," "empathic listening," among others.

Although there is much about this exercise that is not new, its importance in heart-to-heart communication merits repeating. The following principles are tried and true. Read them, practice them, and watch your intimacy shift from ordinary to extraordinary:

1. *Listening involves hearing.* If you're thinking about what you're going to say next, you're not hearing your partner and you're not listening.

2. *Communication must be from the personal "I" perspective.* If you begin sentences with "you always" or "you never" it encourages a defensive or reactive response.

3. *Sex is a way of communicating with each other.* People who listen empathically to their partners and give clear messages to their partners are on their way to becoming great lovers.

4. *There are no right or wrong feelings.* If one of you laughs during a particular movie and the other doesn't, who is "right"? You've probably heard someone say, "Why are you laughing? It's not funny." Feelings vary and reflect your personal reality. Each reality must be respected. When you deny another's feelings, it's natural for them to feel slighted and unimportant.

HOW TO BEGIN

1. **The first thing to do when you're involved in a reactive battle is to** *Stop.* This is by far the hardest of all three steps. Each person wants to get his point across and stopping is a challenge.

2. **Then one of you begins as the sharer while the other is the listener.** *Look* at your partner. (Don't do this in the car. The car is a terrible place for intimate dialogues. People incorrectly assume they have several hours of time in a car and can use it productively. It rarely works to build intimacy. The reason for this is that you can't look at each other. You also can't have intimate conversations when one person is looking at the television. Shut off the television. Unplug the telephone or turn on your answering machine. Pull up a couple of chairs and look at each other.) This may feel very awkward, but if you want to have sex with this person, you have to be able to look at him or her.

3. **Focus on *one* subject.** If you let one topic snowball into another,

the exercise won't work. Use some self-control and stay on one subject per session.

4. The next step is to *Listen*. This means to listen to the actual words and to your partner's feelings. Not what you *think* the other person is saying or feeling. Listen to the meaning of the words from *their* perspective. Try to put yourself in your partner's position as you listen. This is called enabling empathy and it's easier said than done, I assure you. It's very hard to listen to someone telling you something you'd rather not hear about yourself and to do so empathically! The natural tendency is to interrupt, defend, explain, or protect yourself in some way. But when you deflect the message, you dilute the intimacy. Instead of thinking about your retort, say things like "Tell me more. Is there more? I'd like to hear more about that." Listen attentively until your partner is done.

5. Repeat what you believe you heard and how you think they feel. Ask if you're correct and listen if you're not. When the sharer is done, he or she should thank the listener for listening. The listener also should thank the sharer for sharing. This in not an easy process. It takes effort on both sides and deserves an appreciative comment. Saying "thank you" is an important part of the healing process as we unmask the feelings beneath boredom.

Peter and Susan used this approach to understand each other's feelings. Peter's challenge was to accept Susan's decision to put more time into herself and to overcome his narcissistic disappointment at not always being the center of attention. His task was to become more mature, empathic, and tender, to ask about her day and *listen* to her reply. It wasn't easy for Peter to be empathic, but with perseverance and practice he succeeded. Susan developed patience with Peter as she understood how difficult it was for him to share her. Since they've started understanding one another more, their intimate connection has grown. Loving each other hasn't been boring since.

The next chapter will show you how to identify and bridge the expectations gap in your own relationship.

CHAPTER 20

THE EXPECTATIONS GAP

*I know not anything more pleasant, or more instructive,
than to compare experience with expectation, or to register
from time to time the difference between idea and reality.
It is by this kind of observation that we grow less
liable to be disappointed.*

—SAMUEL JOHNSON, LETTER, 1758

EXPECTATIONS CREATE DISAPPOINTMENT

There's no doubt that our expectations can set us up for disappointment, and that each disappointment represents an expectation unmet. I can still remember asking my father why we didn't have a home as big as my third-grade girlfriend's and his wise reply, "How many of your friends have homes *smaller* than ours? Count your blessings." In a letter to playwright John Gay, Alexander Pope wrote of the "ninth beatitude" as "Blessed is the man who expects nothing, for he shall never be disappointed."

So what's the message here? Are we to expect nothing or forever be disappointed? Of course not. Problems arise when we're unclear about what we expect from ourselves and our partners, when our expectations are unexamined, or when they're accepted as immutable truths.

Expectations emerge from a range of formative sources, including the teachings of our family and cultural norms, our religious beliefs, what we learned in school from teachers and peers, and countless outside influences. As we develop, they continue to evolve and are shaped by popular mythology, political ideology, the media, and a host of other contemporary sources.

We have expectations about everything that matters to us. But the expectations that upset relationships are those that represent "desirable conduct" for intimate partners.

Imagine you're in the express checkout lane at the grocery store. It's late and you're tired. The store is crowded with the before-supper rush. You have only three items and find yourself counting the items in the cart of the person ahead of you. He has more than twenty items—eight over the allowable limit! You feel miffed. Your expectation is: We should all play by the rules—this isn't fair. The "violator" in front of you, obviously, has a different set of expectations. Perhaps he expects every person can push the limits once in a while, or six cans of the same product "don't count" as separate items, or he's in a hurry and has a sick child at home, so it's okay. His expectation may be that everyone should be more flexible. What if Ms. Rigid-rule-observer were married to Mr. Laid-back-flexible? Think of the struggles they'd have! The truth is that these couples *do* marry each other and many of them wind up in my office complaining about their boring sex lives.

WHEN EXPECTATIONS CLASH

Everyone carries with them a raft of expectations about love, sex, marriage, and a slew of other things. Reflecting the standards of your family of origin, you probably have expectations about showing affection, how often (if ever) you should argue, or how your partner would behave "if they really loved you." Because we're individuals, our partners rarely share all of our expectations. Conflict is inevitable. The chasm that grows out of differences in expectations is responsible for a large percentage of the sexual dysfunctions I treat. For the relationship to survive, the chasm has to be bridged.

Unmet expectations *always* precede anger. Think of a time you felt angry and I can guarantee you that someone or something failed to meet your expectations. Unfortunately, because expectations are difficult to recognize, they are often not expressed directly.

Consider this example: Mary comes home with an armful of groceries and finds Max watching a football game on TV. Mary *expects* Max to get up from his easy chair and help her with the heavy load without having to ask. Max, on the other hand, is annoyed at Mary for picking the most inopportune time to go grocery shopping. He *expects* her to know he doesn't like to be disturbed when he's watching football.

Mary, feeling unappreciated and annoyed, walks into the kitchen and drops the groceries on the counter with a loud thump. Max yells from the family room, "Could you keep it down in there? I'm trying to listen to this game." Mary's anger is fueled by his insensitive reply. She had expected Max to ask, "What's wrong in there? Are you okay?" His indifference incenses her even more. She storms into the family room and unleashes her wrath: "If you'd get up off your lazy butt and give me a hand, I wouldn't have to make so much noise." You can figure out how this scenario progresses from there. It ends when Max leaves the house and slams the door.

This example appears to have nothing to do with sex, but it does. Mary and Max came to see me because (you guessed it) "the romance had left their relationship." They were unaware that their unexpressed expectations were destroying their intimacy.

If You Loved Me You Would . . .

When it comes to expectations, most people assume there's very little variation. After all, isn't it obvious that if Max loved Mary he'd naturally want to help her with the groceries? But Max believes if Mary loved him she'd be considerate of his free time. Expectations aren't truths, but we act as if they were. And, of course, we believe that *our* expectations are the correct ones. There is, however, generally more than one side to every story.

The most important point to remember when you're hurt, angry, or feeling rebuffed is that your partner is entitled to his or her own expectations. You may not agree with them, but that's beside the point. I understand that it's difficult to empathize with your partner's point of view when you're fuming, but that's the challenge. When we're angry, defensiveness replaces openness, intimacy becomes overshadowed by incessant bickering, and sex (assuming you still have sex) will be perceived as boring.

Switching Expectations to Wishes

One way to resolve unmet expectations is to *convert your expectations to wishes*. Instead of thinking, "I expect him to help with the groceries," you could think, "I'd like him to help or would appreciate his help with the groceries." Saying to yourself, "It would be nice if X or Y happened," leads to a very different emotional outcome than *expecting* X or Y to happen. It also creates different emotional climate around the event.

Using the "Stop, Look, and Listen" format presented in the previous chapter, Mary and Max shared their lists of expectations but expressed them as wishes. Mary told Max that she'd appreciate some assistance with the groceries, and Max told her he'd appreciate some uninterrupted time while watching his favorite sports events. Hearing expectations phrased as "wishes" makes them much more palatable.

Max agreed to help with the groceries, if Mary would shop at a different time. This seemed like a reasonable compromise to Mary. By sharing expectations in a nonblaming manner, it was easy to work out a solution. I also suggested that Mary thank Max for his help and Max thank Mary for doing the shopping. It had been a long time since they had remembered to treat each other courteously.

Next Mary and Max explored dozens of expectations that had been plaguing the relationship. They discovered they each had an unspoken list titled "If you loved me you'd . . ."

Mary's list went like this:

If you loved me you'd:

- Help in the kitchen without my having to ask.
- Spend more time at home than with "the guys."
- Never be late.
- Notice a new hairdo or outfit and compliment me.
- Rub my back when I announce that I've had a hard day or offer to make me a cup of tea.
- Not expect *every* sexual experience to end with intercourse or your ejaculation.
- Spend more time touching me in places besides my breasts and genitals.
- Put down the newspaper or shut off the television when I'm trying to have a conversation with you.
- Make time for my family and friends.

- Show me more affection.
- Want to make love more often.
- Never look at other women when we're together.
- Give me a kiss in public.
- Hold my hand when we walk down the street.
- Give me a present without any particular occasion.
- Never forget my birthday.
- Never give me a major appliance for Valentine's Day.

The last item on her list stemmed from a fight they'd had the previous Valentine's Day. Max had surprised Mary with a microwave oven wrapped in a red ribbon! He'd expected she'd appreciate the effort and expense involved. When Mary saw the microwave she was speechless. How could Max consider a major appliance to be an appropriate Valentine's Day gift? Max was stunned at Mary's reaction. After all, he shopped around for just the right model because he wanted Mary to have an easier time in the kitchen. He'd saved for months to buy the very best model and felt crushed that his efforts were unappreciated. But all Mary "expected" on Valentine's Day was a romantic card or a flower.

Needless to say, Max's "If you loved me" list was very different from Mary's. It went like this:

If you loved me you'd:

- Be less critical and appreciate my efforts even if we disagree.
- Respect my time with my friends and not insist I spend all my free time at home.
- Overlook some of the small things and cut me some slack.
- Understand I'm not intentionally ignoring your new hairdo or outfit, I just have trouble with "details."
- Be less critical of what I wear when we go out together.
- Not expect public displays of affection.
- Reach out to *me* more often sexually.
- Wear something besides that old nightie to bed.
- Look as pretty around the house as you do when you go to the office.

- Watch erotic movies with me once in a while.
- Experiment with sexual fantasy.
- Include oral sex more often in our lovemaking.
- Tell me what you'd like sexually.
- Not overemphasize birthdays or anniversaries and just know that I love you.
- Know that I show my love by working hard for you and the home.
- Not interrupt me when I'm watching sports on television.
- Not schedule my weekends before we talk together.

These divergent lists gave Mary and Max lots to discuss. They decided that it was much better to compromise than to be constantly arguing. By following the "Steps to Resolve Boredom" in the next section they arrived at a new level of intimacy and understanding.

And what do you think happened to their romance? When they stopped arguing, they remembered what they loved about each other and their passion became stronger than before.

BRIDGING EXPECTATIONS: THE CURE FOR BOREDOM

Annoyance dampens the most intense ardor. After you eliminate the negative feelings that create the boredom, it's easy to find ways to put the fun back into sex.

The cure for boredom is rarely as simple as "Try a few new positions!" If that were the case, the countless books offering thousands of suggestions promising to make sex sizzle would be flying off the shelves. Think back to the times you've read "ten tips guaranteed to make him beg for more" in some popular magazine. Do you remember how you responded to the suggestion that you paint his body with chocolate sauce and slowly lick it off? If at the time you were reading the article, you were feeling annoyed because he forgot your birthday or didn't call to say he'd be late for supper, I doubt the chocolate sauce idea appealed to you.

STEPS TO RESOLVE BOREDOM

. . . .

1. IDENTIFY YOUR UNMET EXPECTATIONS ABOUT INTIMACY

Begin by setting aside thirty minutes for you and your partner to brainstorm *separately* about your expectations. Write what you expect from each other when it comes to love, sex, and intimacy. This isn't as easy as it sounds. To give you a few ideas, I've listed some expectations I hear frequently from my clients. Read through them and see how many you share:

I expect my partner to not criticize my "few extra pounds" if he/she really loves me.

After marriage, I expect to not have to work so hard to impress my partner—I should be able to "be myself."

I expect him/her to be ready for sex when I am and not to turn me down.

I expect him/her to tell me I'm attractive, give me little presents, make me feel loved.

I expect her/him to look happy to see me when I come home.

I expect her/him to want to spend free time with me.

I expect our relationship to come before his/her friends or hobbies.

I expect him/her to confide in me.

I expect him/her to be my best friend.

I expect him/her to be sensitive to my feelings.

I expect him/her to appreciate what I do and to tell me so.

I expect to hold hands when we walk down the street.

I expect outward displays of affection. It's not enough for me to know I'm loved, I like to see evidence of it.

I don't expect him/her to find other men or women sexually attractive after we're married.

I expect him/her not to fantasize about anyone else.

I expect him to be satisfied with our sex together and not "need" to masturbate.

If we're at a party, I don't expect him to leave me unattended or dance with someone else unless I'm already dancing.

I expect him to have an erection if he sees me naked.

I expect her to get "wet" and be turned on when I kiss her.

I expect her/him to make noises during lovemaking.

I expect her/him to initiate oral sex.

I expect her/him to enjoy giving and receiving oral sex.

I expect him/her to look into my eyes when we're talking to each other.

I expect him/her to not interrupt me when I'm reading, watching TV, or (fill in the activity).

I expect lovemaking not to be work; it should be effortless, spontaneous, and fun.

I expect that after we're married we don't have to compliment each other as often as we did while dating.

I don't ever expect him/her to be too tired to make love.

I don't expect to have to say I appreciate my partner's cooking, hard work in the yard, or whatever—it should just be understood.

I expect him/her to make time to love me—go on special dates, weekends away—without my having to ask.

I expect him/her to put as much time and energy into our relationship as he/she puts into his/her job.

I expect him/her to always be kind and never to be critical.

I do not expect arguments.

I expect complete honesty.

I expect my partner to just *know* what I want sexually.

I expect an erection to last as long as we want it to.

I expect we will have orgasms together.

I expect my partner to be interested in sex whenever I am.

I expect sexual inhibitions to decrease over the years.

I expect my partner to be open to sexual variety (erotic films, toys, and/or light bondage).

Once it's complete, exchange your list with your partner. You now have a ready-made map to the heart of your lover.

....

2. CORRECT YOUR MYTHS AND MISCONCEPTIONS

Sometimes expectations are the product of our myths and misconceptions about sexuality. A number of the items on the preceding list are myths. That erections should last as long as you want, that we should *always* be interested in having sex, that all *good sex* ends in orgasm, and that inhibitions decrease over the years are examples of myths that create unrealistic expectations.

In some cases inhibitions increase over the years. Wild or kinky sex may be acceptable during courtship, but some couples have the expectation that after they're married or have a family, more "conservative" sex should be the norm. When lovers get married or have a family, some of them feel uncomfortable with the freer sexual experimentation of earlier days. If you still long for hot sex on the beach, but he only wants to be intimate beneath the covers, you may be facing a difference in your expectations about what "normal married sex" should be.

But don't assume this is true for every older couple. Some find their inhibitions decreasing and sexual interest rising as they mature and as the freedom to make love is unhampered by the responsibilities of parenting and/or career.

Myths can set up a pressure to perform that often undermines your natural erotic response. A number of years ago, there was a lot of talk about multiple "vaginal" orgasms. I got dozens of calls from couples wondering if something was wrong because the woman "just had one orgasm—and the orgasm only happened with oral sex or clitoral touching and *not* during intercourse." Instead of feeling liberated by multiple orgasmic potential, many women who had previously felt satisfied with one orgasm now worried that they were "dysfunctional."

We now know that the early Freudian view that vaginal orgasms are somehow more "mature" than clitoral orgasms is incorrect. Whether an orgasm is a product of nipple stimulation, clitoral or vaginal pleasuring, or fantasy alone—an orgasm is an orgasm. Enjoy it! By correcting myths and misconceptions you can prevent needless stress and worry from interfering with your sexual pleasure.

3. SEVEN STEPS TO "MENDING WOUNDS"

Couples rarely face their own expectations, let alone share them with one another. There's less risk of exposure and limited vulnerability when you say, "Our sex life has gotten boring." But in order for boredom to be corrected, the feelings buried beneath it must be unearthed one layer at a time.

A cautionary note: when you begin your personal expedition to uncover the *real* issues underlying your boredom, take it slowly. Some couples are so excited about getting to the bottom of things that they underestimate the fragility of the relationship and barge full speed ahead. Like a miner anxious to find that vein of gold, they put on their helmets, gather their picks and shovels, and start their excavation before evaluating the soundness of the mine shaft.

The goal of the "mending wounds" exercise is to clarify expectations and deepen intimacy. Before you begin, you and your partner should agree to cooperate with each other and *listen* to each other's feelings. Make sure the sessions have time limits and are focused. Use the "Stop, Look, and Listen" approach on page 255 and agree to be sensitive to each other's perspectives. Think this process through as if you were building an addition onto your home. You don't randomly knock down walls before you know where the support beams lie. Remember, the purpose of the "mending wounds" exercise is for self-disclosure and increased intimacy, *not* to see whose expectations are more correct.

A. *Begin by expressing any expectations you set:*
"I expected you to come home from work on time, like you promised."
B. Next, *express your anger, annoyance, or disappointment when your expectations are unmet using "I" statements:*
"I feel angry when I feel less important than your other responsibilities."
C. Next, *share the hurt, sadness, or other feelings beneath the anger:*
"I feel hurt (sad, alone, rejected, disappointed, frightened, scared) when I think I don't matter to you."
D. *Rephrase your expectations as wishes:*

"I wish you would or I'd appreciate it if you would call me if you're going to be late."

E. *The listening partner clarifies:*

"Are you saying you'd like me to call you if I'm going to be late?"

F. *Empathize and reverse roles:*

Show your understanding of your partner's feelings, then reverse roles—listening partner becomes the sharing partner and steps a–f are repeated.

G. *Grant one wish:*

Agreeing to try a compromise.

The interaction may sound something like this:

A. "I understand you expect me to be home when I say I will and that you feel angry and unimportant if I don't call when I'm going to be late. From my perspective, I expect to have the freedom to be late once in a while without being blamed and criticized. I sometimes have a last-minute detail at the office that might detain me or get caught in traffic and come home later than I had planned."

B. "When you expect me to rigidly conform to your time standards, I feel controlled and resentful."

C. "I also feel hurt that my trustworthiness is questioned and sometimes I feel like a child being punished for violating the curfew. When this happens I feel injured and don't feel like making love."

D. "I wish you would trust me and be a bit more flexible."

E. At this point, the new listener clarifies:

"Are you saying you'd like more freedom, that things come up that are unanticipated, and you feel controlled and resentful when I get angry at you?"

F. Empathize:

Share any new perspective or understanding that may have emerged and express whatever regret you honestly feel. For example: "I never knew you felt like a child or didn't make love with me because you felt hurt. I'm sorry. I didn't mean to make you feel that way."

G. Each person agrees to "grant" the other's wish and take a step to repair the problem:

This is the process of negotiation and putting some action behind your promises. It takes maturity and a willingness to compromise.

One partner may say, "I'll call you if I'm going to be more than fifteen minutes late."

The other says, "Thank you. I'll reduce the intensity of my anger and try to be more flexible in how I handle lateness."

....

4. RECOGNIZE THAT IT TAKES TWO TO MAINTAIN A PROBLEM

Long ago, I learned from Masters and Johnson-trained therapists Philip and Lorna Sarrel that "there's no such thing as an uninvolved partner." Neither partner is *solely* responsible for a sexual problem. Sex occurs within the context of a relationship, and the *relationship* shifts through the action of each of the participants. Either partner can change the balance in the relationship by trying out some new behaviors.

If you feel too angry to "mend your wounds" go to Chapter 21 and write your Last Erotic Love Letter. It is a dramatic way to cut through misgivings and recapture the essence of your love. You may think that exercises are too contrived or simplistic, but I can assure you that if you put in sincere effort you'll see results.

It takes an inordinate amount of patience and control to follow an exercise step by step, and the last thing you want to do when you're angry is be reasonable! Old habits die hard. But if you want to create a more loving and more passionate relationship, you have to begin to make some changes in your style. Although the exercise may feel awkward at first, if you stick with it it will become second nature before long.

GLORIA AND PARKER

Parker, forty-one, a mechanical engineer, and Gloria, forty, a high school science teacher, have been married sixteen years. When they first came to see me, their initial complaint was painful penetration. Although Gloria had seen several specialists, she had no success resolving the excruciating pain and burning she experienced during intercourse. The results of her gynecological examination were essentially within normal limits, with the exception of some mild vaginal spasm around the insertion of the doctor's speculum. Gloria was diagnosed as having vaginismus, an involuntary spasm in the outer one-third of her vagina that made penetration uncomfortable for her.

Gloria's symptoms had begun about three and a half years ago. At that time Parker had taken a new job that required him to be out of the country about seven to ten days each month. The job paid well, but it led to a major change in their lifestyle. Parker had promised her it would be for only a year, but three years later he was still with the same company. The firm was considering Parker for an executive promotion which would demand even more time overseas. Gloria was pleased about the promotion and the increase in Parker's salary, but resented his time away from home.

There were other changes in their lives. Since Parker was gone so much, Gloria had decided to finish her master's degree in education and had taken up karate in the evenings. Out of necessity, she assumed more of the tasks previously done by Parker. She paid the bills, dealt with the lawn service, and did some odds and ends at home. In a way, Gloria enjoyed her newfound self-sufficiency, but not the solitude.

Parker sensed her unspoken disapproval and felt unsupported in his climb up the corporate ladder. He had increased his income to six figures, but didn't feel appreciated.

On the weekends he was home, sex had become obligatory and much less spontaneous. They had so little time together, they had begun to have sex even when they weren't "in the mood." Gloria would respond when she was clearly uninterested because she feared what might happen to their marriage if she refused him. It was during one of these weekends that the symptoms of vaginal pain and dryness began. As the months progressed, the discomfort increased. They tried lubricants and creams, but the pain only worsened with each attempt at intercourse. They called me for an appointment.

Therapy focused on re-creating honesty. As they expressed their unmet expectations and disappointments, Gloria allowed her sadness and anger to emerge. Parker revealed his disappointment at feeling unappreciated. They both acknowledged they'd been going through the motions sexually for some time. Gloria admitted that she had suppressed her anger at Parker and tried to pretend all was well. "We had so little time together, I didn't want to ruin it." She had gone ahead with intercourse when her vagina was clearly telling her "no."

The more she ignored her body, the more pain she had. Parker could feel her dryness and low arousal and assumed she wasn't attracted to him anymore. He even began to suspect she might be having an affair. Over the months their resentment grew and their passion steadily declined.

This is a clear example of both partners perpetuating their sexual problem. Instead of rushing to use vaginal dilators, the treatment I suggested focused on resolving their mutual hurts and unmet expectations.

Rather than pushing resentment under the rug, they began to share their feelings using the "Stop, Look, and Listen" format. They placed the steps of the "mending wounds" exercise on their refrigerator door and followed them whenever they felt stuck in unmet expectations:

RECOGNIZE EXPECTATIONS I SET

ACKNOWLEDGE MY FEELINGS WHEN MY EXPECTATIONS ARE UNMET

EXPRESS HURT OR SADNESS

REPHRASE EXPECTATIONS INTO WISHES

CLARIFY

EMPATHIZE WITH PARTNER AND REVERSE ROLES

GRANT ONE WISH

Gloria and Parker discovered that they missed each other but had been too busy arguing to notice. They decided to spend time getting reacquainted, before leaping into sex. Parker's business trips and Gloria's outside interests had pulled them apart. They vowed to decrease the distance that had insidiously crept between them.

As they reestablished their trust, they remembered what they loved about each other. Parker's sexual desire returned. He took time to touch Gloria in ways that felt good to both of them. They agreed to focus less on intercourse and more on loving each other.

Women who have learned to ignore the pain in their genitals have inadvertently silenced the messages of their bodies by ignoring their pleasure as well as their pain. Gloria needed to rediscover how to listen to what her body was telling her. Resensitization and empowerment were part of the treatment approach. It was essential that she learn to focus on positive sensations and not do anything that felt uncomfortable.

I also taught Gloria some guided imagery techniques to relax her breathing, stop any negative or distracting thoughts, and replace those thoughts with positive images. And what was Parker to do while Gloria was reestablishing her comfort in her body? He was to focus on *his own* enjoyment and not to worry about the sexual outcome. This was difficult at first, but with practice it became fun.

Gloria and Parker spent the next three or four weekends practicing their sensual closeness. One evening she felt especially turned on and got into the female-on-top position. She slowly slid her vagina down over Parker's penis while focusing on what felt good to her. She tightened and relaxed her vaginal muscles as she relaxed her breathing and imagined a very comforting place. She was delighted that there was no discomfort and that he slipped in easily. As she focused on pleasure and erotic images, the wetter and more turned on she became. Gloria's excitement added to Parker's arousal as their passion built to an amazing climax for them both.

As Gloria and Parker continued to take responsibility for sharing their feelings openly and honestly, their intimacy and sexual passion grew exponentially. The pain on penetration ceased to be a problem and they found themselves wanting sex more often and in a variety of ways. Even though Parker's job continued to take him away from home, Gloria was always on his mind and he made sure he told her so.

CHAPTER 21

SIX INGREDIENTS FOR EXTRAORDINARY SEX

Taking a new step, uttering a new word is what people fear most.

—FYODOR DOSTOEVSKI

- Put Away Old Hurts and Anger
- Assert Your Needs and Respect Each Other's Boundaries
- Break Out of Old Patterns Starting Today
- Treat Each Other Like Company
- Make Time for Each Other
- Focus on Pleasure, Not Measure

INGREDIENT #1: PUT AWAY OLD HURTS AND ANGER

Real learning comes about when the competitive spirit has ceased.

—ANONYMOUS

Becky and Sonny, married six years, were always at each other. The slightest thing would set them off. Two competitive Lions, they spent more time fighting than loving. A typical weekend might begin with Becky washing the ceramic tile in the foyer only to have Sonny walk in from the garage and leave his muddy footprints all over the floor. "Damn it, Sonny, do you have to be such an inconsiderate slob!" Becky would scream. Sonny, not to be demeaned, would up the ante by telling her to go to hell. A sad beginning to a long, loveless weekend.

There's no doubt that an occasional argument can clear the air and release pent-up frustrations. For some couples, an occasional fight can even be sexually arousing. But name-calling and choice expletives aren't part of the formula. There are rules for fighting cleanly and keeping your blows above the belt.

Anger blocks intimacy. We can't change history and the more we dwell on old hurts, the more they become part of our day-to-day experience. Just as each of us is responsible for our own pleasure, the same is true for our hostility.

PENNY AND VANCE

Past hurts interfere with feelings of comfort and safety that are central to building intimacy. Penny and Vance, in their mid-forties, have been engaged in a cold war ever since Vance's affair more than eight years ago. Vance had made the call to me saying, "My wife is never interested in having sex." His assumption was that since the affair was over long ago, it was time to get on with their lives.

"I've been brooding and seething and can't get it out of my mind," Penny admitted at the beginning of our first session. "I felt as though I'd failed as a woman and each time we make love I think of them together. Maybe I don't have sex with Vance because I'm trying to punish him, but I'm also punishing myself."

There comes a point when rehashing an old battle becomes pointless. The victim of the affair, in this case Penny, becomes the victimizer by abusing Vance for cheating on her. Understandable, but unhelpful. There's no easy way to get over hurt, especially a breach of trust. You must just come to a point where you decide to let it go. This doesn't mean that you accept it, condone it, or aren't deeply pained. It just means that you've made the choice to move ahead with your relationship.

TARYN AND SAL

But for negotiation to work and healing to begin, both parties must be willing to put aside their hurt and anger and work toward a common goal. Too many relationships are destroyed as each fights for some "principle." I'm reminded of the divorce of Taryn and Sal, who spent $10,000 in legal fees battling over who would get custody of their vacuum cleaner!

Taryn maintained it was rightfully hers because her parents gave it to her as a shower gift. Sal claimed it was his because he did most of the vacuuming. They battled on and on over this vacuum cleaner, even though they both knew this was absurd. I suggested that they seemed to be having difficulty letting go of each other and chose to stay connected through barbed wire. Anger is, after all, another form of passion. It's not unusual for couples to engage in fighting when they fear intimacy. In the end, the court ordered that Taryn and Sal split the paltry proceeds of less than $150.

Like Taryn and Sal, couples often argue over minor issues that serve as a smoke screen for the real problem. Ask yourself these questions: When I argue with my partner, does each episode have a familiar ring? Does the scene change while the cast of characters stays constant? Do I feel like I'm spinning my wheels and even though "I win" I feel unsatisfied? Instead of an argument about the "toilet seat" thing, perhaps the issue is one of power, control, or an opportunity to pay him back for flirting with my best friend? Unless you identify the *real* issues buried in the tiny skirmishes, you may find yourself endlessly battling to no avail.

Putting away old hurts and anger is crucial to making space for intimacy. There are countless times when couples have asked me for suggestions to revitalize their sex life, but meanwhile they're arguing vehemently over old incidents. And each time they argue, they open the wound once again.

EXERCISES TO PUT AWAY OLD HURTS AND ANGER

Are you a couple who frequently bring up old hurts and angers? Once you've discussed the hurts completely and expressed your individual feelings, there comes a time to let them go. Holding on to hurt indefinitely not only blocks intimacy but is a waste of energy.

IMAGINARY CHALKBOARD

When you've decided you're ready to let something go, imagine writing down your old hurts or angers on a chalkboard and choosing to erase them. Erase each hurt—letter by letter, until they are all gone. Starting with a clean slate can be very healthy for your relationship.

HOT-AIR BALLOON

Another approach I suggest is to visualize placing the hurts into the basket of a hot-air balloon and let it drift into space. Watch it become a speck in the sky until it is out of sight.

THE MELTING POPSICLE

If you're a good visualizer, imagine your hurts as an ice-cream cone or Popsicle melting in the sunlight. As the hurts melt away, breathe in the warmth of the sun and the clean fresh air. With each exhale say, "I let this go."

If it feels too hard to let go of your hurts, try the next exercise. It is a more detailed form of the "mending wounds" exercise on page 267. The purpose of the Anger Inventory is to recognize some self-defeating communication patterns, begin to take more responsibility for your own behavior, and recognize some positive alternatives to arguing.

THE ANGER INVENTORY

1. You and your partner *take two sheets of paper apiece and tape them together* (lengthwise). Divide your sheets into nine columns. Title the first column "things that make me angry." Work separately on each of your lists. Be specific. Don't make a global statement like "when the house is a mess." Instead say, "I'm angry when you forget to wipe your feet when you walk in the door."
2. *Then, in a second column, list the "expectation" that has been violated.* To use the above example you might say, "I expect that I don't have to

tell you to wipe your feet and that since you've been asked you'll comply."

3. *In a third column write the "hurt and other feelings" that emerge out of having unmet expectations.* For example, "When I ask you to do something repeatedly and you don't, I feel hurt, frustrated, and unimportant."

4. *In the fourth column, write "how you usually deal" with your hurt or disappointment.* Again, be specific about what you might say or do.

5. *The fifth column is titled "enable empathy."* This is difficult. *Put yourself in your partner's position and <u>imagine</u> how he or she feels when he hears your comments or experiences your behavior.*

6. *In the sixth column ask yourself, "What am I trying to accomplish with my behavior?"* Am I trying to vent my feelings, hurt or punish my partner, or gain understanding?

7. Next ask yourself, *"What am I <u>actually accomplishing</u> with this behavior?"*

8. In this column, *consider some "NEW options."* List alternative behaviors and ways of dealing with your frustrations.

After each of you has completed this exercise privately, take turns sharing what you have written. As always, use the "Stop, Look, and Listen" format from page 255. Take turns listening and sharing. Always remember to say "thank you" to each other. And don't expect to do your entire list in one sitting. Take your time. Share one or two points at a time so you don't feel overwhelmed.

9. *In the last column, each of you agrees to negotiate one area of disagreement.* If she wants you to do ten things, pick one and make sure you keep your promise.

Letting go of anger goes hand in hand with rebuilding trust. Make certain that you enter into the process in good faith and stick to your commitments.

Remember, this is not a time for rebuttal or for being the "most hurt." Don't get into competition here. This is a time to break out of old communication patterns by respectfully attending to each other. It is an opportunity to start fresh and begin with a clean slate.

SOME HINTS TO DEAL WITH ANGER PRODUCTIVELY

1. *Blaming never solved anything.* Would you rather be right or happy?

2. *Try to hear your partner's point of view.* Don't nod, pretend you're listening, and wait for a lull in the conversation to make your convincing argument.

3. *Don't use words like "you always" or "you never."* Every good student knows that in a multiple-choice exam a question with "always" in it is usually false.

4. *Remember that attentive listening to your partner <u>doesn't</u> mean you agree with their point of view.* It only means that you understand what they're saying given their particular assumptions, feelings, and perspective.

A LIST OF DON'TS

1. *Don't roll your eyes or laugh to undermine or distract your partner* when they are speaking.

2. *Don't interrupt.*

3. *Don't demean,* resort to name-calling, or try to get leverage by dredging up some sensitive information from your partner's past.

4. Above all, *don't threaten* verbally or physically.

5. *Don't say something you'll regret later.* Words matter and once uttered are impossible to retract.

6. *Stop the negative spiral.* If your partner is acting inappropriately, that doesn't justify *your* hurtful retaliation.

7. *Remember what you love about this person* and why you married him or her. This is difficult to do when you're angry, but no one told you this would be easy.

8. *It's okay to use some humor,* but using humor doesn't mean laughing at your partner.

9. *Don't sweat the small stuff.* It isn't worth going to war over who last emptied the dishwasher or why he controls the television remote control.

10. *Enable empathy*—the most important ingredient of all. It's human nature to be self-involved and think of "me, me, me." It takes incredible

self-control to consider your partner's feelings in the heat of an argument, but it is the most helpful thing you can do.

CALCULATE THE RISKS AND BENEFITS

I've found it helpful to suggest that my couples draw up a risk-benefit sheet. Bee couples are very receptive to this approach. For every fight there's a risk and some kind of perceived benefit. List both sides of the tally sheet and then you be the judge of determining whether the argument was worth the risk.

The goal of intimate discussion is to negotiate a better solution. Resorting to old bad habits will only fuel the fire. No sexual technique, vibrator, or negligee will stimulate desire or closeness when there's anger on board. Angry mates don't want to please their lovers. And as you've discovered, no one emerges unscathed.

CHANGING THE BALANCE AND FOCUSING ON APPRECIATION

Once you've defused some of the anger, it's time to build your connection by reminding yourself why you married your partner. This is another one of those exercises that take a lot of ego strength and maturity, but it is well worth the effort.

1. Take two separate sheets of paper, one for each of you.
2. Make a list of all of the things you appreciate or admire about your partner.
3. Think about the way he/she looks, feels, smells, tastes, sounds. Think about what you enjoy doing together. Think about all the positive things that make your partner the person you decided to spend the rest of your life with.
4. Complete these phrases to help you get started:

I appreciate your ....
I fell in love with you because I admire your ....
What I'd like to learn from you is ....

When I first met you, the thing I like the most was ....
One thing I like about you physically is ....
One thing I like about your personality is ....
I really enjoy it when you ....
If we were to break up, or if I were to lose you, what I would miss most
    about you would be your ....
I know I don't tell you often enough that I ....
I love you because ....

Make your list as long as you like. Then take turns sharing it with your partner. Hold hands and look into each other's eyes as you read your list. Start each sentence with an "I" statement. For example: "I appreciate the fact that you're a wonderful mother to our children, your generosity, your beautiful smile, and the way my arm fits so perfectly around your waist when we dance together." You decide how intimate to make your list.

After you hear your partner read his or her list to you, find some way to say "thank you."

HELP—MY RELATIONSHIP IS OVERDRAWN!

Appreciation statements make your relationship stronger. Think of your marriage as if it were a checking account. Each deposit is an appreciation statement and each withdrawal is a criticism. When we're dating we make lots of deposits. Each compliment, bouquet of roses, loving gesture, and thoughtful note results in dividends. You build your emotional equity with tenderness, respect, and kindness. Most couples amass a fortune in goodwill when they're dating.

Think of criticism, rudeness, impatience, and selfishness as withdrawals from your account. It's simple mathematics—if your withdrawals exceed your deposits, your account will be overdrawn.

To get your emotional checkbook into the plus column and generate a healthy return for your investment, you must change the negative/positive ratio so that you make at least *three times* as many deposits as withdrawals.

Is your relationship criticism-focused? Are you insensitive to each other's needs? If so, your relationship will soon be overdrawn. Intimacy doesn't flourish in unfriendly settings. Before we can talk about extraordinary sex, you must get your emotional balance out of the red.

MAKE A WISH LIST

Experiencing extraordinary sex becomes its own reward, but, as with all good things, it takes some effort. It's the little things that really make the difference. Remember that appreciation list? It's now time to write your wish list. Make a list (as long as you can) and complete this sentence:

I wish you would (do or say) ....

Specify when, how often, and any other features of the wish that are important to you. For example: "One time during the next week, without my asking, I'd like you to come home and greet me with a big hug and a smile."

Make sure you don't use this list as a way of being critical with your partner. ("I wish you wouldn't be such a slob" is NOT what is intended here.) Something like "I wish you would take me out to dinner one time over then next two weeks" or "I wish you would climb into the shower with me and wash my back" is more like it.

Make your requests reasonable, timely, and not overly burdensome. For example, don't ask your partner to paint the house this weekend or do a special striptease every night. The more reasonable the wish, the more likely it will be granted.

Make *three* wishes and the rules are that your partner will agree to grant you *one* wish of his or her choosing. Don't be greedy. One wish granted is a great start.

When you agree to grant your partner's wish, treat this as a sacred bond. It's vitally important that you not disappoint your partner. It's better to renegotiate the terms than to blow off the entire deal. If you don't feel you can make dinner three times next week, negotiate to two times, but then make sure you keep your word.

Part of what's happening in this exercise is caring enough to listen to your lover and showing them they're worth some effort.

INGREDIENT #2: ASSERT YOUR NEEDS AND RESPECT EACH OTHER'S BOUNDARIES

Communication can definitely be sexy. Sexual initiative is about taking equal responsibility for sexual pleasure. Communicating needs, hopes, and erotic desires is central to experiencing your vital connection and extraordinary sex.

When you're making love, if something is especially pleasant or uncomfortable it's important to let your lover know. Most people say, "I assumed he could tell I was uncomfortable from my body language or facial expressions—what do I have to do, paint him a picture?" The answer is an emphatic yes. When partners are involved in their own passion of the moment, they may not be attending to your subtle or even not so subtle nuances.

Most couples find it easier to be clear about their preferences and expectations *out of* bed than *in* bed. They'll tell someone if their cigarette smoke is bothering them, or if they feel someone's driving too fast, or if they're annoyed because someone cut into the ticket line as they waited patiently. It's human nature to self-protect and to self-assert, but somehow this gets lost in the bedroom.

In our naked vulnerability, it's more difficult to reveal our preferences. There's a risk of upsetting the mood or dampening the enthusiasm, but withholding honest communication can be deadly.

Dishonesty destroys intimacy. It's amazing how many people justify "faking" pleasure during sex. If you start faking orgasm or faking what you like early on in your relationship, when will you stop? Taking the initiative requires sexual confidence, which is really a state of mind. It's about having the courage and self-awareness to be honest about who you are and what you want in and out of bed. The pulses and the minuses. The earlier you're honest, the better. But it's never too late to begin. Honesty is at the heart of genuine intimacy—not just with your partner but with yourself.

NO MATTER WHERE YOU GO, THERE YOU ARE

There is a Sufi tale called "The Red Lion" that tells of an Arabic prince who finally decided to face his fears. The prince had tried to run away from three different lions until he realized that wherever he went, there was always another lion waiting for him. Once he confronted his fear of lions, he obtained his freedom.

This story calls up for the reader the liberating possibilities of facing one's feelings. Until we meet our feelings head-on, we waste immense energy attempting to evade, obscure, or defend against them.

Imagine this scene: You're standing on a crowded bus and someone steps on your foot. You assume it was done accidentally and try to ignore the action. A few seconds later, the same person steps on your foot again. This time you're becoming perturbed, but you suppress your annoyance. When the same event happens for the third time you lose your patience and turn to the person, ready to tell him off. What you see is an old man carrying a white cane and accompanied by a Seeing Eye dog. What happens to your anger? The anger subsides as your assumptions are corrected, but your foot is still throbbing.

This example illustrates two important points. The first is that our assumptions structure our expectations. And second, whether something is intentional or unintentional, it can still result in pain.

The other half of self-assertion is self-protection. Respecting each other's boundaries. Letting your partner know when you're hurt, especially when the hurts are small, will dilute the intensity of anger and enhance the intimacy between you. Too many couples don't resolve issues when they are relatively minor, allowing them to fester until they eventually erupt.

Saying, "I was hurt by that comment" or "I'd like it if you wouldn't correct my grammar in public" is an important part of being sexual. Honest communication involves risk taking and vulnerability on the part of the sender, and concern on the part of the receiver. Couples who have extraordinary sex are experts at correcting mistaken assumptions and caring enough to apologize when they're wrong.

WAYNE AND ABBY: A CASE OF MISTAKEN ASSUMPTIONS

Many people, even those with basically good sex lives, operate under mistaken assumptions about what their partners really desire. Following the birth of their second child, Wayne, a dominant Lion, was interested in resuming sex with his wife, Abby, a shy, retiring Bear. The last trimester had been a difficult one for her and they hadn't had intercourse in nearly three months. Wayne had been patient, but was coming to the end of his tolerance. Masturbation had been a good temporary outlet for him over the dry spell, but he eagerly looked forward to the "real thing."

One evening, after six-week-old Meredith was finally asleep, Wayne initiated lovemaking. Abby was a bit nervous but tried not to show it. After all this time, she was worried about disappointing him. It's been Abby's style to put her own feelings on hold and focus on pleasing Wayne.

He reached out to her and his touch felt wonderful. Abby surprised herself with her body's responsiveness. They kissed passionately like long-lost lovers. When it came to penetration, however, Abby felt some discomfort. Wayne asked, "Is everything all right?" Abby said things were fine.

As he penetrated, she felt dry and tight. It's common for women in the postpartum period who are breast-feeding to experience some vaginal dryness. But again, being true to her Bearness, Abby was silent about her discomfort.

Wayne was too aroused to notice Abby's dryness. He ejaculated inside of her and, physically satisfied, drifted off to sleep, but Abby was awake a good part of the night. Her genital area burned and she felt sore from the friction.

Three days later, Wayne approached her again and the scenario was identical. Again, Abby kept her discomfort to herself. After a few more uncomfortable episodes, Abby began to avoid sex. She used the typical complaints of "headache, fatigue, or backache" because she didn't want to tell Wayne the truth. Her fear was that he'd get angry and take it personally.

By the time they came to see me, Abby had developed hypo-desire and was rarely interested in sex. Meredith was now six months old and was sleeping through the night. Despite the fact that they had much more time alone together, sex continued to be infrequent.

As difficult as it was, Abby had to learn to assert her needs and protect her boundaries. I suggested she incorporate a water-soluble lubricant into their lovemaking and that she not have penetration until she felt ready.

When she finally got the courage to tell Wayne about her vaginal discomfort, he was relieved. He had been puzzled by her lack of sexual interest, but now everything made sense.

The next time they made love, Abby brought out the lubricant and asked Wayne to run it under warm water to remove the chill. Wayne put the lubrication on Abby gently and lovingly. He added some playful cunnilingus to further lubricate her with his saliva. Abby applied some of the same lubrication to Wayne's penis. It felt wonderful to him and he got a firm erection. Then she caressed his scrotum, the inside of his thighs, and the shaft of his penis. Being more active in showing Wayne what she enjoys is something new for Abby. She's been accustomed to having Wayne make all the moves.

When Abby was ready, she gently held his penis and moved it back and forth across the opening of her vagina in ways that felt good to her. She stroked his penis along her clitoris, along the large and small lips surrounding her vagina, and across her vaginal opening again. Abby established a pace that was comfortable for her and Wayne cooperated fully.

When she was ready, she assisted Wayne in inserting his penis until it was completely inside of her. She made certain to be sensitive to her body's signals. Abby told Wayne that she would let him know if anything was uncomfortable from now on. So far, so good.

With Abby in control, she was able to relax and really enjoy sex with Wayne for the first time in over six months. Over time she was able to feel comfortable with Wayne assuming a more active role.

The next time you make love with your partner, pay attention to the feelings that are especially pleasurable and make sure to tell your partner if anything is uncomfortable. Using verbal or nonverbal communication, show him or her how you like to be touched. Vary the pressure, location, or intensity of touch. Put your hand on his hand and move it in a way that feels nice to you.

If you can't be honest and direct with your lover, who can you be honest with? Practice the following exercise to increase your ability to assert and self-protect.

EXERCISES FOR INGREDIENT #2: "I" STATEMENTS AS INTIMACY ENHANCERS

"I" statements are frequently recommended by therapists as an excellent way to express your feelings without blaming or inviting defensiveness from your partner. Although using "I" statements involves the risk of rejection, they are certain to increase your intimacy.

Imagine this example: You see an old friend and she says, "We really should do lunch sometime soon." How do you feel? Do you feel a personal connection? Do you really feel she wants to have lunch with you?

Now imagine this invitation instead: "I'd love to have lunch with you next week. Can you make it?" Much more intimate, isn't it?

Couples usually communicate indirectly by saying, "Let's go to the movies" or "What would you like for dinner?" or "Would you like to fool around?" or they may say, "You never touch my breast right" or "You're always too rough with me." Instead of making "you" statements, try to phrase your statements starting with "I." Say, "I'd like it if you'd brush your lips across my shoulders" or "I'd like it if you'd stroke my hair." It's a much clearer way to communicate.

Over the next week, make an effort to express some "I" statements to your partner and you'll notice an immediate improvement in your intimacy.

Practice using "I" statements. Complete the following sentences and share them with your lover:

I feel happy when ....
I feel sad when ....
I feel safe when ....
I am afraid that ....
I look forward to ....
When I'm hurt, I react by ....
What I'd like to change about myself is ....
What I need most from you is ....
What I like best about you is ....

Take turns sharing and listening. These sentences are only meant as conversation *starters*. Feel free to let the conversations unfold. Make sure to listen attentively and respectfully when your partner is sharing and thank one another for their gift to you.

INGREDIENT #3:
BREAK OUT OF OLD PATTERNS STARTING TODAY

The world of reality has its limits;
the world of imagination is boundless.

—JEAN-JACQUES ROUSSEAU

Newton's theory of inertia states that objects at rest stay at rest, and objects in motion stay in motion. Many couples share a benign inertia, a blissful boredom, each being afraid to upset the tenuous balance. The most difficult move to make is the first move, but once it's made you establish a momentum.

We are creatures of habit. Many old habits can be comforting, but some are damaging. Each day we shower and towel off the same way, comb our hair the same way, and drive to work the same way. There's no danger there. But unfortunately most of us also have sex the same way and at the same time of day. Once we figure out a "formula" for making him or her orgasm, we wear it out.

Laziness and fear of failure are at the heart of diminished spontaneity. Instead of putting in the energy it takes to tune into yourself and your lover, we rely on old standby techniques.

Angelica, a twenty-five-year-old actress, has been married for only four months. Her husband, Neal, a thirty-year-old writer of screenplays, thinks things are "fine" between them. "I'm not sure what's wrong with me," said Angelica. "Neal is a good lover, but I feel so sad when we make love. The tears run down my cheeks after I have an orgasm. I can't describe it but I feel *replaceable.*"

Angelica revealed that she feels interchangeable with any other vagina. "It's as though I'm lying next to a person who doesn't experience me as a unique human being."

How does this happen? It begins when curiosity is replaced by complacency. Instead of looking at every little freckle or marveling at the cute dimples on her butt, you switch to automatic pilot and touch automatically. Going through the motions makes you feel mechanical and your partner feel like a machine.

Sexual routines can begin as early as the honeymoon. He figures out how to give her an orgasm and she figures out how to give him an ejaculation and that's it. The mystery is over. If you're not careful, you'll begin to treat each other like objects of gratification, and not lovers. This objectification separates partners from their intimacy and from their vital connection. When couples feel replaceable, not unique, sex loses its vital connection—the mind, body, and spiritual union that makes sex extraordinary.

MY BREASTS BETRAYED ME

Donald, a thirty-five-year-old Lion, and Kate, a twenty-nine-year-old stay-at-home Bear/Bee and mother of three, have been married ten years. Donald, a commercial airline pilot, flew fighter jets in the Air Force. Over the last two years Donald has become concerned that their sexual relationship is going downhill.

"Kate seems so cold to me," said Donald. "I try to reach out and make love to her, but she doesn't seem interested, especially when I touch her breasts. She just pulls away."

Kate sat quietly at first with her face turned away from Donald, but then spoke. "It's your temper. Whenever I don't give you what you want, you blow up at me. I'm afraid of you and the kids are afraid of you."

Donald was trained to be tough. His father was a career military officer, and Donald grew up as an "army brat" moving from barracks to barracks. He had to learn to make friends quickly and let them go just as fast. Penetrate and withdraw.

"When you want sex, I feel I have no choice but to give you what you want," said Kate.

Donald looked at her in disbelief. "I thought you *liked* the way I make love to you?"

"Not all the time," answered Kate. "I haven't been honest with you."

From their individual sexual histories, I learned that Kate was born in the Bahamas and had six brothers and five sisters. When she was thirteen years old, her uncle sexually molested her. "He touched my breasts, but not down below," said Kate. "He used to babysit for me and when I'd go to bed he'd lie down next to me and start fondling my breasts. I pretended to be asleep. He told me if I ever told anyone he'd kill me or hurt my mother. I was really scared.

"When I was fifteen, I heard he was killed in a car accident. I felt so guilty, but I wept for joy." Kate sobbed as she spoke. "I never told my mother or anyone else because I was afraid they'd blame me." Kate had also kept this secret from Donald.

Two years ago, Donald and Kate had a baby boy. Their third son. Kate breast-fed him and during the breast-feeding had an orgasm. She felt terribly guilty. Memories of her uncle flooded in.

"I felt that my breasts had betrayed me," she said. "All of these years I'd felt numb in my breasts, and now my baby was making me have these terrible feelings."

Kate stopped breast-feeding, but didn't say why. From that time on, she shut off her sexual feelings toward Donald and wouldn't let him touch her breasts.

Kate was completely unaware how the sexual molestation had played itself out.

The first thing I did was to tell Kate that as many as one-third of all women experience pleasurable sensations and even orgasm while breast-feeding. Oxytocin, a hormone that aids in uterine contractions, is released when the baby sucks, helping the uterus to return to its prepregnancy size. I also commended her on her attempts to protect herself from her uncle's advances by feigning sleep or numbness. Unfortunately, sometimes the arousal mechanism gets stuck in the "off" position and is difficult to turn back on without reexperiencing the unpleasant feelings associated with the initial incident.

Donald was unaware of all of this. He had been blaming himself for not being a good lover to Kate. I encouraged Kate to be truthful with Donald and share her secrets.

Much to her surprise and relief, Donald was supportive and loving. They practiced the "Stop, Look, and Listen" technique, and Donald empathized with his wife's painful history. Now, instead of taking Kate's lack of desire personally, he understood.

They put genital sex and breast touching on hold, and Donald agreed that Kate would decide when to initiate. They interrupted their old patterns, and Kate took the time she needed while Donald gave her abundant love.

Within a few months, the flames of passion returned. Donald and Kate began to make *love* for the first time in a very long time.

SWITCHING PLACES

This exercise will give you an opportunity to see things through your partner's eyes and break out of old patterns.

Ask yourself these questions: Who is the usual initiator of lovemaking? Who is usually on top? Who takes the lead and moves things from gentle caressing to more passionate exploration or penetration? Who is more verbal, demonstrative, or appreciative?

This exercise will challenge your ability to reverse roles and take on your partner's character. It may be a stretch, but it will open your eyes to a whole new set of options.

To structure this experience, take two sheets of paper, one for each of you. At the top, write three headings. Beneath the headings list one or two of your typical behaviors when you make love and one or two of your partner's usual behaviors. Agree that the next time you make love, you'll reverse roles.

My Usual Role	My Partner's Usual Role	My Agreement
I wait to be invited	He invites	Next time we make love, I'll initiate
I prefer sex that's intense and passionate	He likes it slow and sensuous	Next time I'll slow it way down!
I usually listen to my lover talk sexy	He usually talks sexy to me	Next time, I'll be the one to say some "naughty" things

WRITING YOUR LAST EROTIC LOVE LETTER

Another exercise is writing your last erotic love letter. In these technology-intensive days of E-mail, fax, and voice mail, there are times when only a written letter will do. Letters are lasting evidence and can be read and re-read as a testimonial of the past. Written words can shed light on our innermost feelings and express them with amazing power.

The instructions for this exercise are to imagine that you're driving alone along a quiet country road. Suddenly you encounter a severe blizzard. Your wipers get caked with ice, you lose visibility, and skid into a ditch. The snow is rapidly accumulating and begins to cover your car. The gas tank is nearly empty and the temperature is falling. You have no cell phone and begin to fear you may not survive.

You think of your partner and the last moments you had together. Next to you on the seat are a few scraps of paper and a pencil. Write your last erotic love letter to your special someone. Share what they mean to you and what you've always wanted to say. Tell them what you want them to know, what you'll miss, and what you hope they'll remember about you. This could be your last communication before your death.

Although this is a difficult exercise, the couples who have entered into it seriously have found that it has helped them break out of old patterns and become aware of what they really mean to one another.

In a crisis, we are drawn together. Some people who have lost a loved one or have had a near-death experience say they are forever changed. It would be impossible to live our days with this kind of intensity, but this exercise helps to shake you out of your routine.

Write your letters separately and then read them aloud to each other. Sincerity is important. Be yourself and express your feelings naturally. Don't be afraid to let your emotions come forth. It doesn't have to be long—here, as always, it's quality not quantity that counts. Make sure to thank your partner for this precious gift.

The following are examples of erotic love letters from Michael and LouAnn:

My love,

I'm afraid this may be the last time I can touch you with my words. If it is the last time, then it should also be the song of each moment that

I have been with you. What is my life? It is the source of my breath and the beater of my heart. God gives us but one moment and guarantees no other. If I wait for the next or pine for the last moment, I will have lost this one.

As I sit here, reflecting on our time together, I regret all the wasted moments. Times when I should have loved you, instead of being at the office earning more money. I reflect on your beauty and on the love I feel for you and on how much I will miss you. Together we melt into the moment. I know I have not told you enough how much I love the softness of your skin and those deep brown eyes. After twenty-eight years, looking into them takes me back to the very first time I saw you at your brother's house. When I look at you, fire ignites my heart. I fear that I haven't told you this enough, and I hope that you get this letter.

My love for you is really about how we can be separate and together at the same time, and how we play in that space of difference and sameness. Our love is about this magic as well as the beauty of your elegant neck, the brilliance of your smile, how your body feels beneath mine, and the sound of your voice, all at once sweet child, scarlet temptress, songbird, and scholar. It is about how you make an idea, an omelet, or a kiss, into an experience of Eternity for me.

If I should live, my pledge to you is to cherish each moment as much as humanly possible, and never again to willfully choose work over play with you, my sweet LouAnn. This pledge is now and forever.

Yours,
Michael

Dearest Michael,

I'm so cold and afraid. There's little daylight left, so I must write quickly. My fingers are getting too numb to hold this pencil. What a fool I've been. I feel so alone right now. You have always been the most important person in my life and I know that I haven't told you that. Instead of spending time with you, I've wasted so many precious moments doing foolish inconsequential things.

More than anything else, I want you to know how important you've been to me. Your patience, compassion, support, and friendship. You are my dearest friend. Forgive me for the stupid things I've said in anger and my failure to be sensitive to your feelings. My selfishness often gets the best of me. I'm sorry for turning away from you so many times in bed. I wish I hadn't done so.

It's funny how we don't appreciate what we have until we're about to lose it. I have so many regrets. I regret not telling you that you're the most important person in my life. I regret not making love to you more often. I regret not opening myself to you more completely. I regret not kissing you one more time before I left on this trip.

You are the one who has made me feel worthwhile and I'll always be grateful to you for that. Thank you for sharing your love with me.

Forever,
LouAnn

INGREDIENT #4:
TREAT EACH OTHER LIKE COMPANY

Surround yourself with people who respect and treat you well.

—CLAUDIA BLACK

An essential ingredient in extraordinary sex is to remember to periodically treat each other as well as when you both first met. This is no small task.

Many people treat strangers or their pets better than their partner. If we bump into someone on the street, it's polite to say "Excuse me." This politeness is unfortunately absent from many long-term relationships. There's a myth that once you're in a committed relationship, you can relax, kick back, and finally *be yourself.* For some partners this translates into a lack of consideration. They believe that once you're a committed couple you can make rude digestive noises, slather yourself in cold cream before going to bed, forget to brush your teeth, and still expect sex to be scintillating!

When we have company over for dinner we make sure things look lovely. We seve the meal on our best china, put the good towels in the guest bathroom, put flowers on the table, light candles, have the right mood music playing in the background, and prepare our most delicious meals. We usually put on our party attire, greet our guests warmly, and make sure the television is shut off. During the evening, if one of our guests tells a joke we've heard before, we listen attentively. If the phone should ring during dinner, we'll probably let the answering machine pick it up.

Do you treat your lifelong partner as well as this? If your answer is "yes," congratulations! You're in the minority. Instead of saving the best for our guests, let's treat each other like company.

This point is beautifully illustrated by a story of M. Scott Peck. He recounts a tale of a rabbi and an abbot who became friends. One day, before taking his leave, the rabbi tells the abbot, "Even though only a few monks remain in your monastery, the Messiah is one of you." In the months that followed, all of the monks wondered whether the rabbi's words were true. They pondered whether the rabbi referred to Father Abbot, their leader, or Brother Thomas, a truly holy man. Perhaps it was Brother Eldred or Brother Philip? As they considered who the Messiah might be, the old monks began to treat each other with a new and deep respect. After all, one of them might be the Messiah!

Maybe it would be unrealistic and too much of a stretch to treat each other like company *every* day. After all, we don't have company every day. But what about once a week—or once a month? You decide how often and then stick by your plan.

Another way to make one another feel special is to recapture the magic of the early days of your courtship. One way to do this is to start "dating again."

THE DATING GAME

If you follow the steps to this exercise to the letter, you're sure to have a special evening.

Ask your partner out for a date. The person who invites plans the evening. Plan your wardrobe as carefully as you did when you were dating. The right tie, the perfect fragrance, the special underwear. This takes some planning, but dress at a neighbor's house and knock on the door. It adds to the excitement.

Throughout the evening treat each other as if you were dating. Remember? Ask questions about your partner, their interests and ambitions. Most of all look at them when they speak and really listen to what they say. If you feel moved, hold hands or walk arm in arm.

If the date is a hit, you may kiss your partner good night at the door or invite him in for a nightcap.

GWEN AND SPENCE: LIVING AFTER CANCER

Gwen and Spence find that luxuriating in a bubble bath together is the perfect prelude to their special evening. They've discovered that the warmth of a shared bath can be one of life's simple pleasures.

Gwen and Spence decided to treat each other like company after Gwen's recent breast cancer surgery. "A catastrophic illness has a sobering way of drawing your attention to the ticking of the clock and changing your priorities," said Gwen. "Spence and I are determined not to waste one more precious moment."

Instead of working themselves into a frazzle and taking one or two weeks of vacation each year, Gwen and Spence take fifty-two days of vacation a year—one day a week. Their day is Wednesday. "We're both busy executives but we've promised ourselves to come home early on Wednesdays come hell or high water!" they say with a smile.

They set out their best dishes, bring home fresh flowers as a centerpiece, dance to their favorite song, "As Time Goes By," and feed each other grapes, strawberries, and other sensual foods. I know this sounds unbelievable, but Gwen and Spence are a *real* couple in their fifties and they make this adventure come alive every week.

Not everyone wants to put the same amount of planning or detail into their special evening and that's okay. It doesn't mean you should dismiss the whole idea, however. Maybe you can begin in a more modest way. Instead of planning an entire evening, set aside an hour to treat each other like company. Can you spare an hour?

Increase the sensuality of the moment by surrounding yourself with sights, fragrances, sounds, foods, experiences you love. If the spirit moves you, make love to each other as if it were your last time together. A disquieting thought, but it's certain to raise the temperature several degrees.

Take time to explore each other lovingly and attentively. Experiment with a variety of strokes and textures, including feathers, fabrics, rose petals, lavender. Gwen gathers rose petals and sprinkles them on their rug. "It makes me feel like the heroine in a romance novel." She laughs. "Spence makes love to me with every fiber of his body. It really does feel extraordinary."

This couple's determination to have extraordinary passion is inspiring. In their love and devotion to one another they've discovered endless possibilities for making sex unforgettable.

COMPLETE THE FOLLOWING SENTENCES AND DISCUSS THE WAYS YOU EACH WISH TO BE TREATED LIKE COMPANY:

1. If I wanted to treat my partner like company I would

....

(For example: I would take his coat when he walks through the door, serve a glass of wine, have his favorite meal ready.)

2. If I wanted to be treated like company, my partner would

....

(For example: He'd hold out my chair when I sat down at the table, bring me fresh flowers, listen to my conversations with interest.)

Then pick a date on the calendar, circle it, and make sure you practice treating each other like company on that night.

INGREDIENT #5: MAKE TIME FOR EACH OTHER

Look and you will find it—what is unsought will go undetected.

—SOPHOCLES

The most common excuse for not being more loving is "we're too tired or too busy for sex." By not making time for lovemaking, couples cheat themselves and their partners out of life's most memorable times. Frankly, after all is said and done and you're facing the end of your life, will you regret not having spent more time at the office? Probably not. Many of us foolishly believe that we'll make time for loving tomorrow, but tomorrow never comes.

This principle is portrayed by the Aesop fable "The Dog and the Shadow." A dog who had stolen a large bone was carrying it off to enjoy it without interference. As he crossed the bridge, he saw his reflection in the pool below. Thinking it was a dog with a larger bone, he snarled to grab it and dropped his own bone in the water. The dog went away hungrier than ever.

How many of us grab at shadows and then wonder why we feel so lonely and unsatisfied with our lover? When couples construct their lives so that they don't make time for passion, they lose the substance of their emotional intimacy. I tell couples to consider the epitaphs we might read as we walk through a cemetery: "Beloved mother," "Dearest father," "Loving husband," or "Cherished wife." Never do we see "John Jones, largest shareholder of IBM."

When I'm confronted with a couple who continually protest that there's just no time for loving, I'll ask the following question at the risk of being maudlin: "If you each discovered that you had only three months to live, how would you spend that time?" Invariably, partners say they would spend the time with those they love and perhaps travel together. Never, in all of my twenty-five years of practice, has anyone ever said that they'd spend their last hours on this earth buying new real estate or closing an important business deal.

CREATING AN OASIS FOR INTIMACY

If we wait for a time when there are no work pressures or outside distractions before we make love, we may be waiting for a very long time. Each of us needs to create an oasis for intimacy in our busy lives. Do you have time for a six-second kiss or a five-second embrace? That's a total of eleven seconds. What do you do at a red light? Do you sit there staring ahead waiting for the light to turn green? Why not give your partner a kiss or squeeze his hand and say something sexy? When you see couples kissing in the car ahead of yours, do you assume they must be kids in love or on a date? Why make that assumption? Follow their example! When you're in a restaurant, instead of sitting silently and reaching for the bread basket, why not reach for your partner's thigh under the table!

If sex is to be kept exciting and fresh, it should not become another chore. Where does lovemaking fit in on your priority list? After the dishes are washed or the garbage is emptied? During the late show or before the eleven o'clock news? Doesn't your relationship deserve more than sex sandwiched between two commercials?

You can clearly see that when I tell you to make time for each other, I'm only talking about a few moments of well-placed attention. All it takes is motivation and follow-through.

Making time for each other and creating an oasis for intimacy is critical to keeping sex fresh, vital, and extraordinary.

Try the following exercises to "spice up" your appreciation for your lover and enliven your erotic connection:

THE SPICE JARS

This is a great way to bring more pizzazz into your time together. Designate two jars marked "his" and "hers" as your *spice jars* and put them on the kitchen counter (or in the bedroom if you wish). Fill your jar with scraps of paper containing your wishes. Be creative and let your imaginations run wild. Some examples are: "I'd love a twenty-minute back massage," "Surprise me with breakfast in bed and . . . ," "Play strip poker with me," "Perform any sexual act I want for three minutes," "Lick the back of my knees," "Serve me dinner wearing only your briefs," "Leave a romantic note on my pillow," "Neck with me at the movies"—you get the picture.

Whenever you'd like a little excitement, make sure you're partner is agreeable and reach into his or her spice jar to select one of their erotic wishes. If you chance on something that you feel uncomfortable doing, that's okay. You can reach in again until you find something that's acceptable to you. The fun part of this is that you know it's something your partner has requested, so there's no mind reading or fear of rejection.

The point is to spice up your relationship, stretch your security zones, and introduce some new imaginative opportunities to your usual sexual repertoire.

SEX MARKS THE SPOT

This is an exercise that will break the monotony, but will take some planning. It's a sexual "treasure hunt" that I call a "pleasure hunt." Start with a message that gives the first clue. It can be scrawled in lipstick on the bathroom mirror or taped to the front door. When your partner follows the last clue, you'll be waiting as the ultimate prize.

Bonnie and Fitz play "sex marks the spot" and go on a pleasure hunt at least once a month. They take turns writing the clues. One of Fitz's favorite times started with a Post-It on the microwave that told him to go to the refrigerator and open it. Inside there was a bottle of champagne labeled "get two wineglasses out of the cupboard." The wineglasses had instructions to go to the third drawer in Bonnie's lingerie chest. Fitz found a pair of silk briefs with instructions to put them on and meet Bonnie in the family room.

Bonnie had arranged a blanket in front of the fireplace and had a basket of toys and sensual goodies waiting to be sampled.

Other couples enjoy playing blind man's bluff and take their partner to a surprise getaway. Can you imagine the look on your neighbor's face when he sees your husband blindfolded next to you in the car?

PLAYING DOCTOR

Did you ever play "I'll show you mine if you show me yours"? Children are insatiably curious about so many things, including their bodies and what feels good to them. Unfortunately, many of us grow up thinking it's dirty or wrong to feel pleasure in our genitals. This can lead to a shutting down of our natural pleasure responses. "Playing doctor" reawakens healthy curiosity.

Make yourself comfortable and take some time to really look at your lover. Looking can be very erotic. After touching with your eyes, touch with your fingertips—touch with the sensitivity of a blind person, as if you were reading braille. Take time to lovingly "examine" all of your partner. See what you can discover.

If you feel more comfortable wearing some clothing at first, that's fine. Set the stage so you feel relaxed and let your imagination lead you.

MAGIC CARPET

For those couples who enjoy acting out a fantasy, this is a perfect sensual escape. The only limit to your adventure is your imagination. Perhaps Hawaii is your dream escape but your budget won't cooperate. No problem—get creative. Buy two pineapples, some paper flowers to string together for your lei, some Hawaiian music, and *voilà!* Hawaii! It can be lots of fun to choreograph your getaways. Think of how easily you can transform your living room into an Italian bistro or a French patisserie. And only your imagination will limit how you decide to enjoy your pastries!

AFTERNOON DELIGHT

Arrange to meet at home some afternoon to spend some time together. If your budget can handle it, meet in a hotel with a large Jacuzzi and order room service.

CREATE A PLEASURE CHEST

Another simple idea to bring some passion into your usual routine is to build a pleasure chest together. Go shopping for your favorite lotions and make sure you both like the fragrances. The shop owners may not be delighted that you're sampling all their wares, but it's lots of fun. Buy a large basket and fill it with your selections: scented candles, incense, CDs or tapes, sensuous oils or lotions, favorite lingerie, erotic poetry or videos, vibrators, or body massagers. Keep your pleasure chest close by so you'll have everything you need for sexual bliss at your fingertips.

INGREDIENT #6: FOCUS ON PLEASURE, NOT MEASURE

Life is what happens while you are making other plans.

—JOHN LENNON, 1980

Ron and Amanda have been planning their Labor Day vacation for months. Both of them are highly organized Bees with a carefully developed itinerary.

Amanda tends to be less obsessive than Ron, but has a large dose of compulsivity nonetheless. They've each completed their respective chores in preparation for the trip. Stop the mail, kennel the dog, hold the newspaper delivery, ask the neighbor to put out the garbage, water the plants, and turn on the lawn sprinkler—one by one, they've crossed the items off their enormous lists. Lights off, timer on, windows locked, security system armed, garage door down, and they're finally off.

Ron and Amanda haven't been away together for almost a year. As they pull out of the driveway, map in hand, they worry that they've "forgotten something" but decide to leave to "beat the traffic."

Instead of taking the back roads, Ron opts for the superhighway. Unfortunately, everyone else seems to have the same idea. The roads are jammed with vacationers and they wind up in bumper-to-bumper traffic. "Should we take an exit and explore some antique shops?" they consider. But no, no time. Their vacation awaits.

And so it goes. Instead of taking the scenic route and enjoying the countryside, Ron and Amanda rush to their predetermined vacation destination. The end of this story is all too familiar. They arrive at the hotel, exhausted and tense, unpack their bags, and declare the official "start" of their vacation. As they open their luggage to put on their swimsuits, dark clouds begin to roll in. They turn on the weather report to hear "rain for the next three days." Their plans for swimming, boating, golfing are dashed. According to them, their vacation is "ruined."

The same scenario occurs for them sexually. Unless things go *exactly* as scheduled, sex doesn't happen. Both have lengthy to-do lists that have to be completed before they're in the mood for sex.

"We seem to be having sex less and less often," Ron told me during our first session. "The kids have to be asleep. I can't have an early business meeting. We need to both take a shower. We need at least forty-five minutes, and I can't feel rushed." Amanda has an equally daunting list: "Dinner dishes washed and put away, kids' homework done, fresh linen on the bed, and Ron *must* shave." With this list of prerequisites, it's a wonder they managed to have sex at all! Do they ever enjoy a furtive unplanned romp in the hay? Not this couple.

Ron and Amanda are more interested in measure than pleasure. Instead of allowing themselves to be immersed in the pleasure of the moment, they get distracted by a host of structural and contextual "requirements" which rob the experience of its goodness. Intent on doing things "by the book," they forgot the real purpose of their time together. Instead of thinking of their rainy vacation as a miserable failure, they could have seen it as a time to sleep late, explore a museum, eat at a different restaurant, or share some intimate conversation.

The assignment I gave Ron and Amanda was to practice absorbing themselves in pleasure. To notice the subtleties of lovemaking and to put aside their voluminous lists of "shoulds."

Thich Nnat Hanh, a Vietnamese Buddhist monk, speaks about living fully in this way: "Even when you are walking along a path leading into a village, you can practice being fully awake . . . if you are awake you will experience the path, the path leading into the village. You practice this by keeping this one thought alive—I am walking along the path, the path leading into the village." He instructs us to open our hearts by considering each step with infinite wonder and joy. *(Being Peace,* 1987.)

Now, I'm not suggesting that we all become Buddhist monks to have extraordinary sex, but *focusing* on joy is central to *experiencing* joy. Unrealistic overly rigid *concepts* of the "perfect" vacation, anniversary, or orgasm block the pathways to pleasure. Whether it's the strings of a Mozart concerto, a beautiful sunset, or the feel of your lover's skin, being fully present is at the heart of bliss.

APPROACH SEX AS AN EXPERIENCE, NOT AN ACHIEVEMENT

Think about the language we use to describe sex: *achieving* hot sex, *having* orgasms, *making* her climax, *getting* erect or turned-on. Where's the pleasure?

Many of us think of sex as something we do *to* one another instead of something we enjoy *with* one another. If you and your partner are caught up in this mind-set, it might help to think of sex in a different way, like dancing—I've always felt that dancing was an excellent metaphor for sex. Many years ago Alan Watts said, "We don't dance to get to the other side of the dance floor." The purpose of the dance is simply to dance.

Another achievement we strive for is the "perfect body." The following exercise has been helpful in addressing this concern.

MIRROR MIRROR

Mirror mirror is a wonderful exercise to reduce the tendency of measuring our bodies against some standard. It's often difficult to accept and love our bodies, especially if they fall short of the ideal. Women and men have expectations about body size and shape that affect the ability to receive and enjoy being touched.

I suggest that couples take a good long look at themselves. It may sound silly, but try it. What do you focus on? Do you immediately look at your flaws and imperfections or can you find areas that you like? If you immediately say, "My rear is too big" or "My penis is too small," ask yourself, "Who says?" and "Too big or small for what?" Whom are you allowing to define your ideal proportions?

Learning to cultivate a body-positive attitude is essential to enjoying extraordinary sex. Think about how proud parents show off photos of their children. To them, these are the most beautiful children in the world. That's because they love them. Do we treat ourselves as kindly? I suggest you look at your body through the eyes of a loving friend or parent.

Some couples will stand in front of the mirror together. Initially it may feel awkward or uncomfortable, but it's a good way to enhance your intimacy. Take turns telling each other what you like about the other's body. If you feel too embarrassed being completely nude, leave on some articles of clothing at first. Dim the lights or light candles. Most important, don't argue with your partner when they say, "I love your buns." Just say "thank you."

ISAAC AND HIS STOPWATCH

Isaac, an unmarried forty-year-old international marketing consultant, arranges for an appointment with me to "ask me some sex-related questions." As he walks in, I think, "Hmmm. Well dressed, nice-looking, just the right amount of cologne, and a warm handshake . . . what kind of sexual questions does he have?"

"I know this will sound foolish," he begins, "but I just had to ask an expert. I can last two minutes and fifteen seconds before I ejaculate and I've got to know if this is normal."

"How do you know?" I asked. "Do you keep a stopwatch by your bed?" He laughed nervously, but I wasn't trying to be funny. "Is sex pleasurable for you?" He looked puzzled, as if he were thinking, "What does pleasure have to do with how long I can last?"

Sitting with his limbs folded in a rigid posture, Isaac seemed self-conscious and uncomfortable. He described feeling sexually inhibited with Charlotte, his current partner. "I'm afraid that she's not having an orgasm because I ejaculate too quickly."

Like many men, Isaac was focused on quantity, not quality.

"The size of a penis or actual length of penetration is less important to sexual satisfaction than what goes on in your mind," I tell him. "It's relatively easy to learn to control the speed of your ejaculation through the stop-start method or other well-known techniques. What you're missing is pleasure."

Isaac agreed. Since he was an expert at noticing his erection and the time of ejaculation, I suggested he take this attention to detail and focus on other things. "Pay attention to the way Charlotte's skin feels, her smell, taste, and warmth. For one week, I'd like you to focus only on your pleasure." I also gave him instructions to practice the stop-start approach found in Bernie Zilbergeld's book *The New Male Sexuality*.

Not only did Isaac learn how to delay his orgasm; he discovered something more important—his focus on enjoying Charlotte deepened his own pleasure, *and* hers.

A goal-oriented, detailed approach spells success in business but usually leads to failure in the bedroom. When your goals overshadow pleasure, they dampen sexual enthusiasm and divert your attention from what matters.

We're a society that loves to compare and evaluate. We have rating systems for everything from restaurants and hotels to mutual funds and films. It's natural to ask, "How good was it this time?" Instead of focusing on measure and wondering if she had a five-star orgasm, focus on your own pleasure and you'll heighten the passion for both of you.

EXTRAORDINARY SEX TRANSCENDS EVALUATION

When sex is extraordinary, it transcends evaluation and measurement. The choices you make about what to think about or what to notice are directly related to the intensity of your arousal. Instead of playing ophthalmologist with each other—"Is it better this way or that way? clearer, sharper, brighter?"—you need to trust your partner to let you know what they want. In the meantime, just relax and enjoy your intimacy.

In my sex video *Ordinary Couples, Extraordinary Sex,* Hue, forty-eight years old, gave her partner Larry this sage advice: "Slow down as much as you can, then cut it in half, and you'll be in the right vicinity for extraordinary sex."

Focusing on pleasure, not measure, demands a cognitive readjustment. We hear it and say, "Sure, that makes sense." But then we get distracted and go back to the quantitative approach: longer, harder, and wetter. I guarantee that if you change your focus, and immerse yourself in pleasure, you'll have better sex than you ever imagined possible.

Another Aesop fable that's appropriate here is "The Lioness and the Vixen." An assortment of animals boast about their large families. A Lioness listens carefully, but keeps silent. The shrewd fox, who has had a litter of seven, asks the Lioness, "How many offspring do you have at birth?" "Only one," replies the Lioness quietly. "But that one is a *Lion!*" The moral of this story is identical to the message of this ingredient:

It's quality, not quantity, that really counts.

CHAPTER 22

SIX PREREQUISITES FOR SEXUAL SUCCESS

*It is possible to believe that all the past is but the
beginning of a beginning, and that all that is and has been is
but the twilight of the dawn. It is possible to believe that
all the human mind has ever accomplished is but the dream
before the awakening.*

—H. G. WELLS, 1902

Unless we live in a hermetically sealed jar, we know that all things change, nothing stays forever different. New-car smells fade away much too soon and annoying door dings mar the showroom finish.

As soon as you purchase your new cellular phone, your neighbor brandishes his smaller, lighter, more sophisticated model. Your powerful new computer is incredible, but if you just wait another month a speedier, more efficient one will be available.

There's a thrill that accompanies newness. The first crocus that heralds spring. The first kiss that awakens those early genital stirrings. The first love to steal your heart. Your first time with a new partner. But as we've discussed, "monkey sex" brings fleeting joys. Those who are obsessed with novelty may find themselves bedding and even wedding many partners in search of that new and improved orgasmic release.

And despite the undeniable passion that can accompany a new partner, most of us find serial monogamy an unsatisfying alternative to lifelong intimacy with our chosen soul mate. The greater challenge is to keep intimacy fresh and inviting over the years.

When couples ask me, "What's your success rate?" I tell them that it's *their* success, not mine. I give them the information, but the actual work is up to them. I have, however, identified six behaviors that are common to all clients who learn how to have Extraordinary Sex:

- **Motivation**
- **Commitment**
- **Facing your fears**
- **Daring to go first**
- **Seeking to understand**
- **Practicing often**

SUCCESS FACTOR #1: MOTIVATION

Motivation is that inner drive that moves you forward. It is an interest in trying something different. It means that you have a desire to make this relationship work and are willing to place it at the top of your priority list. If you're motivated to experience extraordinary sex and deepen your intimacy, you must be ready to put in the necessary time and work to make it happen. Yes, I said work. Where did we ever get the idea that we have to work for so many things in life, but not for intimacy? This is one of the greatest fallacies plaguing couples I treat. Somehow they got the idea that work ended after the courtship phase. Now that they're married, they think they can *finally* be themselves.

One of my clients summarized it this way: "I put on a business suit in the morning, make sure I'm on my best behavior all day, and need someplace to let it all hang out!" He thought he could come home, let down his hair, and say or do whatever he felt. He could burp without excusing himself, fail to be attentive or respectful to his lover, and the marriage would stay vital. Wrong.

Without motivation and a willingness to make a change in yourself, intimacy and sexual passion will soon become distant memories.

SUCCESS FACTOR #2: COMMITMENT

Motivation is only the first step. What happens when things don't go according to your plan? It seems like a great idea to make love more often, but it will only remain an idea unless you make it happen.

Your greatest power is the power of choice. Commitment means deciding to hang in there when the going gets rough. It doesn't mean bailing out with a new cutie as soon as the initial lust fades. When you're committed to your partner, you're determined to do whatever it takes to improve your relationship.

Commitment is a personal statement of your willingness to follow through with your vows to love each other until death. When you make that commitment, you're not saying, "I'll commit to you unless you lose your job, or you gain weight, or until someone more attractive comes along."

I marvel at how hard some couples work to save their marriage while others contemplate divorce as soon as the going gets tough. To evaluate your own commitment, ask yourself, "How determined am I to make my relationship better?" Rate your response on a scale of 0 to 5. I've found that couples who rate themselves at level 4 or higher tend to be more successful in therapy.

SUCCESS FACTOR #3: FACING YOUR FEARS

Remember, intimacy can be scary. It is something we simultaneously need and fear. We underestimate how difficult it is to be naked in body and soul. Revealing ourselves to our lover means risking the pain of rejection.

Sex becomes extraordinary when it goes beyond the physical to include the totality of ourselves. Without true intimacy, superficial sexual excitement fades rapidly.

Be on the look out for excuses like "We're too busy or too tired for sex." They're often just cover-ups for the fear of becoming intimate. When you're reluctant to be intimate, you may hear yourself saying: "It's late," "The kids aren't asleep," "I have a business meeting early in the morning," and so on. But it only takes a moment to look into your lover's eyes and say, "I love you." Excuses are so commonplace that we actually begin to believe them.

Let me ask you this, if you discovered that you won the lottery, would you be too tired to go get your prize?

Resolving the need/fear dilemma is at the heart of opening to extraordinary sex. *Great sex doesn't create intimacy; it grows out of it.* There is considerable risk in giving your body, heart, and soul to another—but the potential payoff is enormous.

SUCCESS FACTOR #4: DARING TO GO FIRST

Michael and Sara were childhood sweethearts and have been married for fourteen years. After years of struggling to get Michael through medical school and residency, they finally purchased their dream home in southwestern Connecticut complete with hot tub, tennis court, and au pair quarters. Now Sara, a part-time interior decorator, spends most of her time raising their two children, Amy and Joseph, while Michael, a successful Manhattan endocrinologist, evaluates and treats patients with hormonal problems. It's ironic that his specialty is the treatment of low or absent sexual desire, because that is now *his* problem.

For although he is respected by his patients and liked by his friends and has attained his picture-perfect home, all is not well. When he's not at work, he's either tending to his prize rose garden, perfecting his golf swing, or entertaining his friends in grand style. He's doing anything *except* making time for intimacy with Sara.

What went wrong? It's difficult to know which came first, but when Sara began to feel neglected by Michael she started to eat. At first the eating comforted her, but soon it got out of control. Michael began to complain about her weight, and the more he complained, the more she ate. Both Sara and Michael felt angry, hurt, and betrayed. Sara expected Michael to make the first move. "I just want him to spend some time at home and reach out to me sexually. Why should I bother to lose weight if he won't make love to me anyway?" Michael told me that he'd reach out to Sara. "But only if she loses some of that weight!"

Michael and Sara, in their mid-thirties, were trapped in a typical Mexican standoff. Each one was waiting for the other to make the first move.

Henry Lewis Stimson, a former U.S. statesman, was once quoted as saying, "The only way to make a man trustworthy is to trust him." When relationships have intimacy problems, there has frequently been an erosion in trust. This leads each partner to justify their position and deflect blame onto the other. Unless one person is willing to let go of being right long enough to make a positive difference, however, the relationship is destined to repeat its history. Dare to go first.

SUCCESS FACTOR #5: SEEKING TO UNDERSTAND

Seek to understand rather than to be understood.

—ST. FRANCIS OF ASSISI

Think of your last argument with your lover. What did you argue about? Maybe you were upset because these days he rarely tells you he loves you? Or you were annoyed that she spends hours talking on the telephone with her best friend? You may argue because her snoring keeps you awake all night, or because he asked you to shed those extra fifteen pounds.

Now think about *how* you argue. If you're like most couples, you probably make a detailed case on why his or her behavior frosts you. Before you can finish your point, you're probably interrupted by your partner's attempt to deflect, defend, or counterattack. No doubt this stimulates the launch of your next missile, and so it goes until the more articulate, persistent, or determined "prevails." But what did you win? In most instances, very little.

When Vicki and Chuck came to see me they said they wanted to liven up their sexual relationship, but each time they came to the office they were fighting about one thing or another. Once they fought because Vicki accused Chuck of making the ice cubes too small, and Chuck accused Vicki of not replacing the orange juice when she was the last one who finished the previous container.

As soon as one problem got solved, another would emerge in its place. One evening Vicki put her leftover meat loaf in the refrigerator expecting to have it for lunch the next day. To her surprise, Chuck had gotten up for a midnight snack and had eaten it. They fought for days about "his lack of consideration" and "her controlling behavior."

In all of their struggles, there was an unspoken theme: Do my feelings matter to you? When Vicki felt inconvenienced by Chuck's ice cube tray habit, she was asking, "Do you care that I'm upset?" When Chuck became annoyed at not having orange juice for breakfast, he was saying, "Do you care that I'm inconvenienced?"

It's natural to want to know that our feelings matter. If we were to be perfectly honest with ourselves, we'd admit that we're all fighting for *one thing*—to be understood. The problem is that *when we simultaneously struggle to be understood, there's no one left to understand.*

How many times have you said or thought, "He doesn't understand what I'm feeling?" During your next disagreement, what if your lover said, "Gee, honey, I didn't know you felt that way," or "Tell me more about how angry I made you today." Wouldn't that take the wind out of your sails?

You can't open your arms to your lover if they're folded across your chest protecting you. When you're busy making your case, it's hard to be receptive to your partner's point of view. Enabling empathy happens when you let go of your own position long enough to embrace your partner's point of view.

Carl Jung said, "If one does not understand a person, one tends to regard him as a fool." As each of you tries harder to understand than to be understood, the wisdom of loving will replace the ignorance of acrimony.

SUCCESS FACTOR #6: PRACTICING OFTEN

In the late seventies, Dr. Bill Masters advised his trainees, "Tell your couples that twenty-four hours must not go by without some sensual touching." We thought this was a fairly rigid prescription, but his sage advice has proven true. Couples who practice their intimacy skills with regularity and frequency are most successful in maintaining their progress years after therapy has come to an end.

Although one romantic weekend is a good start, don't assume it will permanently carry you to new erotic heights. By making time for *daily* loving, you'll create an environment where passionate intimacy becomes a way of life.

MAKING SEX EXTRAORDINARY AND KEEPING IT THAT WAY

By now I hope you realize that every one of us can have extraordinary sex. It only takes a willingness and a commitment to bring intimacy into your relationship.

Before I close I want to say a few words about children. Many of my couples tell me, "Sex went down the drain after the children came." There's no doubt that little ones impact on sexual spontaneity. But I'm a firm believer that they benefit from seeing their parents hug and kiss openly and often.

Too many couples don't hesitate to criticize their mates or call each other derogatory names in front of their kids. For some puzzling reason, they feel less comfortable about openly expressing affection. I am certain that if children saw more love and less hostility between their parents, they'd grow up to be better lovers.

So, while it's important to reserve the more passionate kissing and groping for behind closed doors (and don't forget to use your bedroom locks!), teaching our children respect for our partners and the importance of daily affection is vital to their emotional well-being, and to ours.

IN ENDING

I'd like to leave you with a story. The writer is anonymous.

There was once a wise old man who could answer any question, no matter how difficult. One day, two young people decided they were going to fool the old man. They planned to catch a bird and take it to the old man saying, "Is what we have in our hands alive or dead?" If the man says "dead," we'll turn it loose, and it will fly away; if he says "alive," we'll crush it.

They caught a bird and went with it to the old man. They said, "Is what we have in our hands alive or dead?" The wise old man considered them and smiled. Then he said, *"It's in your hands."*

It's hard for me to end. I hope that I've given you enough advice to feel comfortable beginning your own extraordinary sexual journey. Each of you will do it differently. Lion, Bear, Bee, and Otter will each undertake this challenge with their own unique flair.

There are no right or wrong ways to have extraordinary passion. The boundaries of extraordinary sex are infinite and for that reason will stay forever new. The future is in your hands. My blessings to you for a joyous adventure!

I have witnessed countless couples transform their relationships in only one weekend. Hundreds of thousands more have benefited by watching my instructional video series, *Ordinary Couples Extraordinary Sex,* and putting some of the suggestions to work.

If you have attended one of my workshops or have seen my videos, I'd love to hear your success stories.

For those of you still "wishing and hoping" that things will get better on their own, I invite you and your partner to join me for a couple's seminar that will change the way you relate to one another forever.

For information about seminars and videos or to share your experiences with me, please write me at:

Dr. Sandra Scantling's Seminars
P.O. Box 174
Farmington, CT 06032